SO YOU NEED TO
WRITE
A BUSINESS
PLAN!

JEROME S. OSTERYOUNG

Jim Moran Professor of Entrepreneurship
Professor of Finance
Director, Program in Entrepreneurship
Executive Director, Jim Moran Institute for Global Entrepreneurship

and

DIANE L. DENSLOW

Lecturer in Entrepreneurship
Director, Small Business Institute
Associate Director, Jim Moran Institute for Global Entrepreneurship

College of Business
Florida State University

THOMSON
™
SOUTH-WESTERN

Australia · Canada · Mexico · Singapore · Spain · United Kingdom · United States

THOMSON

SOUTH-WESTERN

So You Need to Write a Business Plan! 1e

Jerome S. Osteryoung and Diane L. Denslow

VP/Team Director:
Mike Roche

Executive Editor:
Mike Reynolds

Developmental Editor:
Elizabeth Thomson

Senior Marketing Manager:
Charlie Stutesman

Production Editor:
Stephanie Blydenburgh

Manufacturing Coordinator:
Sandee Milewski

Senior Design Project Manager:
Michelle Kunkler

Cover Designer:
Paul Neff Design

Cover Illustration:
© Artville, Inc.

Printer:
Transcontinental Printing

For more information
contact South-Western,
5191 Natorp Boulevard,
Mason, Ohio 45040.
Or you can visit our Internet site at:
http://www.swcollege.com

Library of Congress Control Number:
2002112765

ISBN: 0030315336

TABLE OF CONTENTS

FORWARD

This business plan text will be a book that will teach you how to write a business plan. It has many examples and exercises to show you how to go about this process. Honestly, (stole this word from the politicians), there will be nothing new in terms of content in this book, rather the newness of this text will be on the process of teaching you how to prepare a business plan. Throughout the text you will be shown many examples (both good and bad) from actual business plans. End of the chapter experiential exercises, a worksheet for each business plan section, and web resources augment the text. The exercises and worksheets will reinforce the material in the text and the resources will show you how much material on the web that there is to assist you. Additionally, on the financial portion of the plan, we will take you through the foundation of financial statements and how to prepare statements for a business plan.

Throughout the business plan book, we will provide examples from a product oriented company, a service oriented company, and a retailer. With this triad, we should be able to cover the majority of the issues that are unique for business plans for specific types of industry. Unfortunately, we will miss certain industries such as bird watching and alligator wrestling (a Florida tradition).

As business plans are not the most lively subject, we will use humor throughout the text to make the book more vivid and interesting (not much humor yet in this write-up but we are trying).

This book is written for two different audiences: entrepreneurs who are starting a business and students who are learning about business plans. If you are starting a business just disregard the experiential exercises, as this is for student usage.

After reading and studying this book, you will have a good overview of what a good business plan looks like and how to develop it. If you complete the worksheet at the end of each chapter as you progress through the book, you will have the basis of your business plan upon completion of this book.

The sample plan that is used throughout this book is based on an actual business plan for Warm 'n Safe Bottle. Although Warm 'n Safe Bottle represents a manufacturing firm, their planning process can be applied to any business. Regardless of the type of business you will need to address issues of marketing, management, and finance. The appropriate section of this plan is included at the end of each chapter and should be read as a model plan. Reading a model plan will help you to understand what each section of the business plan should include.

If at any time you should have some questions about the structure of the business plan, please feel free to write to us at jostery@cob.fsu.edu or ddenslow@garnet.acns.fsu.edu

CHAPTER 1
BUSINESS PLAN BASICS

WHAT IS A BUSINESS PLAN?

So you decided to buy this book on your own or were coerced by a professor to purchase it for a course. Whatever the reason, we hope you will enjoy it and benefit from the material provided. If not, this book makes a great starter for a fireplace. If you decide not to burn this book, hang on to it for some fun, as this book will try to bring some life to the incredibly dull but vitally important subject of business plans.

Welcome to the world of business plans or really, business planning. Business planning is the most important thing a business can do, right after earning a profit, making sure that bills get paid, and having a great Christmas party. By far the success of a business is related to its planning.

> *"You can always amend a big plan, but you can never expand a little one. I don't believe in little plans. I believe in plans big enough to meet a situation which we can't possibly foresee now."*
> Harry S. Truman, former U.S. President

When we are talking about business plans, we are talking about big plans. It is the future of the business laid down on paper so others can see and comment on it. Sometimes this is not a very pleasant process, but rather a necessary evil.

A business plan is very simply the future business strategy laid out in an operational format. What do we mean by this? Every entrepreneur has some pretty definite ideas of where he or she would like to take their business, e.g. sales growth rate of 20% for 5 years, capture 5% of the market, make a net profit of $1,000,000. **The business plan is the description of these goals and the process of their attainment.** These goals should incorporate your values as an individual because you will exert great effort in pursuit of them and you need to feel strongly about them or you will not continue in the attainment of them.

Now writing a business plan is no fun, of course unless you are reading this book at the same time. Many entrepreneurs, who are asked to make a choice between torture and writing a business plan, would opt for the torture. However, with a little bit of humor it can become invigorating and almost fun. In many ways it is the attitude that you have that determines how you progress through this process. If you go into writing a business plan with the thought that you are being forced to go through this tortuous process, then it will be a battle. However, if you go through the process of writing a business plan with the thought that you are going to be putting down on paper your dreams and aspirations, it will flow much

Actually , business planning comes BEFORE having a great Christmas party!

more easily. Additionally, if writing the business plan is broken down into segments it will not seem like such an overwhelming task.

WHY WRITE A BUSINESS PLAN?

Most entrepreneurs have to be forced to write a business plan. In most cases either a bank needs the business plan in order to provide a loan or a potential investor needs a business plan to determine whether to fund the business. However, having a business plan in place and one that is updated yearly is one of the most critical elements for the success of the business. A business plan is like a road map in that the more closely you follow it, the faster you will get to your destination. Additionally, when you detour from your intended route, the business plan will be a resource to alert you to a change in direction. If you were going to take a trip across the United States, you would have to plan the trip in terms of the roads that you would take and the distances between stops along the way to your destination. You would need to identify detours along the route, calculate your estimated travel time, and where you will stay (unless you are very adventuresome and are willing to take a chance that there will be lodging available at the various stops along the way). Clearly you have to plan for this trip and if you do not plan, then you may encounter unexpected problems. Sometimes just by going through the process of writing a business plan, the entrepreneur is able to envision ways of dealing with potential problems.

Having a business plan that is updated yearly is one of those lifelines to a business that helps to guide it through some very difficult times. Frequently we see entrepreneurs who are momentarily lost, regain their course of direction and inspiration by looking back on the business plan and seeing how far they have come. It is important to rewrite the business plan annually because the business environment changes; there may be new competitors that will impact your business or new regulations. The plan needs to change to adjust to these changes. Additionally, you will be able to incorporate information about your customers as you have more experiences with them.

One of the major benefits of writing a business plan is that you will have the opportunity to get to know and understand your industry and your particular market in depth. This is important because even a limited amount of information in these areas can make a significant difference to the success of your business. The real value of a business plan is the decisions that it influences such as potential sales for a particular market segment and how to compete in that segment.

One of the biggest problems for entrepreneurs is how to deal with competition. Waiting until competition hits is **not** the way you want to deal with competition. Just look at the businesses that sat around and let Wal-Mart eats their market share. Most entrepreneurs have found that the thought process to develop the business plan and addressing competition in the abstract (has any one ever

---

Paradigm shift: consider Business Plan writing as recording dreams

Pay Attention: knowledge of your industry will improve your business success!!

seen abstract?) has helped them to deal with competition when it comes. The business plan is a neat way to focus on some upcoming problems and try some what-if strategies in the safety of your mind.

Normally, there are two general times to prepare a business plans. One is when you start your business and the other is when need some money to finance your business. Unfortunately, most entrepreneurs only write a plan when they are required no matter how much they are preached to as to the value of the business plan.

WHO ARE THE USERS OF BUSINESS PLANS?

When writing a business plan, it is really, really important to understand to whom you are writing. The business plan that is written for internal uses is going to be a lot different than the business plan written for external purposes.   Is it unethical to have two different forms of business plans? Some people might say yes, then again some people might say yes to everything. However, having two business plans is really addressing the needs of each of the users of the business plan in a way that they will find most beneficial. Writing a business plan is akin to writing a resume in that you need to write it with a specific audience in mind. The internal business plan is written as guide for the internal workings of a business and is written with a great deal of specificity (there we go again with big words again). Some of this specificity will be dealing with the organization of the business to accomplish its plans. The external business plan is used to raise funds and needs to have a sales pitch spin to it in order to try to entice the user to invest in your business.   Some of the major differences between the two types of plans are shown below.

	REALLY Important: Know to whom you are writing the plan

External Business Plan	Internal Business Plan
1. Focuses on provider of funds	1. Focuses on the internal operations
2. Is a form of selling document	2. Purpose is for implementation
3. Explains the concept in detail	3. Briefly goes over the concept
4. Emphasis on marketing and finance objectives	4. Emphasis on quantitative
5. Highlights management	5. Highlights the objectives to be accomplished

Bankers and investors are the typical users of the business plan that is written for external purposes. The banker's goal is simply to have the loan repaid which means that they are looking for information in the business plan indicating that the business is able to keep up a loan repayment schedule, that there are tangible assets that can be sold to repay the loan, and the owner's personal guarantee and personal assets. An investor's goal is to have a high rate of return on his investment. That means that he is looking for indications of rapid growth, strong potential in the market, and a solid management team in the business plan.

HOW DO YOU GO ABOUT WRITING THE BUSINESS PLAN?

Writing a business plan can be daunting. How do you go about doing this? Well you could go have a couple of beers and think about it or you could buy a computer program to help you write it. However, both of these approaches suffer from a common malady of not being effective (whatever effective means-- have you noticed that every time you read about a government or an executive, "this being effective" or "that being effective" is mentioned, but no one defines this concept?)

Words to look up:

Specificity
Effective

Obviously having a few beers is going to make you feel pretty good but will deter you from working on the plan. A computer program is not recommended as they use a template approach and most outsiders who look at these plans get turned off very fast by seeing a business plan that appears to be canned. Additionally, any business is going to have unique attributes that a standard computer program will not be able to capture. However, they can be used as a resource to direct the writer of the business plan to the areas that need to be addressed.

One approach is to take some time everyday to work on the plan. Just plan on scheduling one to one and half hours a day for about four weeks to get the plan written. However, if you are in a time crunch this will not work and you need to speed along the process. What seems to be most effective (that e word again) is to figure out how much time you have and then allocate a sufficient number of hours to get the plan written. A good rule of thumb (what is so special about a thumb?) is to allow about 40 to 60 hours to write, revise, and finalize the draft of a business plan. Some plans are going to take significantly longer. The more complex the business, the longer the time it is going to take especially for those firms that sell or service multiple product lines. The business plan needs to sufficiently cover the relevant information and substantiated with data while at the same time being clear and concise.

What seems to work best for most individuals is to complete certain sections first and then complete the other sections. The two critical sections of a business plan are the marketing section (how are you going to sell the darn things) and the financial section (where are you going to get the money to build the darn things). These two sections are the key parts of the business plan and we will talk extensively about these areas in Chapters 7 and 10 respectively. In addition to the marketing and financial sections, the section on the management team is also extremely important. Funding sources want to know that the management team has the education and experience to do what they say they are going to do.

In starting to write a business plan the first section to be written should be the marketing section, as that will allow you to visualize how you are going to sell and distribute your product or service. Additionally, this section develops the revenue forecast for your business plan. The revenue forecast is the anticipated sales for the business over the next five to seven years.

The second area to concentrate on is the financial section. With section, the forecasted or proforma statements are produced. These statements are the income statement, balance sheet, and cash budget. These statements are discussed in length in Chapter 10. When these two sections are completed the rest of the stuff (another technical term) can be added later.

> **Two Critical Sections:**
> Marketing and Financials

CHAPTER SUMMARY

A business plan is a necessary requirement in order to run your business effectively. A business plan (let's use BP from now on) is a written planning document that lays out the methodology to meet the firm's goals and objectives. Every business actually needs two plans, one for internal purposes and one for external purposes. It is the business plan that others evaluate when they consider the decision to invest in your business. When starting to write a plan it is best to begin with the marketing section followed by the financial section.

CHAPTER APPLICATIONS:

1. Find an entrepreneur who did not write a business plan and determine how it impacted his/her business.

2. Interview an entrepreneur of a business that wrote a business plan prior to starting. Find out the value of the plan to him/her.

3. Write a paragraph describing your personal reasons for wanting to start or expand your business. Consider your entrepreneurial skills.

RESOURCES

Jim Moran Institute for Global Entrepreneurship
http://www.cob.fsu.edu/jmi/
Site has a section on developing business plans including guidelines, elements in a business plan, sample plans, and additional resources.

U.S. Small Business Administration (SBA)
http://www.sbaonline.sba.gov
Site provides a considerable amount of information on business including how to start a business, writing a business plan, grants, loans, etc.

Service Corps of Retired Executives (SCORE)
http://www.score.org
Provides assistance to businesses. Online consulting allows you to ask a question of an expert in your industry.

Small Business Development Center (SBDC)
http://www.sbdcnet.utsa.edu/sbdc.htm
Sponsored by the SBA. They provide seminars and assistance on starting and growing a business, writing a business plan. Locate the center nearest you on this site.

Business Opportunities Handbook: Online
http://www.busop1.com
Lists business opportunities and articles on running a small business.

CHAPTER 2
DEVELOPING A MISSION STATEMENT:
A CRITICAL ELEMENT IN DEVELOPING A BUSINESS PLAN

In the first chapter we defined a business plan as the future plans of the business articulated on paper. In this chapter we will discuss a very critical (what is not critical in a business plan?) element in developing a business plan. This element is developing a mission statement for the business.

DEVELOPING A MISSION STATEMENT

"Once there was an old sea captain who was soliciting shipmates for his greatest embarkment ever. He managed to gather an entire crew of men willing to go off to sea. He huddled them together on the deck of his ship and began to delegate responsibility among the crewmen when one of the ambitious sailors asked, "Captain, where exactly are we going?" Confident in his own sense of direction and impeccable navigation ability, the captain replied, "Just do the job I assign you and leave the rest to me."

One night, a storm hit the small vessel tossing it about on the waves. One hard hit sent the captain into the mast and unconscious on the deck. When the storm calmed, the crew began to argue about where they should direct the ship not knowing the direction that the captain desired to take. Unable to agree on a common direction, the crew divided, took lifeboats from the ship and abandoned the captain.

The captain made two fateful errors. One was walking on the deck of the ship in the middle of a raging storm, the other was not sharing with his crew his expectations and mission of the voyage. In the business world, it is also important to establish a common purpose so that all employees and clients of the business know exactly where they fit in and where the company is going. Just as man has always striven to define a purpose for existence, so should businesses ask themselves "Why are we here?" and establish a mission statement." (1) by Jeff Foxx in Business Leader online

When writing the mission statement, it is important to bring a significant number of employees into this process. If the employees are expected to buy into these statements then it is only fair and reasonable for employees to have a voice in producing this statement. Whenever you can provide opportunities for employees to feel vested in your business, they will become much better employees.

The mission statement is **probably the most important element** in the business plan. It defines the underlying goals and objectives of the firm and states them in a very clear fashion. It includes the markets that are served and the benefits that are offered. Usually it is less than fifty words. Many people have said that writing

> **Did you get that?**
> The Mission Statement is very important to the BP

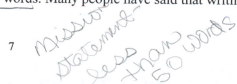

7

a mission statement is analogous to painting a complete picture on the head of a pin! It is not critical that the statement be fifty words but rather the critical aspect is that it needs to be brief and to the point. Some business owners could go on and on as to what their business does, and we all have known some of these individuals, but a well written mission statement <u>clearly and succinctly articulates</u> this.

Oftentimes firms have their mission statement plastered over all the walls of their business so employees can understand what the organization as a whole is trying to do. It is good vehicle, almost like a mantra, to make sure that everyone inside a business as well as those outside clearly understand what the business is about. A clearly articulated mission statement can also direct future decision-making. It is a guide to aid decision makers in the business to stay on task and not get diverted by the latest opportunity if it is not in alignment with the mission of the business.

Some of the basic attributes of a mission statement are:

1. **It is very succinctly written, normally less than 50 words.**
2. **It establishes your company's purpose and what it does.**
3. **It specifies where you want to take your company.**

While these three statements are helpful, the following is a list of items to include that have a much higher level of specificity.

1. **Who are and who will be your customers?**
2. **Where does your firm compete?**
3. **What are your company's products or services?**
4. **What is your company's basic technology?**
5. **What is your firm's commitment for growth and profitability?**
6. **What is your firm's attitude towards its employees?**
7. **What are your company's basic core beliefs**?

Okay, okay, we have been going on about mission statements so now you want to see some examples. Just for fun, here is one off of the Dilbert page on the Internet (we would give you the site but about the time this book is published the site will have changed location seven times).

| WHAT are they saying????? | **Our challenge is to enthusiastically coordinate economically sound intellectual capital while continuing to assertively restore low-risk high-yield data for 100% customer satisfaction.** |

Comment: Obviously, this is not how you want to write a mission statement as it really tells you nothing about the company.

8

Mission Statement for a Service organization:

The following is a mission statement by the American Red Cross:

The American Red Cross, a humanitarian organization led by volunteers and guided by its Congressional Charter and the Fundamental Principles of the International Red Cross Movement, will provide relief to victims of disasters and help people prevent, prepare for, and respond to emergencies.

Comment: Notice in this mission statement it states what type of an organization it is (humanitarian) and how it guided plus what it is and will do "provide relief to victims of disasters and help people prevent, prepare for, and respond to emergencies."

Manufacturing businesses:

Dell Computer has an interesting mission statement:

Dell's mission is to be the most successful computer company in the world at delivering the best customer experience in markets we serve. In doing so, Dell will meet customer expectations of:

- **Highest quality**

- **Leading technology**

- **Competitive pricing**

- **Individual and company accountability**

- **Best-in-class service and support**

- **Flexible customization capability**

- **Superior corporate citizenship**

- **Financial stability**

Comment: This statement is very general.

Otis Elevator has this mission statement:

Our mission is to provide any customer a means of moving people and things up, down and sideways over short distances with higher reliability than any similar enterprise in the world.

Comment: Notice how they define their market as the entire world and they define very clearly what they do (in terms of movement) and the quality of their

> Are you getting the idea?? If not there are more examples.

Add to my plan

products (higher reliability than any similar enterprise in the world). It would have been preferable for them to add a statement about growth and profits as well.

Microsoft has the following mission statement:

> **Since its inception in 1975, Microsoft's mission has been to create software for the personal computer that empowers and enriches people in the workplace, at school and at home. Microsoft's early vision of a computer on every desk and in every home is coupled today with a strong commitment to Internet-related technologies that expand the power and reach of the PC and its users.**

Comment: Microsoft's mission statement is really vague and not really helpful in ascertaining what they plan to do. It is very glib and lacks specificity. A mission statement such as this would not be of much value to someone who might be considering investing in your business.

The mission statement for Bombardier is:

> **Bombardier's mission is to be the leader in all the markets in which it operates. This objective will be achieved through excellence in the fields of aerospace, rail transportation equipment, recreational products and financial services. All Bombardier units must meet the needs of their customers and markets as well as reach and maintain world-class performance. They must also create added value in order to sustain their own growth and achieve a superior level of economic return to shareholders.**

Comment: Bomadier's mission statement is well done as it talks about being a leader in all markets in which it competes. Of course, it is assumed that being a leader means you have the largest market share of any competitor.
The mission statement of this business specifically mentions the market in which it competes, the type of service they will perform, growth, and shareholder return.

Mission Statement for a Retail Business:

The mission of the Safari Falls is to provide the most valuable and memorable dining experience to its customers.

This mission was also supported by the company's long-term vision, which is to be the leader in meeting the dynamic changes of customer needs, tastes, and personal requirements.

Comment: Although the mission statement establishes the purpose of the company it fails to provide information regarding the customer, specific type of dining experience, commitment to growth, attitudes toward their employees, and the core beliefs of the company.

Writing a mission statement takes a lot of work to get the wording just right. Try to show your proposed mission statement to others to get as much feedback as possible. Show it to your wife, kids (not your pet animals as they may tear it up) employees, bankers, and even the much maligned lawyers. Include the mission statement of your business in the executive summary and in the first part of the business plan.

Hear Ye Hear Ye
Here is our mission statement

CHAPTER SUMMARY

The business plan rests on some fundamental tenets that must be enunciated in a very clear fashion. The mission statement must be clearly articulated so that outside investors can easily see where you intend to take the business. The mission statement is a statement that specifies the firm's core beliefs and strengths.

MISTAKES TO AVOID IN THIS SECTION:

➢ Being too vague
➢ Being too detailed and lengthy
➢ Failing to indicate the purpose of your company and where you want it to go.
➢ Failing to get input from employees in your business

END OF CHAPTER APPLICATIONS:

1. Read the following mission statement and note at least three areas for improvement.

Mission Statement of a community technology center planning and implementation company:

To provide governmental bodies and agencies with cost effective planning, design and implementation of community technology centers congruent with designate computer literacy objectives.

2. Write a mission statement for your business using the worksheet.
3. Read the mission statement of the Safe-Temp Bottle Plan as a model statement.
4. Interview an entrepreneur of a growing company and determine if they have written a mission. Why or why not?

RESOURCES

Business Online
http://businessonline.org/info/mission.html
Provides assistance in writing a business plan.

ABC News
http://abcnews.go.com/sections/business/YourBusiness/sbb990519.html
Provides information on building the perfect mission statement

Business Leader online
http://www.businessleader.com/bl/sep96/shared.html
Provides information on why a mission statement is needed and how to develop it.

BizPlanit
http://www.bizplanit.com/vplan/mission/mistakes.htm
http://www.bizplanit.com/vplan/mission/ basics.htm
Another site with information on creating a mission statement.

Model Plan: Safe Temp Bottle, Inc.

Vision Statement

The vision of Safe-Temp bottle, Inc. is to be the market leader in design, creation, and manufacturing of baby bottle products in the United States through efficient use of cutting edge technologies.

Mission Statement

Safe-Temp Bottle, Inc. is increasing the quality of baby bottle products to the public in Northwest Florida and is setting the standard for affordable baby bottle products.

Use for developing mission statement

Mission/Vision Statement Worksheet

MISSION--Describe your business's position regarding the following:

Who are your customers and where will your firm compete?

_____
_____
_____
_____
_____

What are your company's products or services?

_____
_____
_____

What is your company's basic technology?

_____
_____
_____

What is your firm's commitment for growth and profitability?

_____
_____
_____

What is your firm's attitude towards its employees?

_____
_____
_____

What are your company's basic core beliefs?

_____
_____
_____

VISION

Where would you like to take your company?

_____

_____

_____

_____

CHAPTER 3
DECIDE ON A LEGAL STRUCTURE

The form of organization you select will need to be included in the BP. You can just mention the form of organization in The Business section of the business plan if your business is not complicated in the manner in which it divides up ownership. Entrepreneurs have a variety of alternatives under which to operate their businesses. When you start a business you need to determine if you will structure the business as a sole proprietorship, general partnership, limited partnership, limited liability company, or as a corporation. How do you determine which legal structure to select? There are a number of options to consider and some trade-offs may be necessary in selecting a form of business organization. There are no right nor wrong choices but some of the considerations in selecting a form of ownership include: organizational costs, liability and risks you are willing to assume, continuity of the business, transferability of ownership, income taxes, your need for capital, and management control. An especially important factor in considering the legal form of an organization is its relationship to income taxes. You may want to obtain the advice of an attorney and tax accountant before you make a final decision. There are four main ways to organize the business: the sole proprietorship, the partnership, the corporation, and the limited liability company. Remember, the legal structure that you select will determine your ability to raise capital, how your business will be taxed, the amount of personal liability you will have, and the amount of paperwork required. Let's take a look at the four most common forms of organization:

> Make sure you consider these factors carefully

I. SOLE PROPRIETORSHIP

A sole proprietorship is defined as a business owned and controlled by one person. Most small businesses are run as sole proprietorships and often start as such. However, it may have employees. The business is not legally considered a separate entity, but rather a part of the proprietor's personal identity. Both personal and business income taxes are reported on the personal income tax form. However, it is recommended that separate bank accounts be established for business and for personal financial matters. This is the most common form of business organization due to the ease of start-up and the relative freedom from government regulations and paperwork. It is also the least expensive and least regulated business legal structure. Basically, it can be started by obtaining a business license and securing a location. The owner (proprietor) has total management control over the business but he is at risk for personal liability incurred through the acts of the owner's employees or agents. You need to consider whether the business will be exposed to any potential lawsuits such as customers injured on the premises or from products sold by the business. If you determine to be a sole proprietorship talk about your abilities and experience in the business plan and include your resume.

> Most common form: Simple and Inexpensive

Note that you will need to be forthright about any areas in which you will need assistance and specify where you will obtain it.

ADVANTAGES OF SOLE PROPRIETORSHIP

➢ Start-up Ease
Starting a sole proprietorship is simpler then a partnership or a corporation. This process has less legal restrictions and demands less capital.

➢ Financial
A sole proprietor has control over where profits are distributed. Income from the business is taxed as personal income and as a result is not subject to double taxation. Financial information does not have to be shared with the public.

➢ Proprietary Control
The owner has control and decision making ability over all aspects of the company. This enables the owner to respond quickly to the changing needs of the company.

DISADVANTAGES OF A SOLE PROPRIETORSHIP

➢ Unlimited Liability
The sole proprietor is personally responsible for all business debts. These debts may exceed the total investment in the company and personal assets. The sole proprietor is also responsible for personal injury to all who come in contact with the operations of the company or the company's products and services.

➢ Limited Life
The life of the company is limited to the life of the owner.

➢ Limited Size
The company's growth, experience and knowledge are limited to the capabilities of the owner.

➢ Financing
It can be difficult to obtain long-term financing.

Be aware that Partnerships can be troublesome

II. PARTNERSHIP

The Uniform Partnership Act defines a partnership as "an association of two or more persons to carry on as co-owners of a business for profit." Basically, the partners own the business assets together and are personally liable for business debts. There are two types of partnerships: the general and the limited. An important aspect for both of these partnerships is the Partnership Agreement. The Partnership Agreement is often implemented from the beginning of the start-up process. This early implementation is highly recommended.

GENERAL PARTNERSHIP

In the general partnership the owners agree on how much capital each will contribute and how the profits and losses will be divided as a vital part of the formal partnership agreement. General partners are both personally liable for the partnership's debts.

LIMITED PARTNERSHIP

A limited partnership requires that at least one partner manage the company and be personally liable for the debts of the partnership. The limited partners are not held personally responsible and risk only their investment in the company unless they participate in the management and hold decision-making control of the company.

PARTNERSHIP AGREEMENT

Starting a partnership has the advantage of quick start-up, fewer legal requirements then a corporation, and shared talents and responsibilities. Starting a partnership also means that, in-order for the business to work, each partner must be honest, healthy, capable and compatible. If you have formed a partnership, you should explain why the partners were chosen, their experiences, and how they will complement your skills and abilities. The Partnership Agreement can help define the relationship, each partner's role, responsibilities, and accountability. Explain the reasoning behind the terms of your agreement. The following is a brief outline for a partnership agreement:

> Don't skip this—it's really important.

Name and formation of the partnership
Address of partnership
Names and addresses of partners
Statement of fact of partnership
Statement of business purpose
Life spans of partnership
Amount invested by each partner
Sharing ratios for profits and losses
Salaries
Authority
Partners' rights regarding finances
Specific duties of each partner
Settlements of disputes
Sales of partnership interest
Death of a partner (dissolution and winding up)
Provision for protection of surviving partners
Provision of dissolution and distribution of net assets
Partnership restrictions
Distribution of the profits and financial responsibility for any losses
Provision for partners to exit

ADVANTAGES OF A PARTNERSHIP

➤ Ease of Formation
   Legal requirements are few compared to a corporation
➤ Growth and Expansion
   Sources of capital and credit, skills and experience and decision making potential are increased.
➤ Motivation
   Partners are motivated to work together, share talents and grow the company
➤ Focus
   Each partner is able to focus more of their time and attention on aspects they are most interested and talented.

DISADVANTAGES OF A PARTNERSHIP

➤ Unlimited Liability
   The partners or unlimited partner is personally responsible for all business debts. These debts may exceed the total investment in the company and personal assets. They are also responsible for personal injury to all who come in contact with the operations of the company or the company's products and services.
➤ Problem of Continuity
   The Partnership is dissolved upon death of a partner or if partners withdraw.
➤ Control
   It is important to make sure the partners' work habits, goals, ethics and general business philosophy are compatible.
➤ Law of Agency
   Partners are bound by the Law of Agency, which holds both partners liable for the actions of the other for business purposes.

III. CORPORATION

There are two forms of corporations: a C corporation and an S corporation. These corporations are formed by filing Articles of Incorporation with the Department of State, and stockholders electing the board of directors.

As defined by Chief Justice John Marshall of the United States Supreme Court, a corporation is "an artificial being, invisible, intangible, and existing only in contemplation of the law." In short, a corporation is a distinct legal entity separate from the individuals that own it. The owners are not personally responsible for the debts and risks of the company and they risk losing only their investment in the corporation.

The C Corporation

A standard corporation is taxed by the federal government as a separate legal entity. The income of the corporation is taxed and then the income of the owners is taxed. In your BP give detailed information on the corporate officers including their skills, reasons selected, and what they will bring to the company. A copy of the charter should be included in the Supporting Documents section. The C-corporation is the only business form that permits multiple forms of stock. Thus, this form of organization is usually the one that most venture capitalists require since they want a superior position in the event of liquidation. Venture capitalists usually want to hold preferred stock whereas founders and key members of management hold common stock.

ADVANTAGES OF A CORPORATION

- ➤ **Limited Liability**
  Owners are only liable for the fixed amount of their investment in the corporation.
- ➤ **Ownership is Transferable**
  Shareholders can sell their ownership shares.
- ➤ **Growth Potential**
  Equity capital can be raised by selling additional shares of stock or long-term bonds. Securing long-term financing from lending institutions is much easier as well because corporate assets can be used to secure loans.
- ➤ **Centralized Management**
  Owners are able to delegate authority to hired managers.
- ➤ **Knowledge Base**
  The Corporation is able to use the experience and skills of many individuals.

DISADVANTAGES OF A CORPORATION

- ➤ **Government Regulation**
  Extensive government regulations require reports.
- ➤ **Expense of Incorporation Process**
  They are expensive to form and maintain. Costs that are unique to the corporation include fees to set up the corporate structure, the expense for legal fees and paperwork, and the costs of stockholder's meetings.
- ➤ **Taxes**
  The income of the corporation is taxed and then the income of the individuals is taxed.
- ➤ **Security**
  Financial statements are public information and can be viewed by competitors.

The S Corporation

This form of organization affords the same legal protection as a Corporation. The key difference is that corporations are taxed differently. Shareholders are able to absorb all corporate income or losses as partners and report it as individual taxpayers. The profits or losses are passed through to individual shareholders and income on their individual income and tax returns. This is particularly good for a business that anticipates initial losses but long-term profits since is could start out as an S corporation which would allow the shareholders to deduct losses on individual tax returns. The business could later be changed to a C corporation when it becomes profitable.

ADVANTAGES OF AN S CORPORATION

Taxes
The S Corporation is not obligated to pay federal corporation income taxes; therefore double taxation is eliminated. Income and loss are passed through to shareholders in proportion to their stock ownership.

Limited Liability
An S Corporation provides investors with much greater protection from personal liability. Note that if you require outside funding, most investors prefer dealing with an incorporated entity.

Ownership is Transferable
Shareholders can sell their ownership shares

DISADVANTAGES OF AN S CORPORATION

Limitations on Number of Shareholders
No more than 75 shareholders are permitted all of whom must be individuals or estates (partnerships and corporations cannot be shareholders in an S corporation). The shareholders cannot own more than 80% of the voting stock of another entity.

Restrictions on Stock
Can issue only one class of outstanding stock.

Taxes
The shareholder's deductibility of losses is limited to the shareholder's basis resulting from capital contributions or loans from the shareholder.

Government Regulations
There are strict requirements regulating not only the structure of the S corporation but also it's membership and operation.

LIMITED LIABILITY COMPANY (LLC)

The LLC is a fairly new form of business legal structure. It is an unincorporated association with or without perpetual duration (this depends on individual state statutes), having two or more members (individuals, corporations, partnerships, trusts, etc.). In a LLC the owners are called members (not stockholders or partners) and their ownership interests are known as interests. Basically it is a blend that gives the owners of the business protection from personal liability that is afforded to the corporation and the ability to pass through taxation as in the partnership structure. Usually an Operating Agreement (created by the members when the company is first established) sets forth how the LLC will be operated, how profits and losses will be shared, and the rights and obligations of the members.

ADVANTAGES OF A LLC

➢ **Ownership**
The number of members or their status is not restricted (unlike the S corporation). An unlimited number of individuals, corporations, and partnerships may participate in a LLC.
➢ **No Restrictions on Stock**
 The LLC can issue more than one class of stock that have different rights (The S corporation is limited to one class of stock).
➢ **Loss Deductions**
The owners do not assume liability for the debts of the business and any losses can be used as tax deductions against active income. (Loss deductions are more limited under an S corporation).
➢ **Liability**
No member, manager, or agent of an LLC will have any personal responsibility for the liabilities of the LLC. However, the assets of the LLC are subject to the claims of its creditors.

DISADVANTAGES OF A LLC

➢ **Limited Use**
The use of an LLC is restricted. It cannot be used for professional services such as an attorney, accountant, or insurance agent.
Also since the LLC is relatively new, there is limited case law.

> ➤ **Transferability Restrictions**
>
> There is not a uniform code as to what happens when an owner dies, retires, or resigns. There are restrictions as to transferability of ownership interests. For example, the transferee of an LLC membership interest will not be admitted as a new member of the LLC unless all other member give their consent.
>
> ➤ **Continuity**
>
> Unless the business is continued by unanimous consent of the remaining members, the LLC can be dissolved in the event of death, resignation, expulsion, bankruptcy or dissolution of a member.
>
> ➤ **Limitations in Obtaining Financing**
>
> To take on venture capital or do an IPO the LLC like the S corporation will need to convert to a general corporation.

The form of organization you choose does not have to be permanent. If the circumstances of your business change, you can change the form of your business. For example, you may start out as a sole proprietorship and change to a corporation as the business grows. However, in selecting the proper business form it is important to consider how the form will meet the present as well as anticipated future needs of the venture in terms of such areas as external financing, tax considerations, continuity, etc.

CHAPTER SUMMARY

There are various forms of organization structure. The appropriate choice for your business should be determined by the amount of liability that you are willing to assume personally, tax considerations, continuity decisions, organizational costs, and tax considerations. The form of organization chosen can be changed at a later time as needs of the business change. If you plan to make a change, note why you would change, and how it would benefit your business.

*[handwritten margin note: * If more change this note would you change]*

CHAPTER APPLICATIONS:

> ➤ For your business list the critical issues in selecting a form of organization.
> ➤ Research the main forms of organization in more detail and present a case as to the best form for your type of business.
> ➤ Determine the best form of organization for the following business, note the critical deciding factors for this type of business.

Yuppie Pups Dog Day Care provides a service much like a child day care center only for dogs instead of children. Just as you would a child, dog owners drop off their precious puppies while on their way to work and retrieve them in the evening on their way home. While at the day care, the dogs would have the freedom to run and play in an atmosphere complete with the comforts of home including furniture, toys, and social interaction. Dogs have the freedom to choose between indoor fun and supervised outdoor play, all while receiving the companionship of dog lovers as well other canines.

Yuppie Pups Dog Day Care's core competencies include highest quality care and service for its clients and their owners. By understanding our customers' preferences, Yuppie Pups has developed the concept to exceed their expectations therefore insuring the business's success. With a convenient location and additional services such as grooming, overnight care, and weekend care, Yuppie Pups has strongly positioned itself to take advantage of the northeast Tallahassee niche market.

MISTAKES TO AVOID

➢ Trying to cut costs versus making an appropriate decision.
➢ Failing to consider all relevant issues.
➢ Making a decision but failing to reevaluate after business has been up and running.
➢ Failing to obtain the advice of an attorney if unsure of implications for your business.

[handwritten: include note from Dave Hickman]

RESOURCES

Tax Guide for Small Business
http://www.irs.ustreas.gov/prod/bus_info/index.html
Information on taxes for small businesses.

WSJ StartUp Journal
http://www.startupjournal.com/partners/incorporate.html
Information on LLC's and incorporating your business.

Corporate Agents Inc.: The Business Incorporating Guide
http://www.corporate.com
Information on incorporation.

Small Business Law Center
http://www.courttv.com/legalhelp/
Links to legal resources for entrepreneurs.

Biz Filings Incorporated
http://www.bizfilings.com/index.html
Provides information for determining a legal form of organization.

Form of Organization Worksheet

Effective date of organization_____

Format selected_____

Name(s) of owners_____

Assess the financial resources available to fund your business._____
_____

Determine the amount of time you are willing to spend on paperwork._____
_____

What are your future plans for the business?_____
_____

Assess product liability and other liabilities for your business._____
_____

How important is limiting personal tax liability?_____
_____

How much money are you willing to spend starting your business?_____
_____

Do you work well in a team environment?_____
_____

Are you willing to share authority?_____
_____

CHAPTER 4
GUIDELINES FOR DEVELOPING A FEASIBILITY STUDY:
A PRELIMINARY STEP TO WRITING A BUSINESS PLAN

You need to carefully and fully think through what you are going to do before you write a business plan in a rigorous fashion (this is not something that you wear).

After you have the mission and vision statements for your business plan nailed down, then the next step is to:

a. Start to write the business plan?
b. Just start the darn business?
c. None of the above?

Well you nailed the correct answer if you chose C, as you really do need to do a feasibility study next. A feasibility study is a quick precursor to a business plan that will attest whether the business idea has sufficient potential to spend the time necessary to complete a business plan.

FEASIBILITY STUDY BASICS

Two basic questions need to be answered with this feasibility study:

A. Is there a demand for the product or service?
B. Can that demand be fulfilled on a profitable basis?

The answer of yes to both of these questions means that it is okay to progress on to the full-scale business plan.

Many entrepreneurs want to skip this process. However, if you have to write a business plan for a new business or venture, we implore you to do a feasibility study before you do a business plan! Why? Because you need to verify the concept is viable before you spend the time and money doing a full-blown business plan. Do not worry, any information you gather from the feasibility study will be directly useful in the business plan.

The purpose of the feasibility study is to give you a quick analysis to make sure that you are on the right track (after all who wants to be on the wrong track).

Please note that a feasibility study is not a whole study of the anticipated business – but more like a preview of the business plan that discusses the cogent issues. Therefore the feasibility study should be no more than five pages in length. The following is a suggested (and we mean suggested) outline:

27

I.   A brief overview of what the business is about (1 page).

II. Overview of the market for the product or service and the results of the market analysis (1-2 pages).

III. Competitive advantage of your product or service over the competitor, and the strengths and weaknesses of your competitors (1 page).

IV. Rough Pro formas including the Income Statement that should show the expected level of sales and profit over the next five years.

Please, please remember as you write the feasibility study that the whole purpose for this document is to assist you in assessing whether or not to move on with your business concept. If at this stage it looks as if your idea is not feasible – that is <u>okay</u>. Like most entrepreneurs, you have tons of ideas and the nature of the feasibility study is to ensure that your business concept is a tremendous success. If a few ventures do not "cut the mustard" (ever, wonder why -ketchup isn't the pass word?), this is fine. We all have options and we must be very careful not to fall in love with the first-or second idea that pops into our heads. The primary purpose of the feasibility study is to act as filter or screening device. It is okay to disregard an idea as we are trying to find the best idea, not just the first idea.

We would recommend that you not only limit the pages of this document to five, but that you also <u>limit your time to no more than sixteen hours.</u>

Remain objective
REPEAT:
Remain objective

COMPLETING THE FEASIBILITY STUDY

Okay, how do you get started? Well, the first step is to draft a brief description of the business. Shown below is an example write-up:

Warm 'n Safe Baby Bottle

This new business venture will develop a plastic temperature device to measure the temperature of the liquid in a baby bottle. The device will be a spiral spring looking device (which is patent pending) that fits down the center of an existing baby bottle to indicate to the parent the current temperature of the liquid inside the bottle.

The product currently has superficial competition from the XYZ company which produces a bottle with a device attached to the outside of the bottle and therefore can not measure the temperature of the liquid in the middle of the bottle.

The manufacturing of this product will be out-sourced and the firm will concentrate on sales as an operating expense for the other plastic baby bottle sellers by hiring a sales manager who has the necessary contacts to get the product sold.

The distribution will be done by the contracts with the manufacturer to inventory and ship the products as needed.

Comment: Notice that in the above discussion just the basics of feasibility study are laid out, including some information about production and sales.

The next step in the feasibility study is to do the market analysis. Of course you are saying, "What is a market analysis?" A market analysis is simply the act of ascertaining the demand for the product or service. This is the critical part in both the feasibility study and the business plan. You must show an empirical level (boy are we using big words now), that people want to buy your products or services. We cannot stress how important this step is in the feasibility study. We implore you, we beg you, to do a thorough job in this area as it is so, so important.

> The list is growing:
>
> Specificity
> Effective
> Empirical

Okay, you are convinced market analysis is important, or we have brain washed you, but how do you do this market analysis? Well like most things there are several parts:

1) Look at the health of the industry.
2) Quantify the demand for the product or service.
3) Determine your competitive advantage

LOOK AT THE HEALTH OF THE INDUSTRY

When you look at the health of the industry, you need to consider the industry that you are going to be operating in and assess its viability and future growth. The U.S. Industrial Outlook is a great resource document that assesses the health of numerous industries. Also, you might want to check out the Internet for various sources (check end of chapter resources). Also, please feel free to call your local reference librarian as he or she will be happy to help.

One of the key elements in this section is to ascertain the future growth of the industry. This is important as you do not want to be selling in a declining market if you can avoid this. Clearly you do not want to be in the adding machine business when computers are coming out. However, there are certain exceptions to this. For example, as the market for a product dries up, the result may be more and more opportunities. Remember vacuum tubes for radio (we know that we are showing our ages now). Vacuum tubes were used before we had transistors and resistors. They were glass tubes in which electricity passed in a vacuum to perform some function. As technology changed many people still needed these vacuum tubes and some entrepreneurs were able to earn a bunch of money servicing this shrinking market. However, for most entrepreneurs, you need and we mean you really need to make sure you are going into a growing industry as this makes survival so much easier.

Where do you go to get information on market growth? Most industries put out estimates of future growth rates. Look for these industry publications on the internet as you can find the majority there.

However, if you are not able to find industry information, **do not give up, but persevere.** Here are a couple of alternatives to assist you.

One way to get some quick industry data or growth rates is to look at other firms in the industry and what analysts are saying as to their expected growth rates. Another way is to look at the larger industry than the industry you are trying to find and use this as a surrogate. For example, if you are trying to find the industry growth rate information for a new type of ball that skims the water (Skimmerball) then you will probably have to use pool toys as a surrogate for a pool ball toy. So just enlarge your market definition until you get the necessary data , but do not enlarge it too much. An entrepreneur that we were helping to find an industry growth rate enlarged the market such that he was using the U.S. gross national product as the surrogate for the market of charcoal grills. Clearly he had carried this way too far or had not been diligent in his search. What we are trying to say, and sometimes this is tough, is that market growth rates may not be available for your industry. If so, increase the definition of the industry growth rate such that it is representative of your industry but be careful that it is not too big.

QUANTIFY THE DEMAND FOR THE PRODUCT OR SERVICE

Of all parts of the feasibility study that we have discussed so far, quantifying the demand for the product or service is the most critical. It is this portion of the feasibility study that states what the demand is for your product or service and what people will pay to buy your product or service. One thing you to not want to do is to ask your friends or relatives what they think of your products or services. "Hey Uncle Joe, what do you think of my new baby bottle concept" Uncle Joe might say to take the bottle and shove it. Clearly your friends and relatives are not going to be your friends very long if they give you negative feedback, and at this stage of the analysis you need as much feedback, both positive and negative, as is possible.

> It's really important to get OBJECTIVE feedback so **don't** ask friends and family

It is preferable (mandatory would be a better word if we had eaten our Wheaties™ this morning) for you to do a survey of at least twenty randomly selected people. By random selection, we are not talking about surveying folks just standing in front of the grocery store -- even though this is much easier. Try to get as many varied people (in terms of age, gender, and race) as you can. The written or verbal questions should contain a brief description of the product and at least the following two questions:

1)   Would you buy the product or service? __YES__NO
2)   If you answered yes to the previous question, what would you be willing to pay for the product?

Some other questions to ask would be:

A)   What improvements would increase your desire to buy this product ?
(The more input, the better)

B)   Where would you expect to find this product for sale?
(This helps in planning distribution)

C)   If you did not want to buy this product or service, why?
(This is very important information)

D)   Do you have other comments about the product?

By doing this study of market demand you are verifying that people would consider buying your product. The numbers serve as the basis for ascertaining if you can generate adequate levels of profitability.

What happens, however, if the results are very negative? There could be two problems. First it could mean that the sample of people you surveyed is not representative of the entire market. If this might be the case, then you just need to do another test in a different geographical area. If you do it again, and still find yourself receiving negative responses; then it is time to consider abandoning the project. While this at the time might seem harsh, it is even harsher for you to continue on with the project if people will not buy your product.

It is okay to let go of a good idea that does not have a market. We have seen numerous projects that should have stopped at this point continue on with the entrepreneurs losing all of their money and having to file for bankruptcy. It is better to pull the plug early on a project and devote your energy and finances to other projects that will be successful.

DETERMINE YOUR COMPETITIVE ADVANTAGES

This next section of the feasibility study is divided into two parts. Competitive Advantages and Strengths and Weaknesses of your major competitors.

Competitive Advantages
When determining competitive advantages it is important to lay out what really differentiates your product from your competitors. Some of these ideas could be:

Competitive Factors

A) Quality
B) Features
C) Location
D) Price
E) Service
F) New Application

> **Note:**
>
> **Do not** try to use price as a competitive advantage

Price is not a very good competitive advantage for most entrepreneurs as it does not generate repeat business. Most entrepreneurs want and need to have repeat business. By selling on a price basis you do not generate repeat business. Customers are only interested in price and are not loyal to the business – this is not the type of customers an entrepreneur should be after. When entrepreneurs are selling their products or services, they need to compete on everything but price.

STRENGTHS AND WEAKNESSES OF YOUR MAJOR COMPETITORS

In this portion of the feasibility study you need to list each competitor, their critical attributes and how these attributes relate to your product. Throughout this chapter we have been discussing the baby bottle temperature gauge. Shown below is a list of the critical attributes of firms competing with this product:

1) established name
2) established operations
3) relationships with suppliers

DEVELOP PRO FORMA FINANCIAL STATEMENTS

> The final litmus test: will it make sufficient MONEY?

The last section (finally we get to this) of the feasibility study is the financials. In this section we need to determine the firm's breakeven point and a pro forma or forecasted income statement (Chapter 10 will explain this process in detail). The purpose of this section is to quantify if we can generate a profit off the product or service. While having a demand for the product or service is great, the litmus test of the entire feasibility study rests on the financials. We want to know does it look reasonably promising that the business will make adequate money

The following are two feasibility study examples, one is for a sports store and the other for a furniture company.

Don't have to do for plan

Example: Feasibility Study for "Wild Times"

Market Analysis

Wild Times sells products related to extreme sports in the area of land and water. Our customer base consists of outdoor people that are very active in recreation and outside activities. These numbers that we are about to go through are slightly inflated because of the extreme nature of our products. The average consumer will not shop at our store because the average consumer does not participate in these outdoor activities.

This store attracts consumers from the age of 17 to 45 years of age (AEA). Within Lowen County the Somersville Market consists of 192,493 consumers of all ages. Within the age levels that we will target there are 104,333 consumers. Considering the price of our products, it will eliminate consumers in the poverty level from shopping in our store and participating in outdoor activities. The total number of consumers for our business is possibly 86,597 residents in the middle and upper income brackets.

There are three other local businesses that are in the outdoor retail market. We feel the amount of people that would possibly buy our products and shop at our location will support our business. When you divide 86,597 by four locations it comes out that we would have a potential of 21,649 possible customers. That is if all four stores capture equal share market, around twenty-five percent. We also considered out of the 86,597 possible consumers how many will actual buy something in our store. If we capture ten percent of the potential market that will give us 2,164 customers that will buy something at our store. We expect the consumer to spend an average of 300 dollars a year at our location. With these numbers we expect our net income will be around 649,200 dollars. If we capture 20 percent of our market, our net profits will be 1,298,940. We feel these numbers are accurate with respect to capturing certain market shares. The market potential for an outdoor retail store of this size seems to be obtainable.

The size of the store is an aspect we feel could be a little smaller making the store more likely to succeed. Net profits could possibly support a store this size but with the current market it will take some time before we see substantial profits. With the growth of the Somersville area and the development of the area we feel the potential for this business to succeed will only improve over the years. In the year 2010 Lowen County is projected to have 288,200 residents. Some of this information is inaccurate because of the huge student market in the area. We feel the student market in the area will help our business because students are very energetic and fit into the company's consumer's profile. We do have to take into consideration that the student market does not have a large amount of disposable income. We do feel this market in the long run will improve the chances of our store's success.

Marketing information shows the new era of extreme sports has uncovered a new outdoor market. Manufacturers have seen great amounts of growth in some of their lines because of the travel industry. People are traveling more than they ever used to and there has been a recent 55 percent increase. All these travelers are equipping themselves with outdoor gear from backpacks to hiking shoes. (Agoglia)

The Extreme Sports market is also showing double-digit growth rates. The Sports like snowboarding and windsurfing and roller hockey have brought a large amount of sporting goods companies into business. Old traditional sports are falling to the waste side because the interest's in traditional sports is on the decline. Extreme sport's growth rates are registering in triple digits. There were 1.5 billion in sales in the camping industry. The industry is proposed to keep growing at 11 percent a year with the Baby Boomers retiring and looking to do more outdoor activities. We feel we will capture both markets of the Baby Boomers and Generation X (Simmons).

One article stated to capture the industry design your shop around a concept. People are becoming more sophisticated to and want to go to certain shops to find the products they are looking for. These specialized shops give customers the highest quality of customer service. Our store is going against this idea -- we will have the largest selection of products in the area. Nationwide, it was estimated the outdoor-sports industry was worth 5 billion dollars in 1997. This was up from 4.7 in 1994 the growth was caused by the implementation of concept shops. Concept shops are controlled by manufacturers of certain outdoor equipment. Local retailers are encouraging the growth while concept shops are too restrictive because of the controls the manufacturer has over the owner.

We feel our concept of having many products for the consumer and having everything the consumer wants under one roof will give us a competitive advantage over the consumer. This is the concept this store was founded on and will hopefully lead to success in this market.

Comment: Capturing 20% of that market may be unrealistically high. They do not indicate how they came up with the average expenditure of $300 per visit. They do not indicate the income level of their target market and how this will narrow the original potential of 86,597. They also mention baby boomers as being a targeted market but do not include this in the original market potential figures. They need to watch inconsistencies in their determination of market potential.

Example: Competitive Analysis

Wild Times needs to take into consideration three stores in the local area. We will be selling similar merchandise that these three locations sell. We will be combining all the products that these businesses sell in one location. This will give us a competitive advantage. The three stores consist of the following:

Washout Sports	2415 N. Adams Street
The Boat Dock	1115 W. Osborn Avenue
Sled and Hike	2748 Camden Circle NE

Washout Sports store has many strengths because it is a franchise. Washout Sports has a big advertising and promotions budget. We feel it will be hard to compete with an advertising budget comparable to theirs. The store is located inside the mall and attracts a lot of attention with weekly specials and promotional activities. These specials create low prices that will cause our store to keep prices low. This will keep our profit margins to a minimum is some areas of merchandise. The attendants in the store offer average customer service. Here is where we feel we can over take this competitor. There are times you can't find anyone, or when you do, they do not really know how to help the customer. Our customer service will be very highly rated because of our trained staff. We feel this is what will set us apart from this local competitor. Even with the following circumstances Washout Sports Store will have a strong effect on the success of our business.

The Boat Dock is a small business located on Osborn Avenue. The shop is a business run by an outdoorsman and he does not pay much attention to the books. The business is run very inefficiently by a single entry accounting system. I feel this is where we can better compete with this store. An inefficiently run business can be overtaken more easily than an efficiently run business. The owner only has ideas of how they are doing and goes on gut feelings most of the time. The store concentrates on customer service and I feel this is the only reason it still exists. There are four employees that assist the customers. The employees of The Boat Dock can be very informative and are great sales people by being friendly. The shop helps the customer by running shuttles to local rivers; this gives the customer added value. Customers that do not have vehicles for canoeing or kayaking to participate in the activity go to The Boat Dock because of this service. The Boat Dock also has a schedule of weekend excursions that are guided by the staff. These allow customers to do overnight trips with the help of a guide to make the trip as enjoyable as possible. All these attributes give The Boat Dock competitive advantages over the large non-customer oriented franchises. We will be offering most of these services and will complete directly in the areas of shuttles and trips.

Sled and Hike is a store located on Camden Circle in the Esposito shopping center. The store is about 5,000 square feet and has eight employees. The store has been around for over twenty years and has been located all over Somersville. They feel this is their best location they have chosen (Gayhartt). They offer mid to top of the line outdoor gear. The gear they sell ranges from backpacking, skiing equipment, boots, and sandals. This is just some of the items our store will keep in stock. Sled and Hike has a very customer oriented sales approach. They feel the customer is number one and their training is evolved around this idea (Gayhartt). Their staff is trained on all the merchandise and can be very helpful by pointing the customer in the direction of what product he or she might need. They also know the products and point out the advantages and disadvantages to help the consumer make a decision. We feel their weakness is the lack of gear they stock. There is a limited amount of equipment you can purchase at their store and their merchandise is more expensive. They do have a great location because of the wealth that is located out in the Highpoint area. This will be another strong competitor that we will have to watch very carefully.

Dave's Sporting Goods Store is a store that might have a couple of products that overlap with ours but they concentrate their merchandise on hunting and fishing and we feel this will have a minimum effect on our store's performance.

With these local competitors, we feel we still have many competitive advantages to offer to the consumer. The first will be having all the products that consist with the three stores under one roof. Consumers will be able to shop for all their extreme sports and outdoor equipment needs. We will also have great customer service. Customer service is very important when selling equipment to the experience and inexperienced consumer. We will train our staff to be very informed on products and merchandise that we sell. This will give the employees resources to help the customer and pass along any information the consumer is lacking. We will also have a great location on North Monroe. This will locate us away from the other competitors but allow us to capture the traffic of Somersville Mall. We feel we can attract all of Somersville to come shop at our store located in this area. In our study, we found that people will drive 45 miles to go an outdoors shop. We feel this will help our store become a success and compete in the existing market.

Comment: They have done a thorough analysis of their competition.

Financial Assessment

Searching for a potential business start-up, we were drawn to an area that we both felt very comfortable with, extreme outdoor sports. The market is showing increases in these sports now more than ever. With the possibility for a large demand and profitable future, we decided to invest deeply into building our company from the ground up. The construction of the facility was estimated by G-Man Design Construction to be near $1,000,000. The property for our site is owned by Somersville Land Real Estate, and is priced at $550,000 for the acre and one half. The land and building make up close to 75% of the projected start-up cost, which is between $2,000,000 and $2,200,000. The initial inventory is estimated to be $720,000 (60% of projected sales). Equipment was projected at a cost of $22,000 in comparison with industry norms. From these estimates, the first year will cost somewhere in the neighborhood of $2,122,000.

We were fortunate enough to have investments given to us by our parents. John's parents donated the down payment for the land that ended up being $100,000. Benny's parents contributed the down payment for the land, which was $50,000. Both grants enabled us to capture these loans, both of which have an

11% interest rate. With the amortization of these long-term debts, we were able to spread the debt out.

Comment:
Need to include information on potential profits in this summary. No mention is made of required collateral for these large loans and the monthly costs to service this large amount of debt. (Developing financial statements will be discussed in greater detail in the financial section of this book).

Wild Times <u>Assumptions for Financial Statements</u>

Income Statement:

Sales Revenue was predicted from the population of the target market, and the market share we believe to consume. The traffic count was also taken into consideration for this estimate. In the second year, our sales increased by 10%, and 11% in the third year.

Cost of Goods represents 60% of sales.

Fixed Expenses include salary, payroll, and depreciation. These are affected in the second year due to a 33% increase in the owner's salary. In the third year, the company hires a manager on salary for $25,000/year. The owner's salary takes another increase of 33% in year three also.

Variable Expenses are allocated at 5% of sales for the first year. After the first year, we slow down advertising and calculate variable expenses at 4%.

Interest is accrued from the long-term debt.

Balance Sheet:

Cash is derived from 16% of gross sales.

Accounts Receivable is only 3% of sales. This number is very low because most purchases will be at the point-of-sale with either cash or credit card. However, we will offer financing for our most expensive products. This financing will include a 10% down payment and a customized payment plan.

Inventory will consume 60% of sales.

Plant and Equipment will see increases due to technological integration within the workplace. These fixed assets are 125% of sales.

Accounts Payable are 30% of sales.

Notes payable consists of smaller equipment.

Long-term debt is the decreasing payment of the building and land.

Owner's Equity is the residual value found from the difference between total assets and total liabilities.

Cash Budget:

Purchases were allocated to be 60% of sales.

Accounts receivables were 3% of sales. For these receivables, we demanded 50% of the sale price down, 25% in the following month, and 25% in the final month.

The Cash Disbursements were taken off of the Income Statements and Balance Sheets, as well as the Estimated Start-up Expenses.

Wild Times					
Balance Sheet as of					
31st of December					
		2000	**2001**	**2002**	
Assets					
Current assets					
Cash		$ 192,000	$ 209,440	$ 232,478	
Accounts Receivable		$ 36,000	$ 39,270	$ 43,590	
Inventory		$ 720,000	$ 785,400	$ 871,794	
Total		$ 948,000	$1,034,110	$1,147,862	
Fixed assets					
Plant and Equipment		$1,500,000	$1,636,250	$1,816,238	
Total Assets		**$2,448,000**	**$2,670,360**	**$2,964,100**	
Liabilities and Owner's Equity					
Current liabilities					
Accounts Payable		$ 360,000	$ 392,700	$ 435,897	
Notes Payable		$ 40,000	$ 40,000	$ 40,000	
		$ 14,080	$ 18,040	$ 11,440	
Total		$ 400,000	$ 432,700	$ 475,897	
Long-term debt		$1,350,000	$1,168,440	$1,006,851	
Owner's Equity		$ 648,000	$1,069,220	$1,481,352	
Total Liabilities and Owner's Equity		$2,448,000	$2,670,360	$2,964,100	

Wild Times					
Income Statement for the Year					
Ending December 31, 2002					
Sales Revenue				1,452,990	
Cost of Goods Sold				871,794	
Gross Profit				581,196	
Operating Expenses:					
Fixed Expenses				214,804	
Depreciation					
building				33,336	
land				22,008	
Variable Expenses				58,120	
(4% of sales)					
Total Operating Expense				328,268	
Operating Income				252,928	
Interest Expense				111,589	
EBT				141,339	
Income Tax (34%)				48,055	
Net Income				93,284	

Wild Times				
2001 Income Statement				
(Quarterly)				
	March	**June**	**September**	**December**
Sales Revenue	$ 220,000	$ 352,000	$ 451,000	$ 286,000
Cost of Goods Sold	$ 132,000	$ 211,200	$ 270,600	$ 171,600
Gross Profit	$ 88,000	$ 140,800	$ 180,400	$ 114,400
Operating Expenses:				
Fixed Expenses	$ 43,701	$ 43,701	$ 43,701	$ 43,701
Depreciation				
building	$ 8,334	$ 8,334	$ 8,334	$ 8,334
land	$ 5,502	$ 5,502	$ 5,502	$ 5,502
Variable Expenses				
(4% of sales)	$ 8,800	$ 14,080	$ 18,040	$ 11,440
Total Operating Expense	$ 66,337	$ 71,617	$ 75,577	$ 68,977
Operating Income	$ 21,663	$ 69,183	$ 104,823	$ 45,423
Interest Expense	$ 32,891	$ 32,891	$ 32,891	$ 32,891
EBT	$ (11,228)	$ 36,292	$ 71,932	$ 12,532
Income Tax (34%)	$ -	$ 8,422	$ 19,438	$ 1,078
Net Income	$ (11,228)	$ 27,870	$ 52,494	$ 11,454

Wild Times

Cash Budget 2000

	December	January	February	March	April	May	June	July	August	September	October	November	December
Monthly Sales	$ 75,000	$ 60,000	$ 65,000	$ 75,000	$ 90,000	$ 100,000	$ 130,000	$ 150,000	$ 140,000	$ 120,000	$ 100,000	$ 80,000	$ 80,000
Cash Receipts													
Cash Sales for Month		$ 59,100	$ 64,025	$ 73,875	$ 88,650	$ 98,500	$ 128,050	$ 147,750	$ 137,900	$ 118,200	$ 98,500	$ 78,800	$ 78,800
1 Month after Sale			$ 450	$ 488	$ 563	$ 675	$ 750	$ 975	$ 1,125	$ 1,050	$ 900	$ 750	$ 600
2 Month after Sale				$ 450	$ 488	$ 563	$ 675	$ 750	$ 975	$ 1,125	$ 1,050	$ 900	$ 750
Total		$ 59,100	$ 64,475	$ 74,813	$ 89,700	$ 99,738	$ 129,475	$ 149,475	$ 140,000	$ 120,375	$ 100,450	$ 80,450	$ 80,150
Purchases (60% of Sales)	$ 42,000	$ 45,000	$ 36,000	$ 39,000	$ 45,000	$ 54,000	$ 60,000	$ 78,000	$ 90,000	$ 84,000	$ 72,000	$ 60,000	$ 48,000
Cash Disbursements													
Payments on Purchases		$ 42,000	$ 45,000	$ 36,000	$ 39,000	$ 45,000	$ 54,000	$ 60,000	$ 78,000	$ 90,000	$ 84,000	$ 72,000	$ 60,000
Mortgage		$ 4,167	$ 4,167	$ 4,167	$ 4,167	$ 4,167	$ 4,167	$ 4,167	$ 4,167	$ 4,167	$ 4,167	$ 4,167	$ 4,167
Wages and Salaries		$ 7,000	$ 7,000	$ 7,000	$ 7,000	$ 7,000	$ 7,000	$ 7,000	$ 7,000	$ 7,000	$ 7,000	$ 7,000	$ 7,000
Tax Prepayment					$ 251	$ 1,441	$ 5,011	$ 7,391	$ 6,201	$ 3,821	$ 1,441	$ -	
Utilities		$ 1,000	$ 1,000	$ 1,000	$ 1,000	$ 1,000	$ 1,000	$ 1,000	$ 1,000	$ 1,000	$ 1,000	$ 1,000	$ 1,000
Interest on long-term note		$ 12,833	$ 12,833	$ 12,833	$ 12,833	$ 12,833	$ 12,833	$ 12,833	$ 12,833	$ 12,833	$ 12,833	$ 12,833	$ 12,833
Total Cash													
Disbursements		$ 67,000	$ 70,000	$ 61,000	$ 64,251	$ 71,441	$ 84,011	$ 92,391	$ 109,201	$ 118,821	$ 110,441	$ 97,000	$ 85,000
Net change in cash		$ (7,900)	$ (5,525)	$ 13,813	$ 25,449	$ 28,297	$ 45,464	$ 57,084	$ 30,799	$ 1,554	$ (9,991)	$ (16,550)	$ (4,850)
Beginning Cash Balance		$ 16,000	$ 16,000	$ 16,000	$ 16,000	$ 16,000	$ 16,000	$ 16,000	$ 16,000	$ 16,000	$ 16,000	$ 16,000	$ 16,000
Cash before borrowing		$ 8,100	$ 10,475	$ 29,813	$ 41,449	$ 44,297	$ 61,464	$ 73,084	$ 46,799	$ 17,554	$ 6,009	$ (550)	$ 11,150

41

So You Need to Write a Business Plan!

	January	February	March	April	May	June	July	August	September	October	November	December
Short-term borrowing (payment)	$ 7,900	5525	$ (13,813)	$ (25,449)	$ (28,297)	$ (45,464)	$ (57,084)	$ (30,799)	$ (1,554)	9,991	16,550	4,850
Ending Cash Balance	$ 16,000	$ 16,000	$ 16,000	$ 16,000	$ 16,000	$ 16,000	$ 16,000	$ 16,000	$ 16,000	$ 16,000	$ 16,000	$ 16,000
Cumulative short-term												
debt outstanding	$ 7,900	$ 13,425	$ (388)	$ (25,837)	$ (54,133)	$ (99,597)	$ (156,681)	$ (187,480)	$ (189,034)	$ (179,043)	$ (162,493)	$ (157,643)

Wild Times
Cash Budget 2001

	January	February	March	April	May	June	July	August	September	October	November	December
Monthly Sales	$ 66,000	$ 71,500	$ 82,500	$ 99,000	$ 110,000	$ 143,000	$ 165,000	$ 154,000	$ 132,000	$ 110,000	$ 88,000	$ 88,000
Cash Receipts												
Cash Sales for Month	$ 65,010	$ 70,428	$ 81,263	$ 97,515	$ 108,350	$ 140,855	$ 162,525	$ 151,690	$ 130,020	$ 108,350	$ 86,680	$ 86,680
1 Month after Sale	$ 600	$ 495	$ 536	$ 619	$ 743	$ 825	$ 1,073	$ 1,238	$ 1,155	$ 990	$ 825	$ 660
2 Month after Sale	$ 600	$ 600	$ 495	$ 536	$ 619	$ 743	$ 825	$ 1,073	$ 1,238	$ 1,155	$ 990	$ 825
Total	$ 66,210	$ 71,523	$ 82,294	$ 98,670	$ 109,711	$ 142,423	$ 164,423	$ 154,000	$ 132,413	$ 110,495	$ 88,495	$ 88,165
Purchases (60% of Sales)	$ 48,000	$ 39,600	$ 42,900	$ 49,500	$ 59,400	$ 66,000	$ 85,800	$ 99,000	$ 92,400	$ 79,200	$ 66,000	$ 52,800
Cash Disbursements												
Payments on Purchases	$ 80,000	$ 48,000	$ 39,600	$ 42,900	$ 49,500	$ 59,400	$ 66,000	$ 85,800	$ 99,000	$ 92,400	$ 79,200	$ 66,000
Mortgage	$ 4,167	$ 4,167	$ 4,167	$ 4,167	$ 4,167	$ 4,167	$ 4,167	$ 4,167	$ 4,167	$ 4,167	$ 4,167	$ 4,167
Wages and Salaries	$ 8,250	$ 8,250	$ 8,250	$ 8,250	$ 8,250	$ 8,250	$ 8,250	$ 8,250	$ 8,250	$ 8,250	$ 8,250	$ 8,250
Tax Prepayment			$ -			$ 8,422			$ 19,438			$ 1,078

	January	February	March	April	May	June	July	August	September	October	November	December
Utilities	$ 1,000	$ 1,000	$ 1,000	$ 1,000	$ 1,000	$ 1,000	$ 1,000	$ 1,000	$ 1,000	$ 1,000	$ 1,000	$ 1,000
Interest on long-term note	$ 10,964	$ 10,964	$ 10,964	$ 10,964	$ 10,964	$ 10,964	$ 10,964	$ 10,964	$ 10,964	$ 10,964	$ 10,964	$ 10,964
Total Cash												
Disbursements	$ 84,381	$ 72,381	$ 63,981	$ 67,281	$ 73,881	$ 92,203	$ 90,381	$ 110,181	$ 142,819	$ 116,781	$ 103,581	$ 91,459
Net change in cash	$ (18,171)	$ (859)	$ 18,313	$ 31,389	$ 35,830	$ 50,220	$ 74,042	$ 43,819	$ 10,407	$ 6,266	$ (15,086)	$ (3,294)
Beginning Cash Balance	$ 16,000	$ 16,000	$ 16,000	$ 16,000	$ 16,000	$ 16,000	$ 16,000	$ 16,000	$ 16,000	$ 16,000	$ 16,000	$ 16,000
Cash before borrowing	$ (2,171)	$ 15,142	$ 34,313	$ 47,389	$ 51,830	$ 66,220	$ 90,042	$ 59,819	$ 5,594	$ 9,714	$ 914	$ 12,706
Short-term borrowing												
(payment)	$ 18,171	$ 859	$ (18,313)	$ (31,389)	$ (35,830)	$ (50,220)	$ (74,042)	$ (43,819)	$ 10,407	$ 6,286	$ 15,086	$ 3,294
Ending Cash Balance	$ 16,000	$ 16,000	$ 16,000	$ 16,000	$ 16,000	$ 16,000	$ 16,000	$ 16,000	$ 16,000	$ 16,000	$ 16,000	$ 16,000
Cumulative short-term												
debt outstanding	$(199,510)	$(198,652)	$ 216,964	$(246,353)	$(284,184)	$(334,403)	$(408,445)	$(452,264)	$(441,857)	$(435,571)	$(420,485)	$(417,191)

Wild Times

Cash Budget 2002

	January	February	March	April	May	June	July	August	September	October	November	December
Monthly Sales	$ 73,260	$ 79,365	$ 91,575	$ 109,890	$ 122,100	$ 158,730	$ 183,150	$ 170,940	$ 146,520	$ 122,100	$ 97,680	$ 97,680
Cash Receipts												
Cash Sales for Month	$ 72,161	$ 78,175	$ 90,201	$ 108,242	$ 120,269	$ 156,349	$ 180,403	$ 168,376	$ 144,322	$ 120,269	$ 96,215	$ 96,215
1 Month after Sale	$ 600	$ 549	$ 595	$ 687	$ 824	$ 916	$ 1,190	$ 1,374	$ 1,282	$ 1,099	$ 916	$ 733

2 Month after Sale	$ 600	$ 600	$ 549	$ 595	$ 687	$ 824	$ 916	$ 1,190	$ 1,374	$ 1,282	$ 1,099	$ 916
Total	$ 73,361	$ 79,324	$ 91,346	$ 109,524	$ 121,779	$ 158,089	$ 182,509	$ 170,940	$ 146,978	$ 122,649	$ 98,229	$ 97,863
Purchases (60% of Sales)	$ 48,000	$ 43,956	$ 47,619	$ 54,945	$ 65,934	$ 73,260	$ 95,238	$ 109,890	$ 102,564	$ 87,912	$ 73,260	$ 58,608
Cash Disbursements												
Payments on Purchases	$ 60,000	$ 48,000	$ 43,956	$ 47,619	$ 54,945	$ 65,934	$ 73,260	$ 95,238	$ 109,890	$ 102,564	$ 87,912	$ 73,260
Mortgage	$ 4,167	$ 4,167	$ 4,167	$ 4,167	$ 4,167	$ 4,167	$ 4,167	$ 4,167	$ 4,167	$ 4,167	$ 4,167	$ 4,167
Wages and Salaries	$ 12,000	$ 12,000	$ 12,000	$ 12,000	$ 12,000	$ 12,000	$ 8,250	$ 12,000	$ 12,000	$ 12,000	$ 12,000	$ 12,000
Tax Prepayment			$ 8,076			$ 12,922			$ 16,557			$ 10,500
Utilities	$ 1,000	$ 1,000	$ 1,000	$ 1,000	$ 1,000	$ 1,000	$ 1,000	$ 1,000	$ 1,000	$ 1,000	$ 1,000	$ 1,000
Interest on long-term note	$ 10,964	$ 10,964	$ 10,964	$ 10,964	$ 10,964	$ 10,964	$ 10,964	$ 10,964	$ 10,964	$ 10,964	$ 10,964	$ 10,964
Total Cash												
Disbursements	$ 88,131	$ 76,131	$ 80,163	$ 75,750	$ 83,076	$ 106,987	$ 101,391	$ 123,369	$ 154,578	$ 130,695	$ 116,043	$ 111,891
Net change in cash	$ (14,770)	$ 3,193	$ 11,183	$ 33,774	$ 38,703	$ 51,102	$ 81,118	$ 47,571	$ (7,600)	$ (8,046)	$ (17,814)	$ (14,028)
Beginning Cash Balance	$ 16,000	$ 16,000	$ 16,000	$ 16,000	$ 16,000	$ 16,000	$ 16,000	$ 16,000	$ 16,000	$ 16,000	$ 16,000	$ 16,000
Cash before borrowing	$ 1,230	$ 19,193	$ 27,183	$ 49,774	$ 54,703	$ 67,102	$ 97,118	$ 63,571	$ 8,400	$ 7,954	$ (1,814)	$ 1,972
Short-term borrowing												
(payment)	$ 14,770	$ (3,193)	$ (11,183)	$ (33,774)	$ (38,703)	$ (51,102)	$ (81,118)	$ (47,571)	$ 7,600	$ 8,046	$ 17,814	$ 14,028
Ending Cash Balance	$ 16,000	$ 16,000	$ 16,000	$ 16,000	$ 16,000	$ 16,000	$ 16,000	$ 16,000	$ 16,000	$ 16,000	$ 16,000	$ 16,000
Cumulative short-term												
debt outstanding	$(402,421)	$(405,614)	$(416,797)	$(450,571)	$(489,274)	$(540,376)	$(621,494)	$(669,065)	$(661,465)	$(653,420)	$(635,606)	$(621,578)

Wild Times
2000 Income Statement
(monthly)

	January	February	March	April	May	June	July	August	September	October	November	December
Sales Revenue	$ 60,000	$ 65,000	$ 75,000	$ 90,000	$ 100,000	$ 130,000	$ 150,000	$ 140,000	$ 120,000	$ 100,000	$ 80,000	$ 80,000
Cost of Goods Sold	$ 36,000	$ 39,000	$ 45,000	$ 54,000	$ 60,000	$ 78,000	$ 90,000	$ 84,000	$ 72,000	$ 60,000	$ 48,000	$ 48,000
Gross Profit	$ 24,000	$ 26,000	$ 30,000	$ 36,000	$ 40,000	$ 52,000	$ 60,000	$ 56,000	$ 48,000	$ 40,000	$ 32,000	$ 32,000
Operating Expenses:												
Fixed Expenses	$ 13,317	$ 13,317	$ 13,317	$ 13,317	$ 13,317	$ 13,317	$ 13,317	$ 13,317	$ 13,317	$ 13,317	$ 13,317	$ 13,317
Depreciation												
building	$ 2,778	$ 2,778	$ 2,778	$ 2,778	$ 2,778	$ 2,778	$ 2,778	$ 2,778	$ 2,778	$ 2,778	$ 2,778	$ 2,778
land	$ 1,834	$ 1,834	$ 1,834	$ 1,834	$ 1,834	$ 1,834	$ 1,834	$ 1,834	$ 1,834	$ 1,834	$ 1,834	$ 1,834
Variable Expenses	$ 3,000	$ 3,250	$ 3,750	$ 4,500	$ 5,000	$ 6,500	$ 7,500	$ 7,000	$ 6,000	$ 5,000	$ 4,000	$ 4,000
(5% of sales, Year1)												
Total Operating Exp.	$ 20,929	$ 21,179	$ 21,679	$ 22,429	$ 22,929	$ 24,429	$ 25,429	$ 24,929	$ 23,929	$ 22,929	$ 21,929	$ 21,929
Operating Income	$ 3,071	$ 4,821	$ 8,321	$ 13,571	$ 17,071	$ 27,571	$ 34,571	$ 31,071	$ 24,071	$ 17,071	$ 10,071	$ 10,071
Interest Expense	$ 12,834	$ 12,834	$ 12,834	$ 12,834	$ 12,834	$ 12,834	$ 12,834	$ 12,834	$ 12,834	$ 12,834	$ 12,834	$ 12,834
EBT	$ (9,763)	$ (8,013)	$ (4,513)	$ 737	$ 4,237	$ 14,737	$ 21,737	$ 18,237	$ 11,237	$ 4,237	$ (2,763)	$ (2,763)
Income tax (34%)	$ -	$ -	$ -	$ 251	$ 1,441	$ 5,011	$ 7,391	$ 6,201	$ 3,821	$ 1,441	$ -	$ -
Net Income	$ (9,763)	$ (8,013)	$ (4,513)	$ 486	$ 2,796	$ 9,726	$ 14,346	$ 12,036	$ 7,416	$ 2,796	$ (2,763)	$ (2,763)

Purchase of Land and Building

The acre and 1/2 of land that was purchased off of N. Monroe was quoted at $550,000. The loan was formatted as an amortization loan and called for a minimum down payment of 9%. Benny's parents were kind enough to give the business a $50,000 grant. This was used for the down payment on the loan. The remaining $500,000 was amortized over 25 years with an interest rate of 11%. Here is the amortization schedule for the first 5 years.

Year	Beginning Balance	Total Payment	Interest Payment	Principal Paid
1	$500,000	$75,000	$55,000	$20,000
2	425,000	66,750	46,750	20,000
3	358,250	59,408	39,408	20,000
4	298,842	55,873	32,873	20,000
5	242,960	46,727	26,727	20,000

The building that was erected encompasses 25,000 square feet. This warehouse models a Sam's on a smaller scale. Because of the size, this building cost $40/sq. ft. This factors out to be approximately $1,000,000. The bank requires a 10% down payment on such a loan. John's parents were gracious enough to grant the 10% ($100,000), in order to get the business started. The remaining $900,000 was amortized over 30 years with an interest rate of 11%. The following amortization schedule shows payments for the first five years.

Year	Beginning Balance	Total Payment	Interest Payment	Principal Paid
1	$900,000	$129,000	$99,000	$30,000
2	771,000	114,810	84,810	30,000
3	656,190	102,181	72,181	30,000
4	554,009	90,941	60,941	30,000
5	463,068	80,937	50,937	30,000

Wild Times						
Start Up Expenses						
ITEM				**Range**		
Mortgage (1st month of principal and interest)						
Building				10,000	to	11,500
Land				5,000	to	7,000
Initial Inventory				450,000	to	600,000
Equipment/Fixtures						
Sales Counters (3)				2,100	to	2,800
Signage				1,500	to	2,500
Computers (4)				8,500	to	12,000
Security System				3,000	to	4,000
Office Supplies				400	to	600
Office Equipment				750	to	1,500
Display Racks				1,500	to	3,000
Special Displays				300	to	800
Tags/Labels				40	to	75
Clothing Racks				400	to	1,200
Shelving				3,000	to	5,000
Miscellaneous				500	to	1,000
Licenses/Permits				400	to	600
Grand Opening/Advertising				5,500	to	6,500
Utilities/Phone				100	to	400
Professional Services				2,000	to	3,000
Owner/Operator Salary				3,500	to	4,000
Payroll				3,000	to	3,500
Insurance (1st quarter)				1,200	to	1,600
Miscellaneous				600	to	800
Total				**$ 503,290.00**	**to**	**$ 673,375.00**

Comment: They have been thorough in the development of financials. Need to clarify how they determined variable and fixed expenses in their statement of assumptions.

The following is another sample feasibility study. The previous example was weak in market analysis whereas this study is strong in this area. The previous study did a very good job on the competitive analysis whereas the following study does not do as good a job. Both are comparable on the financial sections.

Example Feasibility Study: ABH FURNITURE CO.

Market Analysis

There are quite a few furniture stores in Arlington but not very many that offer higher end furniture as well as one of a kind merchandise. We do feel that there is an opportunity in this city for our business to be successful. As long as people are buying houses there will be a need for furniture. Furniture styles may change with the times but furniture itself is not a trend and it will be around for a long time. Our market is people between the ages of twenty-five and forty-nine with an income of $35,000+. We feel that this is a good range because most people of this age will be out of school and in salary paying jobs. Our furniture is more expensive than most stores in town so we will be attracting customers with a higher income.

To determine our market potential, we took the percentage of people in Lincoln County between the ages of 25-49 (39.1%) and multiplied it by the MSA population (246,400.) We then took that figure (96,342) and multiplied it by the percentage of households with incomes of $35,000+ (60.7.) We determined that there are 58,479 people in Lincoln County in our age range with the appropriate income. From this number, we used Simmons Study of Media and Market to determine our market potential for furniture. We picked our top six sales items to do these figures: mattress and box spring set, bed frame and headboard, recliners, couch, sofa, or loveseat, dining room furniture, and area rugs. Then to find out the market potential we multiplied the percent of people who purchased these items in the last twelve months by our population figure (58,479.) Once we got that number, we multiplied it by the average expenditure, which was $1000. We repeated those steps for each of our top six items and then added them together. Our final figure for market potential was $7,689,000. The percentage of people purchasing those specific Items as well as the average expenditure came from Simmons Study of Media and Market.

After determining the market potential, we felt very sure that Arlington could support another furniture store. While there may be over fifty furniture stores in the area, our direct competition was a much smaller number. We will discuss our competition further in our competitive analysis. After analyzing the information in our 1990 Census

Data provided by Lincoln County Planning Department, we determined that the best location for our business is in census tract 24.02 between Meridian Road and Thomasville Road. This looked like a promising area for a number of reasons. Our product is not a convenience product therefore it is not imperative that our business be located within a mile of our customer base. However, we do feel that our business should be located in an area that houses as many of our potential customers as possible for their convenience. In this particular area we will be focusing on eight different census tracts. It is from these eight tracts that the following information comes from. Out of the 26,662 people who live in this area 55% are in our target age range. The median household income for these residents is $44,462.37. There are 18,240 housing units in this area and the median home value is $94,075. From the information we have gathered, we believe that there is a substantial market for our product.

Comment: They have done an excellent job in determining and describing their market potential.

ABH FURNITURE CO. Market Potentials

MSA population	246,400
People in Lincoln Co. (age 25-49)	<u>39.1</u>
	96,342
Households with Incomes (35,000+)	<u>60.7</u>
People with Appropriate Income	**58,479**
People with Appropriate Income	58,479
Purchasing Mattress/Box Spring Set	<u>2.70%</u>
	1,579
Average Expenditure	<u>$1,000</u>
Current Mkt. Potential	1,579,000
People with Appropriate Income	58,479
Purchasing Bed frame/Headboard	<u>1.10%</u>
	643
Average Expenditure	$1,000
Current Mkt. Potential	643,000
People with Appropriate Income	58,479
Purchasing Recliners	<u>1.60%</u>
	936
Average Expenditure	<u>$1,000</u>
Current Mkt. Potential	936,000
People with Appropriate Income	58,479
Purchasing Couch, Sofa, Loveseat	<u>5.30%</u>
	3,099
Average Expenditure	<u>$1,000</u>
Current Mkt. Potential	3,099,000
People with Appropriate Income	58,479
Purchasing Dining Room Furniture	<u>1.70%</u>
	994
Average Expenditure	<u>$1,000</u>
Current Mkt. Potential	994,000
People with Appropriate Income	58,479
Purchasing Area Rugs	<u>0.50%</u>
	292
Average Expenditure	<u>$1,500</u>
Current Mkt. Potential	438,000

Competitive Analysis

After looking in the phone book, we found that there were over fifty retail furniture stores in the Arlington area. However, based on our inventory and price range, we were able to narrow it down to seven direct competitors. These seven stores are all represented under the business category of attractive small firms. They carry the variety of merchandise that we plan to offer and their prices fall with in the mid to upper range. Each store also offers similar services, which include such things as special orders, delivery and financing plans to their customers. Based on these facts, we can assume that they will be going after the same target market as us, making them our direct competitors. Therefore, we hope to distinguish our store from the others by offering one of a kind merchandise to our customers in addition to our other inventory. We also plan to keep our advertising budget relatively high so as to compete with places such as Harvey's, Rhetts, and Thompsons, who all have a higher advertising budget compared to the other direct competitors.

The other 43+ furniture stores we considered represented our indirect competition. Like our direct competitors, these businesses all represented attractive small firms. However, they distinguished themselves as our indirect competitors because of their different or added merchandise and their price range. While some of the stores specialized in bedroom furniture, antiques, or unfinished furniture, other included electronics, appliances, carpet, and draperies in their inventory. The other stores, who offered similar merchandise in comparison to our inventory, were able to offer a lower price to their customer base because the products were of lower quality.

In addition to the retail stores in Arlington, we included the Internet and catalogs, such as Pottery Barn and Crate and Barrel under our indirect competition. They set themselves a part from our store because they represent high-potential ventures. We classified them as this because we felt as though they are the companies who are able to reach more people at lower costs and are quick to adapt to the changing markets. The Internet is able to reach almost any target market by offering different sites that have a variety of merchandise and price ranges. The catalog companies set themselves apart by offering a unique product that can't normally be found in retail stores. They also offer a wider range of products by extending their inventory into areas such as the kitchen and bathroom.

In looking at the list of all our competitors, there are no specific companies who we feel are expected to make bigger gains in the market. Instead, we believe the companies who will make the biggest gains are the ones who can read the market the best as the industry changes over the next few years. Based on this information, we needed to find out where the industry was headed. So, we turned to Jill's's Dad, who has owned his own furniture business for over fifteen years. His response was summed up with three words, "leather and microfiber." In a recent article in Home Furnishing News, it stated that the "consumer demand remains high" in reference to leather (Buchanan, 4). The problem is that the mad cow disease is not only affecting the food supply, it is also affecting the amount of hides available. This in turn is helping to push leather prices even higher, which creates a threat that could push "leather upholstery out of the mass market that has made it the hottest category in furniture" (Buchanan, 4). Since predictions only see leather prices increasing, the furniture market can expect two things to happen. The first one being that the lower-end leather competitors will be driven out of the market and the second being an increase in the production of microfiber, an expensive alternative to leather. With over "40 percent of all upholstery sold in Europe" being mircofiber, the US can expect this alternative trend to carry over (Buchanan, 4).

With all this information, we feel that we can still create a unique store that will be able to compete effectively against our competitors. We have selected a great location based on the amount of people and their incomes in the surrounding areas. We feel that we will be able to draw our customers in based on our products and customer service. Consumers will be able to choose from a vast selection of the higher end furniture venders, which will allow us to compete in the ever-growing trends of leather and microfiber. They will also have a selection of one of a kind products, and each individual will be able to custom design their furniture if we don't offer what they are looking for. As for customer service, we feel that it is important for all of our sales staff to be trained and able to offer each customer the best knowledge on the products. With these ideas combined, we feel that we will be able to compete successfully in our target market.

Comment: They have not carefully analyzed the seven main competitors nor reviewed the indirect.

ABH FURNITURE CO. Financial Analysis

With a furniture store in mind, we examined the census data and found a location surrounded by the appropriate target market. We decided on a location between Meridian Road and Thomasville Road and found an 8000 square foot building for lease. The cost was $13 per square foot. We also turned to the newspaper, where we found our warehouse. It is located on Apalachee Parkway and cost us $1575 per month. These items were included in our start-up cost, which totaled $322,841.66. We decided to take out a $400,000 loan to be used towards these costs. South Bank gave the loan to us at a 9% fixed interest rate over six years.

Assumptions

Income Statement:

The current market potential and the percent of the market that we believe we will capture predicted sales Revenue. During our first year of business we estimated that our market share would fluctuate between 1% and 2%. We took into consideration different events during the year where our sales might be down such as Income Taxes in April as well as the Christmas season starting in November. These were two times during the year that we felt our market share would be down because there is not as much disposable income to spend on furniture.

We determined our sales growth to be 5% in our second year as well as another 5% in our third year. Our Cost of Goods Sold is 55%. Salaries and benefits in year one is 10% but then grows to 12% in year two and year three so that we can provide a salary to the owners. This accounts for our decrease in net income.

Our interest comes from a $4000,000 bank note with a fixed 9% interest rate over 6 years.

Our rent for or store is based on an 8,000 square foot store with rent of $13 a square foot. The warehouse we picked was listed as $1575 a month.

Balance Sheet:

Cash was determined as 25% of sales revenue. Accounts Receivable made up for the remaining 75%. This was determined because many of our customers will have open balances until their furniture is delivered.

Inventory consumed 22% of sales revenue. This was based on the square footage of our store and warehouse and how much furniture we can keep in stock. We figure that a majority of our sales will be special order.

Accounts Payable is 45% of sales revenue.

Long-term debt is decreasing payments of our $400,000 bank note.

Owner's Equity is the residual value found from the difference between total assets and total liabilities.

Cash Budget:

Our purchases were 22% of sales revenue.

Accounts Receivable was 75% of sales with a down payment of 25%, and then the remainder was split between the next two months each at 37.5%.

The remaining numbers were taken from our estimated financial statements and start-up expenses.

ABH FURNITURE CO. Balance Sheet

	2001	2002	2003
Assets			
Current assets:			
Cash	$ 311,404.50	$ 326,974.72	$ 343,323.46
Accounts Receivable	$ 934,213.50	$ 980,924.18	$1,029,970.39
Inventory	$ 280,000.00	$ 287,737.76	$ 302,124.65
Total Assets	**$1,525,618.00**	**$1,595,636.66**	**$1,675,418.50**
Liabilities/Owner's Equity			
Current liabilities:			
Accounts Payable	$ 560,528.10	$ 588,554.51	$ 617,982.23
Total	$ 560,528.10	$ 588,554.51	$ 617,982.23
Long Term Debt	$ 333,333.28	$ 266,666.56	$ 199,999.84
Owner's Equity	$ 585,313.77	$ 703,015.92	$ 812,267.85
Retained Earnings	$ 46,442.85	$ 37,399.67	$ 45,168.58
Total Liabilities and Owner's Equity	**$1,525,618.00**	**$1,595,636.66**	**$1,675,418.50**

ABH FURNITURE CO. Cash Budget 2001

January	Februar	March	April	May	June	July	August	September	October	November	December

		y										
Monthly Sales	$76,890.00	$76,890.00	$76,890.00	$61,512.00	$76,890.00	$92,268.00	$107,646.00	$123,024.00	$138,402.00	$153,780.00	$138,402.00	$123,024.00
Cash Receipts												
Cash Sales for Month	$19,222.50	$19,222.50	$19,222.50	$15,378.00	$1,922.50	$23,067.00	$26,911.50	$30,756.00	$34,600.50	$38,445.00	$34,600.50	$30,756.00
1 Month after Sale		$28,833.75	$28,833.75	$28,833.75	$23,067.00	$28,833.75	$34,600.50	$40,367.25	$46,134.00	$51,900.75	$7,667.50	$51,900.75
2 Month after Sale			$28,833.75	$28,833.75	$28,833.75	$23,067.00	$28,833.75	$34,600.50	$40,367.25	$46,134.00	$1,900.75	$57,667.50
Total	$19,222.50	$48,056.25	$76,890.00	$73,045.50	$71,123.25	$74,967.75	$90,345.75	$105,723.75	$121,101.75	136,479.75	$144,168.75	$139,324.25
Purchases (22%)	$16,915.80	$16,915.80	$16,915.80	$13,532.64	$16,915.80	$20,298.96	$23,682.12	$27,065.28	$30,448.44	$33,831.60	$30,448.44	$27,065.28
Cash Disbursements												
Payments on Purchases		$16,915.80	$16,915.80	$16,915.80	$13,532.64	$16,915.80	$20,298.96	$23,682.12	$27,065.28	$30,448.44	$33,831.60	$30,448.44
Rent	$10,241.66	$10,241.66	$10,241.66	$10,241.66	$10,241.66	$10,241.66	$10,241.66	$10,241.66	$10,241.66	$10,241.66	$10,241.66	$10,241.66
Truck Lease	$500.00	$500.00	$500.00	$500.00	$500.00	$500.00	$500.00	$500.00	$500.00	$500.00	$500.00	$500.00
Wages/Salaries	$7,689.00	$7,689.00	$7,689.00	$6,151.20	$7,689.00	$9,226.80	$10,764.60	$12,302.40	$13,840.20	$15,378.00	$13,840.20	$12,302.40
Utilities	$1,000.00	$1,000.00	$1,000.00	$1,000.00	$1,000.00	$1,000.00	$1,000.00	$1,000.00	$1,000.00	$1,000.00	$1,000.00	$1,000.00
Interest on Long-term	$1,654.64	$1,654.64	$1,654.64	$1,654.64	$1,654.64	$1,654.64	$1,654.64	$1,654.64	$1,654.64	$1,654.64	$1,654.64	$1,654.64
Total Cash Disbursement	$21,085.30	$37,101.10	$37,101.10	$35,563.30	$34,617.94	$39,538.90	$44,459.86	$49,380.82	$55,839.58	$59,222.74	$61,068.10	$55,187.04
Net Change in Cash	$(1,862.80)	$(17,878.60)	$(17,878.60)	$(20,185.00)	$15,395.44	$16,471.90	$(17,548.36)	$(18,624.82)	$(21,239.08)	$(20,777.74)	$26,467.60	$(24,431.14)

55

So You Need to Write a Business Plan!

ABH FURNITURE CO. Income Statement - 2001

	January	February	March	April	May	June	July	August	September	October	November	December
Sales Revenue	$76,890.00	$76,890.00	$76,890.00	$61,512.00	$76,890.00	$92,268.00	$107,646.00	$123,024.00	$138,402.00	$153,780.00	$138,402.00	$123,024.00
Cost of Goods Sold	$42,289.50	$42,289.50	$42,289.50	$33,831.60	$42,289.50	$50,747.40	$59,205.30	$67,663.20	$76,121.10	$84,579.00	$76,121.10	$67,663.20
Gross Profit	$34,600.50	$34,600.50	$34,600.50	$27,680.40	$34,600.50	$41,520.60	$48,440.70	$55,360.80	$62,280.90	$69,201.00	$62,280.90	$55,360.80
Operating Expenses:												
Salaries and Benefits	$7,689.00	$7,689.00	$7,689.00	$6,151.20	$7,689.00	$9,226.80	$10,764.60	$12,302.40	$13,840.20	$15,378.00	$13,840.20	$12,302.40
Rent (Store/Warehouse)	$10,241.66	$10,241.66	$10,241.66	$10,241.66	$10,241.66	$10,241.66	$10,241.66	$10,241.66	$10,241.66	$10,241.66	$10,241.66	$10,241.66
Truck Lease	$500.00	$500.00	$500.00	$500.00	$500.00	$500.00	$500.00	$500.00	$500.00	$500.00	$500.00	$500.00
Other Occupancy Exp.	$2,500.00	$2,500.00	$2,500.00	$2,500.00	$2,500.00	$2,500.00	$2,500.00	$2,500.00	$2,500.00	$2,500.00	$2,500.00	$2,500.00
Other Operating Exp.	$11,533.50	$11,533.50	$11,533.50	$9,226.80	$11,533.50	$13,840.20	$16,146.90	$18,453.60	$20,760.30	$23,067.00	$20,760.30	$18,453.60
Total Operating Expenses	$32,464.16	$32,464.16	$32,464.16	$28,619.66	$32,464.16	$36,308.66	$40,153.16	$43,997.66	$47,842.16	$51,686.66	$47,842.16	$43,997.66
Operating Income	$2,136.34	$2,136.34	$2,136.34	$(939.26)	$2,136.34	$5,211.94	$8,287.54	$11,363.14	$14,438.74	$17,514.00	$14,438.74	$11,363.14
Interest Expense	$1,654.64	$1,654.64	$1,654.64	$1,654.64	$1,654.64	$1,654.64	$1,654.64	$1,654.64	$1,654.64	$1,654.64	$1,654.84	$1,654.64
EBT	$481.70	$481.70	$481.70	$(2,593.90)	$481.70	$3,557.30	$6,632.90	$9,708.50	$12,784.10	$15,859.36	$12,784.10	$9,708.50
Income tax (34%)	$163.77	$163.77	$163.77	$(881.92)	$163.77	$1,209.48	$2,255.18	$3,300.89	$4,346.59	$5,392.18	$4,346.59	$3,300.89
Net Income	$317.93	$317.93	$317.93	$(1,711.98)	$317.93	$2,347.82	$4,377.72	$6,407.61	$8,437.51	$10,467.18	$8,437.51	$6,407.61

ABH FURNITURE CO. Income Statement - 2001, 2002, 2003

	2001		2002		2003	
Sales Revenue	$1,245,618.00		$1,307,898.90		$1,373,293.85	
Cost of Goods Sold	$ 685,089.90		$ 719,344.40		$ 755,311.62	
Gross Profit	$ 560,528.10		$ 588,554.50		$ 617,982.23	
Operating Expenses:						
Salaries and Benefits	$ 124,561.80		$ 156,947.86		$ 164,795.26	
Rent (Store/Warehouse)	$ 122,899.92		$ 122,899.92		$ 122,899.92	
Truck Lease	$ 6,000.00		$ 6,000.00		$ 6,000.00	
Other Occupancy Exp.	$ 30,000.00		$ 30,000.00		$ 30,000.00	
Other Operating Exp.	$ 186,842.70		$ 196,184.83		$ 205,994.08	
Total Operating Expense	$ 470,304.42		$ 512,032.61		$ 529,689.25	
Operating Income	$ 90,223.68		$ 76,521.89		$ 88,292.97	
Interest Expense	$ 19,855.73		$ 19,855.73		$ 19,855.73	
EBT	$ 70,367.95		$ 56,666.16		$ 68,437.24	
Income Tax (34%)	$ 23,925.10		$ 19,266.49		$ 23,268.66	
Net Income	$ 46,442.85		$ 37,399.67		$ 45,168.58	

ABH FURNITURE CO.							
Start Up Expenses							
Rent					$ 10,241.66		
Initial Inventory					$280,000.00		
Equipment:							
Signage					$ 2,000.00		
Computers (3)					$ 7,500.00		
Security System (2)					$ 8,000.00		
Office Supplies					$ 800.00		
Office Equipment					$ 1,700.00		
Price Tags					$ 200.00		
Miscellaneous					$ 1,500.00		
Truck					$ 500.00		
Grand Opening					$ 3,500.00		
Utilities					$ 400.00		
Insurance					$ 1,500.00		
Miscellaneous (phone, license, advertising)					$ 5,000.00		
Total					$322,841.66		

Comment: Overall did an adequate job in developing financial statements. There was an error in reporting retained earnings—should be a cumulative figure.

CHAPTER SUMMARY

The purpose of the feasibility study is to determine if there is a demand for your product or service and if the product or service can be provided on a profitable basis. The feasibility study is a precursor to the business plan and is usually five pages in length. The study will help you determine what business you are in, determine your competitors, their strengths and weaknesses, and how you will differentiate your business from theirs. Based upon the information obtained in this study you will determine whether to proceed with the business idea.

MISTAKES TO AVOID:

➢ Failing to adequately assess market potential.
➢ Failing to gather sufficient data to determine an accurate sales forecast.
➢ Failing to complete a feasibility study.

CHAPTER APPLICATION:

✓ Complete the Feasibility Study Worksheet
✓ Read the following business idea and identify key questions that need to be answered.

Business Idea for Coffee Drive Thru

A gourmet coffee drive-thru, like Java on the Road, would meet a much-needed demand in the Mayville area. It would accommodate the consumer's demand for quality products, fast and convenient service. Expresso would capitalize on what consumers with a fast paced lifestyle demand. It would meet the needs of commuters, business people, and suburbanites who are quality conscious consumers or merely want a fresh cup of coffee without the additional hassle of finding parking a and waiting long lines inside a building.

RESOURCES:

U.S. Industrial Outlook
http://www.ita.doc.gov/td/industry/otea/usio/usio95.html
Provides growth trends on various industries.

Business Enterprise Centres
http://www.bec.com.au/becarm/assess.htm
This site provides the opportunity to assess your business idea. It provides a worksheet to assist with the marketing and finance aspects.

Eweb
http://www.eweb.slu.edu/papers2/feasplan/frame.htm
This site provides information on feasibility planning and business planning.

Center for Strategic Planning
http://www.businessinsight.org/index.asp
System offers insight into the business planning process.

FEASIBILITY STUDY WORKSHEET
Business Overview

Describe the product /service stage of development._____
What is unique about it? _____
Describe your product benefits and its limitations._____
_____
Indicate proprietary rights of the business (patents, licenses)___
_____
Describe the production process._____

Market
  Industry Analysis
    Describe the status of the industry._____
    Indicate potential for growth_____
    Describe any trends_____
  Market Analysis
    Identify target market_____.
    Give profile of customer and their unmet needs_____.
    Describe marketing strategy_____
_____.

Competitive analysis
    Identify major competitors and compare in terms of price, quality,
location, product line, exclusivity, reliability, etc. (develop matrix)_____
_____
    Are their businesses increasing , decreasing, or staying the same?___
_____
    How will you distinguish your product/service from your
competition(competitive advantage)?_____
Finances
    Calculate breakeven point_____.
    Develop pro forma income statement and cash flow statements.
     (Write up statement of assumptions for these statements)._____
    Estimate product/service sales and operating costs._____
_____
    Determine financing needs_____
    Calculate start-up costs_____.
    Calculate the Gross Margin and compare to industry averages_____
Final analysis
Given the results of this study should a business plan be written?_____

CHAPTER 5
COMPONENTS OF THE BUSINESS PLAN

In this chapter you will learn about the various sections of the business plan, the purpose of each part, and how to develop an outline for a business plan.

All business plans contain key elements, however the content and organization varies from industry to industry, and certain sections may be more detailed than others depending on the purpose of the plan. Nonetheless all business plans should contain the following sections.

COVER PAGE

The first area that we will discuss is not a section but is important in that it provides the first impression of a business. The cover of the document conveys to the reader the purpose of the document. Given that, the cover should be professional looking, yet be attractive in appearance. A simple layout is preferable with clearly legible font on white paper. It should include the following:

- The name of the company (indicate that it is a Business Plan for this company)
- Logo or sketch of the product/service
- Address of the company (include E-mail address)
- Phone number (important to include so investors can contact you)
- Names, titles of the owners or corporate officers
- Date of the plan
- The number of the copy (e.g. 2 of 20) (Allows you to keep track of the number of business plans out for review)
- Name of the person that has written the plan
- Statement of confidentiality (The contents of this plan are proprietary and not to be duplicated without permission)

Comment: The following cover page is an excellent example of a complete page. Compare it to the subsequent cover page which has a nice graphic but lacks key information including the address of the company, phone number, date of the plan, copy number, and statement of confidentiality.

JKA Unlimited, Inc.
bringing you

January 1997

Business Plan Copy Number 1

This document contains confidential and proprietary information belonging
exclusively to JKA Unlimited

John Kenson
Karl Pfeiffer
Aaron Johnson
Chief Executive Officers

1482 E. Ridgeview Drive
Jacksonville, FL 32203
(904)227-7792

This is a business plan. It does not imply an offering of Securities.

Jenn's Fitness Professionals
BUSINESS PLAN

prepared by:

Susan Jones
Melissa Brewer
Cathy Rolman
Paul Charlton

TABLE OF CONTENTS

The Table of Contents comes after the cover page. Again this is not a main component of the business plan, but it is important to include it to allow the reader to easily determine the information that is available on the business and to quickly access the sections that are of interest. Adding tabs to the various sections adds to the ease of locating sections. The main sections, as well as subheadings, should be listed and should appear in bold print in the order that they appear in the business plan.   Page numbers that correspond to the various sections need to be included. Make sure the Table of Contents is organized and that the pages' numbers correspond with those listed. The following are the basic components that are included in a business plan and would be listed in the Table of Contents:

- ✓ Executive Summary
- ✓ Company Description
- ✓ Marketing Plan
- ✓ Management Team
- ✓ Production
- ✓ Financial Plan
- ✓ Critical Risks
- ✓ Supporting Documents

EXAMPLE

TABLE OF CONTENTS

Pricing
Sales Tactics
Warranty Policies
Advertising and Promotion

Manufacturing and Operations VI.

Management Team VII.

Critical Risk Factors VIII.

Financial Summary IX.

Proposed Company Offering X.

Desired Financing
Offering

Appendix A
Appendix B
Appendix C

Comment: It is difficult to locate sections with the following Table of Contents. It would be preferable to have actual page numbers rather than Roman numerals. It also needs to be in the order described previously.

EXAMPLE:

Table of Contents

Cash Flows   Page 16

Comment: This Table of Contents is adequate, but they need to include more subsections with corresponding page numbers.

EXAMPLE:

Table of Contents

(handwritten notes in margin: "Cover these areas" / "Executive Summary"; "Done before Do again")

Comment: This is a thorough and well organized Table of Contents. However, the business plan is too lengthy.

EXECUTIVE SUMMARY

This section is the first major component of the business plan however it is written last because it is, as its name indicates, a succinct summary of each of the sections of the business plan and cannot be written until each of the other components is written. The key to a well-written Executive Summary is that it is concise (less than two pages) and that it get the attention of its readers. Regardless of whether the business plan is developed mainly for the benefit of insiders or outsiders, it should be an attention grabber.

This is a very important section not only because it appears first in the business plan and is read first, but also it is the key determinant as to whether the reader will read the rest of the business plan. For that reason it can be considered the most important section of the business plan. If you can't get the reader interested in these two pages, then it is highly unlikely that they would search through the rest of your business plan to determine if your idea is worthy of their investment. It is especially important they you convey the market potential for your product, the expertise of the management team, and what the profit potential is for your venture. It is not unusual for the Executive Summary to be distributed by itself to obtain interest in your business by an investor.

> This section is Critical— make sure it gets the reader's attention

 It is important to note that in this section, as well as for the rest of the business plan, that not only interest be generated, but that it be substantiated with data and not consist of fluff or hype. There have been many business plans written that go on and on about how great the venture concept is while having minimal support to indicate that. Even if there was support, hype is a turnoff to a reader—just give them the facts in an interesting format. Although the business plan can be used as a selling tool it does not have to sound like a commercial.

> Just give them the facts and skip the fluff

This section should also include: the company's current status, its products or services, benefits to the customers, the financial forecasts, amount of financing needed, and how investors will benefit. Tell investors exactly how they will be repaid for their investment, whether through operations refinancing or selling stock to others.

THE BUSINESS

Now moving on to the main part of the business plan. In this section include the following components: description of the business, the product or service, and history of the business.

1. Description of the Business

Include such basics as the name of the business (identify special significance of the name, if any), where it is located, the form of organization, industry the business will be in, descriptions of the company's products or services, and pricing strategy. Discuss the potential advantages this venture has over the competition including trademarks, patents, or technical/market advantages.

2. Product or Service

Explain your product or service, that is, tell what the product does and how it will be used, any special features or benefits, and for whom it is designed. Include how your product or service is unique. Also discuss if you are planning to expand your product line with additional products or if you intend to make any improvements in your existing products.

3. History of the Business

Include important background information about the business, when and where it was started, date and state of incorporation, founding shareholders and directors. If there have been any important changes in the ownership or management of the company or in its structure, include that information. For example if your company has changed from a sole proprietorship to a corporation include that information in this section. Include the company's annual sales and profits for the last three years and overall performance to date.

4. Location

Include information on why this location was selected, its proximity to available labor, suppliers, customers and competitors. Provide information regarding wage rates and address the impact of local zoning regulations and local taxes. Also present cost data associated with location factors.

MARKETING PLAN

Requires lots of time and work Whew!!

This section will take a significant amount of time as you will need to address the competition, market potential for your product or service, and the strategy that you will use to reach your market. This is a challenging section to prepare, but also a very important one because the sales forecast that is developed here (based on your market research) is the basis for the rest of the plan. It will determine the size of your manufacturing operation, the amount of capital required, and the marketing strategy.

When evaluating the market for your product you will need to identify and describe your target market including identifying customers and their product/service preference and reasons for purchasing your product or service. Market evaluation also includes conducting research to determine market potential for the product or service, looking at the industry itself to determine trends and growth potential, and assessing the competition. Assessing the competition will involve identifying direct and indirect competitors, comparing them in terms of their strengths and weaknesses, and identifying their respective competitive advantages.

When developing the marketing strategy for your product or service, you will be describing your plan of action to successfully enter and operate in this market. This will require that you identify what customer groups your business will target, penetration goals will need to be set, and pricing and packaging will need to be addressed.

THE MANAGEMENT TEAM

This is one of the most important components of the business plan. Most entrepreneurs think the financials are the most important section, right after the business description (where they spend a lot of time going on about how great the product/service is). They are right about the financial section, however, unless there is a strong management team in place, the venture will probably not attain its stated projections. The bottom line is that the entrepreneur and his/her management team need to be able to make it happen. This is why it is so important to clearly identify the skills and abilities of the management team, their areas of expertise and how that relates to the business, what roles they will have in the company, previous experience and whether they have owned a previous business. Complete resumes should be provided for each member in the Supporting Documents section. This section also needs to address the ownership structure and compensation agreements. Include information on the Board of Directors and outside consultants and advisors as well. Funders are most concerned with the team. They are investing in the management team to guide the business.

> This is the section investors will closely review... so make it look good

PRODUCTION

This section will cover production processes, time schedule, and research and development. In regards to the production processes you will need to cover the methods of production, if you will outsource. Discuss where your product is in terms of development and any research that is being done for its development or improvement.

FINANCIAL PLAN

Although this section is usually toward the end of the business plan it is one of the most important sections of the business plan. Why is that? The financial projections for your business indicate the profit potential for your venture. Typically the financial statements include the income statements, balance sheets, and cash flow statement projections for three to five years. If your business has been operational, then you will need to include income statements for the past three years and balance sheets.

Given the difficulty in making predictions with any degree of accuracy, it is sometimes recommended that the entrepreneur generate three different sets of projections based upon a best case, most likely, and worst-case scenario. Although this is certainly desirable, it is sufficient to produce one set of statements that are based on the most likely scenario.

These statements need to be accompanied with a set of assumptions that explain the basis for the numbers in the statements. It is really critical that you base these numbers on the sales projections developed in the marketing section of the business plan and that they are realistic. Many times entrepreneurs want to inflate these numbers to make their venture appear more attractive, but this is not in their own best interest as they are not only deceiving themselves but also experienced investors who will question figures that seem excessive. The projections should be reasonable.

OTHER IMPORTANT DATA

A great financial plan is Comprehensive and Conservative

This section addresses the time schedule for your plan and the critical risks involved. A timeline chart should be developed that identifies significant milestones in the business with priority for their completion identified. It is important to describe any critical risks that your business may encounter and how you can avoid or minimize their effect on the business. Also discuss situations or circumstances that would cause them to occur or would exacerbate them and how you would respond to them if they should take place. Remember that things never proceed exactly according to plan so developing contingency plans to meet crises and likely problems is a necessity.

SUPPORTING DOCUMENTS

This section should include all of the documents that were referred to in the business plan. It provides the data that is needed to support the statements made in the main components of the business plan. These may be statements regarding trends in the industry, market potential, or the management. Documents most likely to be included are: demographic market documentation, legal contracts, resumes of the owner and members of the management team, articles of incorporation or partnership agreements, organizational charts, and diagrams.

OUTLINE OF A BUSINESS PLAN

The best way to get started is to develop an outline for the business plan and determine what information is needed to complete each section. This book has a worksheet at the end of each chapter that will ask the questions and present the primary issues. If you complete each section as you proceed through the book, you will have the essence of your business plan done. At that point, you will need to convert the question-answer format to a narrative format, but the hard work will have been completed.

The following is a sample business plan outline that will give you an idea of what each section consists of and the areas you will need to address.

I. **Cover Page**

II. **Table of Contents**

III. **Executive Summary**
    A. Business Description
        1. Name
        2. Location and plant description
        3. Product
    B. Market and competition
    C. Management expertise
    D.   Financials
        1.Summary of financial needs and application of funds
        2. Earnings projections and potential return to investors

IV. **Business Description**
    A. Description of the business
    B. Description of product line or services
    C. Proprietary position: patents, copyrights, and legal and technical considerations
    D. History of the business
    E. Opportunities or plans for expanding or redesigning product   or service lines.
    E. Project changes in sales mix, cost, and profit.

V. **Marketing Plan**

    Market Analysis
    A. Description of the total market
    B. Industry trends
    C. Target market

    Competitive Analysis

Market Strategy
- A. Overall strategy
  - B. Pricing policy
  - C. Sales terms
  - D. Method of selling, distributing and servicing products

VI. Management Plan
- A. The management team-positions & responsibilities
- B. Board of directors composition
- C. Organization chart
- D. Resumes of key personnel
- E. Staffing plan/number of employees

VII. Production (if applicable)
- A. Materials
- B. Sources of supply
- C. Production methods
- D Facilities plan/planned capital improvements
- E. Operating plan/schedule of upcoming work for next one to   two years

VIII. Financial Data
- A. Financial history (last five years)
- B. Five-year financial projections (first year monthly; remaining years annually)
  - 1. Income statements
  - 2. Balance sheets
  - 3. Cash flow statement
- C. Explanation of assumptions underlying the projections
- D. Key business ratios
- E. Explanation of use and effect of new funds
- F. Potential return to investors compared to competitors and the industry in general

IX. Other Important Data
- A. Timeline for the business
- B. Critical risks your business faces

X. Supporting Documents

CHAPTER SUMMARY

The key components of a business plan include the executive summary, business description, production, management plan, marketing plan, and the financial statements. However, the entrepreneur should begin developing the marketing and financial sections first.

RESOURCES

Toolkit
http://www.toolkit.cch.com/tools/buspln_m.asp
This site provides a wealth of information on starting a business and writing a business plan.

Wall Street Journal
http://www.wsj.com
This site provides a model to develop a business plan along with sample business plans.

The Small Business Resource Center
http://www.webcom.com/seaquest/sbrc
Site provides assistance with starting and running a business.

MISTAKES TO AVOID

- ➢ Plan that is excessively long; make it thorough but complete.
- ➢ Unorganized arrangement of sections.
- ➢ Lack of supporting documents
- ➢ Failure to include the critical risks section
- ➢ Plan phrased in other than the third person
- ➢ Failure to capture reader's interest.

CHAPTER APPLICATION

1. Interview someone who has started a business within the last five years and determine that amount of planning, if any, was done and this person's position regarding the importance of a business plan.

2. Write out an Outline for your business plan. For each section makes notes about things you want to include. For example, for the product section, note unique features of your product/service. Also note information that you need to obtain (industry data, market data).

3. List persons who will be involved in writing the business plan and establish how often you will meet to work on it.

4. Compare sample business plans from a retail, service, and manufacturing business at http://www.businessplanlans.com Note three differences and three similarities.

CHAPTER 6
THE BUSINESS

In this chapter we will discuss the section of the business plan that presents a description of your business, the product or service that is produced, and the history of the business.

DESCRIBE YOUR BUSINESS

In a previous chapter you learned about writing a mission statement. Sometimes it is placed separately in the plan prior to the Table of Contents or it can be placed at the beginning of this section. As you remember, the mission statement not only denotes the purpose of the business, but also specifies to whom the business is focused. It is absolutely critical that you have a clear understanding of what it is that you do and for whom. The rest of the plan must coincide with this statement.

Although there are specific areas that need to be discussed in this section you will still want to make this section as interesting as possible. (So far, we are not very interesting either). You are relating your business to potential lenders and investors. This is a fairly simple section to complete. Everyone says this! If you are just starting a business and have not nailed down some of the details, you may include information in regards to your plans for those particular areas. For example, if you have not secured a location as of yet, you may include information in regards to your plans for locating the business or the process you plan to go through.

> Make sure they understand what you plan to do.

This section should include the legal name of your business (include any brand or trade names, doing business as, and subsidiary companies, if any). Give the location of the business and any trademarks the company may have on its name or its logo. Also indicate where it will do business. State the type of business (manufacturing, retail, service). Indicate what target customers it is attempting to serve. You will need to state the form of organization (sole proprietorship, partnership, corporation). List the people involved in the business and the roles they have had or will have. In particular, mention who founded the business, when it was started. If the company has changed ownership you will need to discuss the reasons for it. Although you will discuss the key people involved in the business in more detail in the management section, mention their names, positions, and the experience they bring. For example, state that President, John Jones, former Vice President of Marketing for Adams Company, brings twenty years of marketing experience to your company. Mention your current growth strategy and whether that includes expanding into new markets. Include how your product or service is doing in the marketplace and give your sales growth rate if you are an existing business (sales of $2 million this past year which is a 15% increase over the previous year). Also state to whom your product or service is directed. Think in terms of the benefits that you provide rather than what you do.

> This goes for dot coms, too

EXAMPLE: DESCRIBE YOUR BUSINESS

Billy McDonald conceived the EZ Opener in 1998. Mr. Simpson saw a need for a product like this in his personal life. He developed the idea into a drawing and eventually into the prototype we have now. The company was incorporated in the state of Florida in the year 2000. A prototype of the EZ Opener has been developed and there is a patent pending. The company is now in the process of trying to raise money to begin the initial production and distribution of the EZ Opener. The company is currently looking into possible manufacturers of the product so that it will be able to find the facility that will offer them the lowest cost and most favorable credit terms.

Comment: Although the product name is given, the name of the business is not stated nor are the key management persons and their areas of responsibility mentioned. This section does not indicate to whom the product is directed.

EXAMPLE: DESCRIBE YOUR BUSINESS

Bus Builders opened in 1979 as a corporation in the city of Ft. Lauderdale by John Brown. John worked as a marketing representative and national sales representative for one of the country's leading school bus manufacturers before moving to Florida in 1979. Bus Builders started as a one man sales representative company and has grown to a full line sales and service and parts distribution company of 15 full time employees with six product offerings at the present time. Bus Builders and their up and coming products will provide a full line of products statewide.

Comment: This is a thorough description of the business.

THE PRODUCT OR SERVICE

Talk about the product or service including its unique features and its purpose. This is really an important section in that your whole business is based upon the great qualities of your product or service. Describe in detail the characteristics of the product or service and include its cost and where it will be distributed.

Your unique selling proposition

You will want to mention how your product or service differs from your competitors. Discuss sources of your competitive advantage. These could be price, quality, location, selection or service. You need to clearly identify what is special about the products and/or services of your business. Oftentimes business owners will use terms such as "best" or "advanced" but they do not explain what is meant by the term. Do not just say it is superior without saying why it is

superior! Be careful that you do not present the product in an inflated manner.
Remember that you are trying to make it appealing without appearing to be a
strong sales pitch. In other words, avoid the hype.

EXAMPLE: THE PRODUCT OR SERVICE

Magic Film for bathroom coating is a high-tech silicon polymer for coat ceramic,
porcelain, and glass, such as tile, bathtubs, basins, sinks, swimming pool decks,
and glass windows. It forms an anti-abrasive coating that repels dirt and dust,
prevents the adhesion of scum and scale. The barrier repels liquid water, but
allows water vapor to escape from beneath the surface, keeping porous material
dry that prevents mold and fungus to grow. The coating is durable, lasts about a
year, waterproof, high temperature resistant, clear, glossy, and anti-slip for bare
foot contact when wet. It is resistant to chlorine water, oxidizers, acids,
shampoos, detergents, seawater, and UV light.

Magic Film coated surfaces can become slippery if covered with oil, concentrated
soap water, concentrated detergent solution, or other lubricants. The floor coating
of a bathtub can be worn off by abrasive particles. Re-coat the floor part of a
shower every six months, or when the anti-skid property drops. Magic Film
warranty does not include a non-skid or anti-slip property.

Because of surface properties, preparations, applications, we cannot predict how
long this product will last on the floor. Magic Film is warranted for one year for
noncommercial application on all vertical surfaces, if used according to the
instructions.

Comment:
*This was a very thorough description of the product and its warranty. However,
they need to include how this product differs from others (if there is a comparable
product) and how it will be priced and distributed.*

EXAMPLE: THE PRODUCT OR SERVICE

The Morrison's Medical is a ground-based lift, that is designed to lift patients
without using overhead arms and slings, common in existing lifts. The seat of the
lift is connected to two telescopic screws, which allow the seat to touch the
ground and lift the patient to a height of 32 inches. The height of the lift is
adjustable within this range. The lift provides the user with a padded plate to lean
against, arm handles to grasp, and safety straps for security. The arm handles are
interchangeable from front to rear to support a person whether they slide onto the
lift forwards of backwards. The lift is made of a durable plastic, which gives it a
lightweight quality. This allows easy portability, which is a significant
competitive advantage in the current market. The lift is constructed of a

reinforced injection plastic produced by GE Plastics. It is called Noryl, The most outstanding properties of Noryl are its thermal and hydraulic stability and low cost.

Comment: Very thorough description of the product itself but fails to include its cost and how it will be distributed.

EXAMPLE: THE PRODUCT OR SERVICE

Dr. Hendy has been refining Kennel Wash for several years in an attempt to provide kennel owners with a safer, effective, and more efficient way to sanitize kennel stalls. The Kennel Wash technology offers a superior disinfectant with complete deodorization. This represents a revolution in the fields of disinfectants and general hygiene in a one-step process. The patented hydro injection tube allows an even flow and concentration of chlorine through its swirler cap and venturi holes (See Internal Concentration Variables Schematic). This design provides a steady and longer-lasting erosion of the solid chlorine tablet into a liquid. Other features which distinguish this product from other hose-end-sprayers include:

1) *EPA/USDA approved and registered:* Kennel Wash's patented, slow dissolving Endure tablets are registered and approved by both the EPA and USDA.
2) *Kennel Wash is economical:* It is adjustable to various levels of chlorination, depending upon the needs of the user.
3) *A one-step wash down operation:* Kennel Wash provides a continually renewed source of hypochlorous disinfectant throughout the wash down process. Because of this and the "roll-over" effect of the wash down, Kennel Wash, using the Endure tablet can disinfect the environment. Kennel Wash gives the user the simplest, most efficient disinfectant tool available today. Unlike many other disinfectants, Kennel Wash requires no pre-rinse and no potable water rinse afterwards to remove harmful chemical residues.
4) *No batch-mixing:* Because of its "point-of-use" design, Kennel Wash eliminates the need for proportioners, complex metering devices, and batch-mixing of chemicals by your workers. In addition, since there is no batch mixing, the Kennel Wash limits worker liability while enhancing worker safety and shortening the clean-up time.
5) *Stability:* Endure tablets are much more stable than the more commonly used sodium hypochlorite. In dry storage, it loses 5%-7% of its strength per year while sodium hypochlorite can lose up to 50% strength in 90 days.
6) *Non-corrosive:* Kennel Wash's unique ability to dispense calcium hypochlorite (a solid into a liquid) insures controlled pH. Most of the corrosion associated with hypochlorites occurs from the use of sodium hypochlorite (household bleach) and its excessive alkalinity. The self-buffering nature of Endure tablets prevents this high degree of alkaline

corrosion. Control of pH also means a high percentage of the most active chlorine disinfectant, hypochlorous.ion.

7) *No harmful chemical residents*: The active disinfectant provided by Kennel Wash and the Endure tablets disinfects, deodorizes, and performs its function before it ceases to contain oxidizing properties. It is then reduced to a chloride and loses all its disinfectant qualities. Chlorides are inert and natural occurring and environmentally friendly.

8) *Odor control*: With Kennel Wash there are no obnoxious, unpleasant odors. Most odors are ammonia/nitrogen based. Endure tablets, with their 65% available chlorine, provide enough chlorine to "burn through" that ammonia. The low-yield (5.25%) chlorine provided by household bleach is insufficient to "burn through". Instead, the low-yield chlorine forms a bond with the nitrogen and creates chloramines. Chloramines produce the obnoxious, pungent odor many people associate with "chlorine disinfection."

Kennel Wash systems have proven their abilities to safely and economically control canine parvo, feline leukemia, feline panleukopenia, feline calicivirus, HIV aids, salmonella, distemper, rabies, candida, staphylococcus, streptococcus, pseudorabies, and swine parvovirus.

Kennel Wash will be distributed to veterinary practices throughout the Southeast.

Comment: Very thorough description of a new product, purpose and its usage.

Special note about manufacturing businesses:

If you have a product that is manufactured, discuss the stage of development that it is in and give a detailed description of how the product is developed. It would be beneficial to include a flow chart to define the stages of development. At this point you are not concerned about its appeal to consumers but rather its ability to be manufactured economically.

If your company provides a service, state the nature of the service, and how it is provided. Mention your supply source and why they were selected. If you have or plan to start a retail business you will need to include a description of the product(s). Also, include information about your supply sources and why they were selected.

HISTORY OF THE BUSINESS

Begin with the actual startup of the company and tell when it was started and the original location of the business. (You have to start somewhere). Include the form of organization, and, if incorporated, give the state of incorporation. Identify the founding shareholders and directors. If there have been any changes in the ownership or management of the company or changes in its structure, these should be noted as well. Any major achievements or milestones (such as signing

Very big deal to investors

a major contract or obtaining a patent) of the company should be included. (Do not include things like: Name of first employee, year, reason the EPA closed your business, or where the first restroom was located.)

SOME OF THE ITEMS THAT YOU SHOULD HAVE IN THIS SECTION INCLUDE:

1. Date of inception of business
2. Type of business formation
3. Sales growth rates
4. Number of customers
5. Prices charged for products or services
6. Explanation of any profit or losses
7. Marketing strategy
8. Any factors that might have affected the firm's performance (e.g. production problems).
9. Key employees
10. Development of new product

The purpose of this section is to put forth the best, but honest, presentation on the performance of your business. A good deal of time needs to be put into this section as it really is carefully evaluated by potential investors to determine your stewardship of the business. (We hope you are not getting tired of hearing about how much time you need to put into this section.) If your business has a history or if you have been in business for a period of time, it is very important to highlight this.

EXAMPLE: BUSINESS HISTORY:

An investment group acquired TT, Inc., on July 1, 1997. Prior to the completion of the acquisition, TT, Inc., operated as a 30-year-old business with over 3,000 active clients for its primary product, MileageMaster. This product is a multipart, shingled customer log to keep tract of customer service visits and to organize sales tracking process in the motorcycle industry.

The company was founded in 1968 by Jane Black who built the business up to $600,000 per year in revenues. Ownership and day-to-day operations of the company were transferred to Ellen (Jane's daughter) in 1991. They relocated the business from Michigan to Pensacola at that time. Since its acquisition (two years ago), the new management team has grown revenues by 315% with earnings increasing 625%. While the revenue and earnings growth is impressive and a key benchmark of management's recent performance, the precise execution of its business strategy is the key to maximizing its potential in the marketplace. The management team has successfully transformed the old MileageMaster line of products into a customer relationship management system with a national identity.

Comment: This history section is informative, but would be more thorough by including prices charged, explanation of profits, and marketing strategy.

EXAMPLE: BUSINESS HISTORY

Lake Side Cafe is a sole proprietorship owned by Joan and John Green. It is situated on Lake Beatrice in Winter Brook, Florida, and opened for business on October 31, 1997 as a gourmet coffee shop serving the Winter Brook market. Beatrice is a small lake in Winter Brook, Florida with a sidewalk around its circumference. It is estimated that between three and four hundred people visit the lake daily. Surrounding the lake are sixteen independently owned shops known as "The Cottages of Lake Beatrice." These shops offer sales on items ranging from bicycles to import clothing. Of these "Cottages" none offer food or beverages.

Comment:
This history is limited in information that is relevant, but has additional information regarding surrounding shops that is not pertinent to this section. Information regarding their sales growth over time, the number of customers, explanation of profit growth, any new products that have been introduced, and marketing strategy over time would enhance this section.

CHAPTER SUMMARY

The mission statement is stated at the beginning of this section to clarify the purpose and nature of the business. The section contains information about the following: a description of the business, the product or services of the business, and a brief history.

It is important to carefully describe your product or service, to identify the target market for it, and to tell how the business has developed over time. Additionally, it is important to give significant emphasis to any prior history of the business.

CHAPTER APPLICATION

> ➤ Complete the Business Worksheet.
> ➤ Evaluate the Business section of the following business plan. Make five suggestions for its improvement.

Extreme Fitness is a start-up venture that has secured a tentative lease agreement for the perfect site for a downtown fitness center. The site is located only a few short blocks from the capital building. The facility is located in a storefront location right off a busy street and has a high volume of potential customer traffic driving and walking by every day. The high traffic area is the ideal location for easy access to both the state government workers and the private sector working downtown. It assures memberships by many downtown workers since it will be a short walk from any parking garage or office building downtown.

The location in the downtown area is in a street level building next to a parking garage and the garage would be included in the lease arrangement. With the garage having more than 25 plus parking spaces, it is assured that no customer or member would have problems finding a comfortable close range space, especially since most of our customers would already have parking spaces nearby for work. The parking garage would allow our personal training clientele to come in from outside the downtown area to use our facility. The building provides 2,000 square feet of space, more than enough for a personal training studio, shower room and changing room, snack bar and small office spaces. This should be very appealing to persons looking for a close-to-work location in which to workout without having to fight for the hard-to-get parking spaces downtown.

MISTAKES TO AVOID

- ➢ Failing to adequately describe the business.
- ➢ Failing to be thorough in the business history.
- ➢ Focusing only on the current status of the business.
- ➢ Failure to laugh at our sorry attempts to add humor to this text.

RESOURCES

BizPlanit
http://www.bizplanit.com
This site provides resources to assist you in developing your business plan.

WSJ.com Startup Journal
http://www.wsj.com
This site has a mini plan to aid you in the process of writing a business plan and sample plans.

THE BUSINESS WORKSHEET

Describe the Business:
Name of business, include brand, dba.

_____

_____Date of

inception _____

What is the company's mission statement?_____

_____

What is the business's form of organization. (Do you anticipate a change in its

form?)_____

Where is the business located? Has the business changed location?_____

_____

What is the main activity of the business?_____

To whom is the business targeted?_____

_____

Marketing strategy_____

_____

Name the founder and members of the management team?_____

_____

If you have a Board of Advisors, how often do you meet and how many members

does it have?_____

Milestones achieved?_____

Sales and profits for last year? Sales growth rates? Explanation of any profits or

losses._____

_____

Any factors that might have affected the firm's performance._____

_____

Prices charged for products or services?_____

Number of employees?_____

Product or Service
Describe the product/service and include unique features._____
_____

What are the key customer benefits of your product/service?_____
_____

If a product, is it a component of another product ?_____

What protection does your product have (patent, trademark?)_____

If a product, is it ready for distribution, if not, what stage of development is it in
(idea, model, working prototype)?_____

If a product, how will it be produced?_____

History
When did the business start?
_____

What was the development process of this business; what if any, problems
occurred in the process and how were they overcome?_____

SAMPLE PLAN: WARM 'N SAFE BOTTLE COMPANY

THE BUSINESS

The Warm 'n Safe Bottle was first conceived in 1993 by Ryan Addison recognized an existing market for this type product and established the Warm 'n Safe Bottle Company in 1994. The Company will be incorporated in the state of Florida in 1995. The Company has produced a prototype of the product and has a patent pending on the product. The Company is in the process of raising seed capital to finance initial production and distribution. The Company has identified sources to manufacture the product to strict specifications and is selecting marketing representatives to facilitate distribution of product in the United States.

THE PRODUCT

During the past two years, Addison has refined his original design in an attempt to produce a baby bottle that would allow the temperature of an internal liquid to be read visually on the outside of the bottle.

Due to the nature of the product, many design requirements and constraints existed which had to be addressed:
(1)   All components must be non-toxic,
(2)   The assembled product must be suitable for use in a microwave oven,
(3)   The assembled product must be suitable for use in boiling water,
(4)   The temperature indicator must be reliable, accurate and easy to read,
(5)   The temperature indicator must have consistent repeatability,
(6)   The entire product must be dishwasher safe and
(7)   The addition of the temperature indicator must not prohibitively increase the bottle cost.

The latest design has been found to meet all of the design requirements and constraints and a prototype has been constructed.

The Warm 'n Safe bottle is designed to provide an indication of the temperature of bottle contents. The bottle utilizes a special polymer spring, which changes in size relative to the temperature. The temperature indicator uses the same principles as an automobile or home thermostat. The spring expands and turns as it is heated. As the spring is fixed at the base, the top turns indicating the temperature. The bottle temperature is read in the indicator window located in the cap of the bottle. The bottle is designed to give an indication of "feed" between 90 and 105 degrees Fahrenheit, the feeding temperature recommended by most pediatricians. Appendix B gives several views of the product.

The very simple design utilizes only three components: the spring, the stem and the cap. All components lock together permanently on assembly and no fasteners or glues are required. The assembly contains no small parts and is baby safe. All bottle components are made of recyclable plastic providing an environmentally conscious design.

The Warm 'n Safe bottle is designed to provide temperature indication regardless of the heating method. The temperature indicator is designed for consistent repeatability and has a product life of approximately two years.

All components of the Warm 'n Safe bottle are FDA approved. All of the materials utilized have been used in the food industry for over ten years. The materials are dishwasher safe and are easily cleaned. The polymers (plastics) utilized are high impact and have been tested to withstand falls of ten feet.

The Warm 'n Safe bottle has a patent pending status in the United States and once marketability is confirmed, worldwide patents will be applied for.

CHAPTER 7
MARKETING PLAN

In this chapter you will gain an understanding of the various aspects of a marketing plan. This will include understanding how to identify your potential customers, obtain information about the industry, get market data, evaluate your competition, and develop a marketing strategy for your product or service.

IMPORTANCE OF THE MARKETING PLAN

This is a very critical part of the business plan and you need to spend some quality time on this section. Yes, you are going to have to do some serious work to complete this section. However, the results of your work will be of great benefit for the information it provides for you and to the interested reader. This section of the business plan requires you to obtain <u>factual</u> information (hunches and best guesses do not count) regarding the potential of your market and information about your competitors that will prove to the reader of your business plan that your business will have sufficient customers for your product or service. This is important, many entrepreneurs want to skip over this research and never really understand to whom they are trying to sell to and whether there are sufficient numbers to make this a viable business. You must do a thorough job on this section. A potential lender or investor wants to know that despite competition there are enough potential customers for your business for you to be profitable. So take the time to gather information not only about the customer that you have targeted but also about the competition and the industry **before** developing a marketing strategy.

> DO NOT Skip or Gloss Over this section

DEFINING POTENTIAL CUSTOMERS

The first thing you need to do is identify your customers and their buying characteristics. Many entrepreneurs tend to be nonspecific about who their customers are, often saying that everyone is a potential customer. In most cases this is just not true and you need to be specific about who will buy your product or service. When defining your customer develop a customer profile regarding them. This is basically a description of the potential customers. You will need to determine their distinguishing characteristics, these are usually demographic terms such as gender, income level, education, etc. Later in this chapter we will talk about where to get this information. Once you have identified those characteristics you can begin to search for data about their location and numbers. If you have more than one target market you must develop a customer profile for each. Include information about what they want/need from your product/service. This information will help you in developing your marketing strategy. If you have an existing business analyze your current customers, note your major purchasers and identify what they represent in terms of percent of total sales.

EXAMPLE: POTENTIAL CUSTOMERS

The prospective consumers of the Quick Paint Company's Touch-up Paint Kit are college students living in the southeast, Midwest, and Southwest regions, who are in the process of moving. The cities chosen have student populations of over 15,000 and are a dominant feature of the community, much like Summerville. The target population is broken down into two groups—students living in dormitories on campus, and students renting apartments off campus. These demographic features can be found in many regions around the country.

Comment: This section clearly defines the customer that the business will be targeting and key aspects of the market itself.

EXAMPLE: CUSTOMER PROFILE

People between the ages of 30 and 49 made almost one half of all lawn and garden purchases last year, according to <u>Adweek Magazine</u>. There is a growing trend among baby boomers to garden because they feel that it enhances the quality of their home, and it does not cost much to do it. This age group will be the main focus of the Weed Waster because of its labor saving design which will effectively reduce the time and physical effort spent in the garden by the consumer.

Comment: They do not clearly define who are the customers. They mention that 30-49 year olds made half of the lawn and garden purchases but do not say that this is their target market nor do they define the characteristics of this group. They go on to state the trend among baby boomers is to garden, however baby boomers do not fit into the previously mentioned age group. Apparently baby boomers are their target group, but the reason that they gives really doesn't make sense. Additionally they have not described the characteristics of this group.

EXAMPLE: CUSTOMER PROFILE

The All Terrain Stroller's potential customers are the parents and grandparents of children between the ages of newborn to four years old. The income level of the potential customers varies greatly; however, we expect the majority of the sales to come from the upper and middle income families'.

The appeal of our stroller is that it can be used on soft and uneven surfaces such as sand, gravel, or grass. Therefore, our customer is also one that enjoys taking their child to the park, the beach, or some other area that is not typically paved. To summarize, the All Terrain Stroller's customer would be likely to be one that:

- Is a parent, grandparent, or in care of a child between the ages of newborn to about four years old.
- Is in the upper and middle income level.
- Enjoys taking the child outdoors.

Comment: This is a good description of their customer, but could be more specific in regards to age and income level.

INDUSTRY TRENDS

Why is this section important? By examining the industry in which your business operates you will have a better understanding of the forces that will impact your business. As you describe your industry, detail trends and opportunities, and strategic opportunities that exist in your industry. Note the rate at which your industry is growing since this will provide insight into the opportunities for your business. Your goal is to not only show knowledge of the industry but also get the reader interested in the industry and your business. You will want to include data about future opportunities in your chosen industry and where it may be in the next five to ten years. Compare the growth rate for your industry to the Gross National Product as this will give the reader an indication of the current status of your industry. When stating facts such as the industry will grow at 15% annually indicate why this is supposed to happen as this will add impact to the data. Include information on what is currently taking place both nationally and regionally in the industry in which your business is operating.

Discuss your position in the industry and how it may change. Most entrepreneurs look only at best case scenarios for the future, but it is wise to consider less than ideal conditions in the industry and then address how you will change or adapt to the changing industry. If you are a startup business, do not hesitate to seriously reconsider pursuing the business idea if you find out some information about the industry that causes concern. If the industry is changing and you are an existing business, discuss the time and money involved to make the adaptations to remain competitive.

All of the information should be based on facts that are backed up with sources. Although there are numerous resources available in the library you will be able to obtain much of your information on the Internet. (Internet resources are listed at the end of this chapter). If you locate articles that have information regarding your industry you can make reference to them or include quotes from them in the business plan itself. Include the article in the Supporting Documents section of

NO personal opinions: You MUST substantiate all statements

the business plan and make note of its location so the reader can access it if they want more details.

Although you want to focus on the industry as a whole in this section, at least mention the major competitors in the industry and discuss who are the leaders (you will discuss this in more detail in the competitive analysis portion of this section).

EXAMPLE: INDUSTRY ANALYSIS

Although the paint kit industry does not exist, certain aspects contributing to the factors for a potential industry, such as the number of people living in rental units, and the sales of products that the Quick Paint Kit utilizes, (eg. paint and supplies used for minor painting tasks) indicates the demand for these products and the strength of the existing industry.

Comment: Actually this company is part of the painting industry and they should have done research on that industry and included that data in the business plan. They mention that the sales for products that their kit contains indicate that there was a demand for paint and supplies. However they did not indicate trends or any information to support that. This section of their business plan will require a considerable amount of additional work.

EXAMPLE: INDUSTRY ANALYSIS

There are approximately 102 million households in the United States that use household products on a daily basis. The household cleaning industry is comprised of several large manufacturers, most importantly Clorox, Dow, Proctor & Gamble, and Johnson Wax. According to the Department of Commerce, wholesale sales of household cleaning products totaled about $20.8 billion in 1994 and will increase at about 2% per year in the foreseeable future. The Commerce Department defines households cleaning products as detergents and soaps for household, institutional and industrial use (73% of total sales); and polishes and sanitation goods (27%), which includes household bleaches, and industrial disinfectants.

Comment:
This section notes key players in the industry and growth trends. No mention is made of potential new products, possibly there are none at this point in time or they failed to mention them.

EXAMPLE: INDUSTRY ANALYSIS

According to the National Restaurant Association ethnic cuisines are becoming very popular in the United States. Although Italian, Chinese, and Mexican are the most popular ethnic cuisine, other less well known cuisines are quickly gaining acceptance. The restaurant industry projects that by the year 2010 industry sales will be $577 billion with more than 1 million restaurants. 53% of the food dollar will be spent away from home. In addition, the average check per person for full service restaurants will be $10, which is 4.1% more than it has been in previous years. By the year 2000, it is projected that restaurant industry food and beverage purchases should exceed $130 billion. In addition almost 50 billion meals are eaten in restaurants and school cafeterias each year. These findings show that the restaurant industry is still growing and is expected to continue growing over the next 10 years. This means that there will be a lot of business for new entrants into the industry.

Comment: This analysis although brief, provides relevant data about the industry.

DEFINING THE MARKET

In this section you will need to define the market including the total size and determine your target market, that is, the group or groups of potential customers to whom you will direct your business. Examine each market carefully as to overall size, demand, and potential profitability. Determine the market for which the product or service will have the highest receptivity. This will be your target market. By trying to serve every single potential segment you will not be able to satisfy those customers that are most likely to buy as well as you could have if you had focused on certain segments of the market. More importantly you will spend a considerable amount of money trying to reach them all when you would be better off focusing on those most likely to purchase your product. Determining which market segments are most attractive is market segmentation. After the market segmentation process, you can then develop a marketing strategy with a unique promotion, pricing, and distribution mix for each target market.

> Another must: YOU MUST show demand

You will want to identify any changes that may have taken place in the market in recent years including any new markets that may open up which your business could serve, changes in market share, and any changes in demand. Discuss which markets are most important and whether this importance will remain the same over time or change.

This is an important section because it is so critical that you show demand for the product or service. Sufficient demand will determine whether your business idea has potential. Note that any statements you make must be supported with data. Most importantly, make sure that your market share assumptions are realistic.

EXAMPLE: DEFINING THE MARKET

The Quick Paint Company will initially target the Southeast, Midwest, and Southwest regions of the country. Initially there are 43 cities with a favorable demographics, with a total of 44 universities and over one million students. The cities will be targeted in seven phases over three and a half years, one phase every six months. Refer to Appendix C for details.

According to Simmons Marketing Data, 26.4% of people between the ages of 18 and 254 have done some sort of interior painting in the previous twelve months. Based on the 4.3% market penetration of the test phase of the Touch-up Paint Kit, the Quick Paint Company may achieve total sales of 46,785 units per year after the initial seven phases of operation.

Comment:
The plan clearly defines the market area and includes the time frames for reaching those markets. The second paragraph supports this information with statistical data. (We will discuss how and where to obtain this data in the next section).

EXAMPLE: DEFINING THE MARKET

According to information provided by Graco, one of the leading manufacturers of strollers, there are approximately two million strollers sold per year. We estimate that our first year we will capture 1.25% of the total market share. We believe this to be a highly conservative yet attainable estimate. This would give use gross sales of $2.5 million and a gross profit of $750,000 in the first year.

Comment: No information is given as to how they ascertained their share of the market. Aside from one reference to secondary data, none other is given. They need to discuss the shares of the market that the major competitors have. A survey regarding their stroller would have been of value.

GETTING MARKET DATA

Once you have determined who your customers are you can figure out the number of potential customers by doing some market research and then determining what portion of the market you will attempt to garner. The main reasons for obtaining and including this information are that it will help you understand who your customers are and why a customer would purchase your product. It will also improve your understanding of the market as well as that of the reader and more importantly it will lend credibility to the plan in the mind of the reader. Conducting market research is also a way to verify that there is a common need that is not currently being met in the marketplace. Explain how your product or service will fill that unmet need in the marketplace. Don't make the mistake of going ahead with a business idea without knowing that there is a real demand for your product or service.

There are basically two ways to get market data: primary and secondary. To obtain primary data you will need to study consumers directly through surveys, interviews, and observation. Secondary research involves searching for data that has already been compiled from sources such as trade associations, government data, and industry resources. Your search should provide information regarding the demographics of your customer, their buying habits, and reasons for their purchases. You will want to include both primary and secondary data in your business plan. You can do the research yourself or pay to have it done.

SECONDARY DATA

There is a plethora of resources for getting this data with the Internet being the easiest and least expensive means for obtaining it. The public and university libraries have numerous resources available including CD-ROM databases and the reference librarians can assist in locating the needed information. (Sorry reference librarians, now you are really going to be busy at those reference desks.) Most of the data will be in journals, periodicals, private information sources, trade association publications, and government publications. You will be able to obtain a considerable amount of information from the U.S. Small Business Administration (SBA), the U.S. Census Bureau, and the U.S. Department of Commerce, all government resources (their respective web sites are listed at the end of this chapter). Also check with your local chamber of commerce as many have regional data regarding businesses in the area and demographic information. Another source of demographic information is your County Planning Department. If you are an existing business you should be able to get data from your own files such as sales records.

> Reference librarians watch out: here come the business plan writers

Although secondary research is valuable you may have difficulty obtaining data that is current and that exactly fits what it is that you are measuring. Nonetheless, there is a wealth of information available and you will most likely be able to locate most of the information required. Look at Simmons Study of Media and Markets for this information and Survey of Buying Power.

PRIMARY RESEARCH

An additional resource is primary data. It involves actually collecting the data yourself. This can be done through surveys and observation. The benefits of a survey are that they can be done via the telephone, through the mail, or though personal interviews. Research can also be done through focus groups that ask consumers what products they purchase, or get their reaction to the product or service you are intending to sell. After reviewing that information you can focus your business on satisfying a need that is growing in demand. You will want to be first to act on this need so that you can capitalize on the potential growth. Include the information from your research in the body of the business plan with copies of the actual survey and other detailed information placed in the Supporting Documents section of the business plan.

If you are an existing business, you may already have some of this purchasing information in your records. If you have information on consumer purchases you could analyze this data to determine where your consumers are located, types of purchases, and frequency of purchases.

EVALUATING THE COMPETITION

Avoid the common downfall of entrepreneurs in their failure to pay close attention to the competition in their industry. Be realistic and understand that you will have competitors and may have even more if you achieve success. It is well worth the time to take a close look at the competition as you start your business and then to continue to monitor them. Why is that so important? What they do can seriously impact your business and you will want to be proactive in your marketing strategy not reactive. Being proactive requires for you to stay on top of things.

Competitive Intelligence, i.e. finding out what the other guys are doing

A potential entrepreneur must examine the type and the size of the competition. Clearly, it is best to compete in an environment that is not being dominated by other firms. On the other hand, many entrepreneurs would rather compete against a big company over another entrepreneur as the entrepreneur can quickly adjust to changes in the marketplace whereas big firms are slow to do this.

Seven years ago a husband and wife entrepreneur team started a sun tan lotion business from scratch because they fell in love with the business idea of selling sun care products. After seven years they still are not making any money, are in debt over $1,000,000, and are trying to figure a way out. What happened is they went into the business naively without a lot of planning. They tried to compete with Coppertone and other large purveyors of suntan products and never could get national distribution for their products. In simple terms, they just did not do their homework and did not realize the extent to which the big players dominated the industry and the way they would respond to competition (not nicely). If this couple had spent a little bit of time learning about the competition in their industry at the onset of their business, they might (nothing is for sure) have eliminated a lot of the pain and anguish that they have faced over the last seven years.

Do your homework by checking out your competition. Look at their size and how they compete. If competition is based on price you normally do not want to be in that industry. Competing on price yields no customer loyalty. Customers who shop in this market are only looking for the lowest price and it is very difficult to retain this type of customer. Once you get a customer you want to keep them so you do not have to keep on spending marketing dollars to attract new customers. Sure you need to always attract new customers but you want to keep your existing customers so happy that they do not think of leaving. You can only do this if you do not compete on price.

To see the effect of price on competition, just look at the dry cleaning industry. It is fragmented and customers are predominately looking for convenience and price. In this market it would be very difficult to keep and retain a customer on a non-price basis. That is not to say that it would be impossible, but that it would be very difficult.

Examine your direct competitors, that is, businesses that sell the same product or service as you to the same market. Include information on annual sales and also market share statistics if this information is available. Within this group there will be some competitors that represent more intense competition than the others. These are the competitors that consumers compare directly with your product or service when making a purchase decision. These are the businesses that you will want to stay on top of because you may be even asked about them by comparison shoppers, but more importantly because you need to know what they are doing so that you can compete effectively with them. Other less intense competitors also need to be monitored.

Also examine your indirect competition. These are businesses that although they sell to a different target market, offer the same product or service as you. For example, if you own a house cleaning service, and one competitor is focusing on commercial accounts the other one on high-end homeowners. Which ones should you watch? Actually all of them, but obviously you will want to closely monitor the direct competitors. Don't make assumptions as to whom your main competitors are, talk to your customers and ask what other products or services they considered before purchasing yours.

Don't forget to keep an eye out for new competitors or potential competitors. Don't get comfortable, as you must continually monitor current activity. For example a bedding company in a college town was experiencing a decline in sales and profits over a three year period. The reason was that they were in a lucrative market with many college students that needed bedding. Many new competitors had entered the market in that time period, yet the market itself had not grown proportionately. By conducting market research and a competitive analysis, they were able to get a handle on the market and on what their competitors were doing. The result was that they were able to develop a proactive marketing strategy and capture more of the market share.

What type of information will you want to obtain about your competitors? The obvious would be their products or services. Remember that the more you know the better you will be able to determine how to compete with them. Begin by obtaining information on their share of the market, changes in their share of the market, and their target market(s). When evaluating other firms in the industry consider the following:

1. Size of the firm in sales
2. How they compete (e.g. price or service)
3. Quality of the product or service
4. Quality of their customer service
5. Quality of their staff
6. How they market their products or services
7. What makes customers purchase their products or services'
8. Customer perception of them
9. Location
10. Financial situation and resources available to them

You may want to format the results in a matrix for easy comparisons.

Where will you find information about your competitors? A good place to start is by looking in the yellow pages of the phone directory. This will give you a good idea of the number of competitive businesses in the area. You may want to get a map of your area and identify each of their locations to determine proximity to your business. For more information, contact your local Chamber of Commerce as most have data about businesses in the area. Another source of information is the trade association for your industry. If you do not know the trade association check the Gale Encyclopedia of Business and Professional Associations at your local library and then contact the association for your industry. Trade associations compile an impressive amount of data that will be useful not only for this section but also for the market data. Also check with trade magazines, newsletters for your industry since they report on industry trends and industry reports.

Reference librarians: you are safe from the business plan writers on this section

After you have this information call or visit them. You must play detective and ascertain the capabilities of the firms that you are going to do battle with in the industry. Some of the ways to get this information is by looking at the company's web site, talking to customers, contacting trade associations, and posing as a potential customer. This is considered competitive intelligence and you need to realize that they will be checking you out as well. Start with a phone call. When you call, present yourself as a customer seeking information regarding the product/service that they have, price, discounts, etc. An important aspect to note is their customer service. Note how were you treated, did they respond promptly, were they knowledgeable and helpful, what was your general impression of them. After you finish that telephone survey, go and visit the businesses. Note the location and general appearance of the business, customer service, and quality of the service. When you have finished this process you will have acquired a significant amount of useful information that will help you determine how you will compete based upon their weakness and your strengths.

You will want to keep up with what your competition is doing on a regular basis. Note their ads, promotions, new locations, and sales. If they have a web site you will be able to easily monitor new products/services and other information. You can also use the Internet to determine if there are any new competitors. This will help you to adjust your marketing strategy.

EXAMPLE: COMPETITIVE ANALYSIS

Direct competition includes five main growing products that are similar to Easy Sprout's Five Day Garden and are sold on the Internet and or in trade related catalogs. The Sprout Master has a variety of twenty types of seeds, books about natural foods, herbs, and seeds, a drying pantry and a video. The Sprout House also has a variety of approximately fourteen types of seeds, and a sprout bag to grown herbs and sprouts. Another product, The Sprout Green House sells a "sprout green house" liquid kelp fertilizer as well as a recipe book. There are also sprout growing trays and automatic hydroponics sprouter, such as the "Hydro-Sprouter." These products costs range from $12.95 for simple single sprouters to $119.95 for automatic hydroponics sprouters.

Indirect competition includes science related, plant growing projects that may be used in the classroom to educate students about scientific process of growth. Easy Sprout's Garden is directly targeted to children in grades K-4, with a video about Easy Sprout and alfalfa sprouts, a teacher's unit complete with instructions, games, and activities for teachers to give to the students.
Competitor product weaknesses include high prices for sprout growing systems as well as the lack of appeal to children and adults.

Comment: The analysis starts off with a brief description of some of the major competitors but fails to consider the strengths and weaknesses of them.

EXAMPLE: COMPETITIVE ANALYSIS

As of October 1994 there were only two known competitors operating in the same market (the use of microabrasion for dental treatment). Although there are other micro-abraders available, they are priced extremely high. One of the competitors is ADL (American Dental Lasers) of Troy, Michigan. This company manufactures the KCP 2000 and sells their product at a retail price of $18,000. This company was founded in 1993 and had 200 dentists using their KCP unit as of October 1994. The other competitor is Sunrise Technologies of Freemont, California. Their product, Microprep, retails at $12,500, but the number of dentists using their product is unknown. Furthermore, DentuLab, Inc., is the exclusive distributor of the TeethVac.

Genesis Inc. is competing on a combination of both price and service. The KV-1 units have a retail price of $7,995—almost half of its closest competitor. The low price will be one of the key factors in the product's success.

Comment: This competitive analysis gives critical details about the main competitors and how this venture will position itself accordingly.

EXAMPLE: COMPETITIVE ANALYSIS

There are many manufacturers of durable medical equipment that have patient lift product lines. These lifts generally sell from $900 to $5,000 depending on the type of lift desired. Currently the most common lift on the market is a sling type lift with Guardian Products and Invacasre providing the popular lifts. These lifts are typically large and heavy which makes them difficult to move from room to room and often require disassembly for transportation purposes. The majority of the competitors target institution due to the size and expense of their lifts. These lifts are usually too large for in-home use and therefore are not marketed to those users. One type of patient lift used in home attaches to tracks along the ceiling. These lifts sell for approximately $5,000 and do not offer much potential for high growth due to the price. The majority of the competitors have a one year warranty on their lifts with a few companies offering longer warranties only on the main frame of the lift.

Comment: Although they identify the two key competitors they do not delineate the competitors' strengths. They should describe the other direct competitors as well.

EXAMPLE: COMPETITIVE ANALYSIS

The following chart illustrates how Manana's product compares to the competition in several different key areas.

COMPETITIVE ROUNDUP – COMPANY

Restaurant	Manana's	LongHorn Steaks	The Loop
Estimated 1995 Sales $'s	$1.75million	$2.0million	$1.0million
Estimated Share of Market	9.1%	9.1%	9.1%

Rank: 1=Weak to 5=Strong

Greatest Strength	Location	Quality	Salad Bar

Quality	[5]	[4]	[3]
Advertising Effectiveness	[4]	[3]	[3]
Work Force Excellence	[5]	[5]	[3]
Future Potential	[5]	[3]	[3]
Seriousness of Competition	[5]	[3]	[2]

COMPETITIVE ROUNDUP – PRODUCT

Price	[4]	[2]	[4]
Size	[4]	[4]	[3]
Capacity	[5]	[5]	[4]
Appearance	[5]	[5]	[3]
Quality	[5]	[5]	[4]
Full Liquor Bar	[5]	[5]	[0]
Efficiency / Speed of Service	[4]	[4]	[5]
Seating Speed	[4]	[4]	[5]

OBSERVATIONS AND CONCLUSIONS

It appears, from the above information, that Manana's has a strong competitive advantage over the local direct competition. We at Manana's feel that we can serve our target niche in a superior fashion committing to quality service, setting and demanding standards of excellence, and keeping everything simple and direct.

Comment: They did a great job in comparing their competitors in key areas. The rating chart makes for easy comparisons.

COMPETITIVE ADVANTAGE

Although Competitive Advantage does not need to be a separate section it is important to address this in the business plan. Every business must have a competitive advantage. You need to identify what will set your product or service apart from that of your competitors. It could be based upon price, service, features, location, and/or quality. If you have more than one competitive advantage, you will have a better chance of beating the competition. To determine your competitive advantage you need to ask what makes your product better/different and why would a consumer purchase your product rather than that of a competitor? Otherwise your product/service will appear to be nothing special. Explain how you will attain your competitive advantage. For example, if your advantage is service then tell what will make your service better. If based on price you will need to explain how you will be able to make a profit if you sell at a lower price. Considerable care must be given to develop the competitive advantage because it is the reason why customers will buy from you rather than from your competitors. In a new market obviously you will be able to garner share by being early to enter the market and competition is not as challenging. However, it is especially important to do a good job in this section if you are entering a mature market as you will have to obtain market share by taking market share away from your competitors.

EXAMPLE: COMPETITIVE ADVANTAGE

Our competitor's will offer the same basic services and products because they are all the same industry. They all have the same basic specials but simply offer them on different nights. Also, most of the clubs offer different styles in music on different nights and many of the bartenders, bouncers, and overall employee staff can be quite indecorous. In this regard Freedom will differ easily and superbly from all of its competitors. As of right now, a classy high-energy, "Miami Style" club does not exist. Currently no clubs stay open after 2:00 a.m. and no clubs will have an awesome Disc jockey like Freedom shall, and to top it off, Freedom will be one of, if not the only, establishment with its very own unique drink recipes. Our employees will not only be experienced, but also beautiful and give top-notch service. A dress code will be mandated requiring dress pants and dress shirts for men and nice clothing for the ladies. Jeans, tennis shoes, and any other unbecoming attire by anyone will not be tolerated, and that person will not be admitted into Freedom.

Comment: This section does not really tell how this club will benefit from its differences. Also it is difficult to determine whether these differences are real or perceived. For example, is having the best DJ a real or perceived difference? Also, it is not stated whether there is a demand for some of these differences. For example is there a demand for clubs to stay open later or a demand for "Miami Style" clubs?

EXAMPLE: COMPETITIVE ADVANTAGE

Our business hopes to gain a competitive advantage over the competition through specialization, our extensive hours of operation, and our commitment to our pickup and delivery service. When looking at similar businesses around Evansville, most of them provided the same service with the same characteristics. None of these businesses seemed to separate themselves from one another by providing a service that the others were not. Consulting storage facilities in the area, we found only two that specialized in document storage alone. The rest were open to storing anything that would fit on their property or storage unit. All the companies did, however, operate off of a computer system to track inventory. These facilities were protected by either alarm systems or well lit fenced in areas. Our company specializes in the advanced use of computer programs, as well as an alarm system. We have in fact found ways in which to set us apart from our competition. We provide a pick-up and delivery system which will be provided at no extra charge. We also can deliver these documents twenty-four hours/seven days a week. After researching these facilities we feel we can capitalize on this market by offering the highest quality of customer service and our personalized selling techniques. Our personal sell and the relationship we will develop with our customers to service their needs will set us apart from the competition. We feel this will give us a direct competitive advantage over our competition.

Comment: They have thoroughly examined their competition and have developed a competitive advantage that is clearly defined and that will set them apart from their competitors.

MARKETING STRATEGY

Once you have determined your target market you need to develop a strategy to discuss in detail the means that you will employ to get customers to purchase your product or service. You will need to consider costs to implement this strategy.

EXAMPLE: MARKETING STRATEGY

Our objective is to use the National Inquirer to reach our target market and offer our unique T-shirt designs based on the twelve signs of the zodiac. This is based on the 5.15 million readers of the National Inquirer who bought items of clothing from advertisements in the magazine during the calendar year 1991. For the first year of operation we will market/advertise the twelve zodiac designs along with related pendants and hats. For our second year of operation, we assume that customers will have grown accustomed to our advertisement and are more inclined to purchase our products.

Comment: Apparently in the second year of operation, their marketing efforts will level off based on first year sales. This is a very limited strategy and no alternative plans are given if sales are not at anticipated levels.

EXAMPLE: MARKETING STRATEGY

The 24-hour emergency hospital expects to advertise in Winter Brook and the surrounding areas in Orange County. Advertising during the first year will be 0.7 percent of sales. For years two through five, an advertising budget of 0.7 percent of sales is also projected.

In this industry, an internal marketing strategy is just as important in this industry as print, radio, or television advertisement. A survey by Veterinary Economics indicated that 54 percent of pet owners choose their veterinarian based upon recommendations. Also, a satisfied client is 35 times more likely to refer their friends or relatives to a practice than a neutral or dissatisfied client. Exceeding the customer's expectations is the best way to build a client base in this industry. Another strategy to increase the client base is through use of a customized presentation folder. The cover will highlight the name, address, phone number, and logo and inside inserts would describe the practice, its services, and staff. As potential clients call the practice, they will be asked if a folder could be mailed to them. In a recent study, four separate consulting firms tracked the effectiveness of the technique and found that 72 percent of those who received a folder became new clients.

Other strategies include:

- Placing an advertisement in the Yellow Pages of the Orlando phone book under Veterinarians-Emergency Services
- Maintaining a presence on a website, Pet-clinic.com provides an affordable web page creation and hosts services exclusively to veterinary clinics and hospitals.
- Addressing cooperative advertising with companies whose products are sold at the hospital, such as flea medicine or food.
- Emphasizing the women's section of the Winter Brook paper due t the nature of the target market.
- Hosting a grand opening reception with tours of the facility may include

Strategic Partnerships: In order for EmVet to be a successful emergency and critical care referral center in the Winter Brook area, it must partner with other veterinary professionals in the industry. This is due to the consolidation of veterinary clinics and the expansion of the presence of pet superstores. This includes partnering with veterinarians, pet superstores before they become direct competitors, medical and animal suppliers and pharmaceutical vendors.

Comment: This is a well thought out plan and encompasses several methods of reaching their target market. It even gives data to support its strategy.

CHANNELS OF DISTRIBUTION

Discuss how you will actually get your product to the customer or make your service available to the customer. This will involve understanding the purchasing patterns of your customers. You will need to review the various channels of distribution as to their advantages and disadvantages in relation to your target market. Discuss which ones you will utilize and the reason for your choice. Information regarding alternative methods of distribution should be included in the case things do not go as planned.

EXAMPLE: CHANNELS OF DISTRIBUTION

In the early years of Central City Magazine, for a time at least, the magazine must be hand-delivered. The reasons are two-fold. First: the cost of direct mailing. Subscription revenues will – even in the best case – only cover postage costs. Plus, the postal service is quite stringent on the editorial content/advertising ratio. Without meeting their standards for journalistic content, publications won't get the magazine postage discount rate.

So, for at least the first issue – perhaps the first year – this magazine will be delivered door-to-door, if necessary, in order to insure the right people in the target market are sure to get this community magazine. For example, the mayor of Central City, Central City Beach and all the other smaller surrounding municipalities – like Summersville and Valley Dale – and other civic leaders must get the magazine. Every household in Gulf Point and on Pirate's Cove Road (some of the prestigious neighborhoods in Central City) must have this magazine. There are special plastic bags – complete with a hanger for a door knob – that would suit our purposes just fine. Other neighborhoods to focus delivery include: the Cove, Pelican's Point, Lighthouse Point, Wood Brook, Forest Dale and The Refuge.

We would also make sure that members of the Junior League, officers' wives at Nations Air Force Base and Naval Coastal Systems Center have a free copy as well as members of the school board and county and city commissions. Remaining issues may be distributed at rental agencies serving the Sea Way and Sunnyside community, who frequently visit surrounding areas like Central City and Summerville while on vacation.
For the first issue, we will include a short note that explains that this is the inaugural issue, which will be handed out to those mentioned above and in many other neighborhoods, and that we've already begun on the next issue, which will be published in April. They will be encouraged to call and subscribe during the

next few months in order to insure prompt delivery of their next issue. We will also cross-reference members of the community that may be in mind for "must have " issues. If we determine that we haven't reached these people in our neighborhood canvassing, we can look them up in the telephone book and deliver one to them. Individuals on the "must have" list would be individuals of high community involvement who could easily spread the word about our new magazine.

In the future, when the magazine is more established and greater subscriptions can offset the cost of mailing, distribution will be primarily by mail. However, to some retail outlets and other locations like the Marriott, doctor's offices and excess copies going to schools, our own vehicles will be used for transporting the magazine, in an effort to reduce costs.

As mentioned above, we will sell magazines at local grocery stores and newsstands on a consignment basis. For example, if we take 500 magazines to Publix, and they make 50 percent on every sale, and sell all the magazines, Publix will make $687 just for making room on the magazine rack.

Comment: They have done a good job describing how they will get their product distributed.

PACKAGING

When developing the packaging of your product or service you need to be concerned with reflecting the values of the target market. It is imperative that you understand who your target customer is so that you can design packaging that will attract him/her to it. This is true of service businesses as well because packaging represents the way the business communicates its uniqueness to customers. Most customers make a decision on the packaging and not the product. It is also important that your packaging effectively communicate the position of your company, i.e. its unique set of values.

PRICING

In this section you will need to discuss not only the price you will charge for your product or service but also how you determined that price. When determining a price you need to set one between the price floor and ceiling. Price floor is the bottom price but it must include a profit. The ceiling is determined by your market. Basically it is the highest amount a customer will pay. To establish a price consider the quality of your product or service and the image that you are trying to project. Look at your competitors. Discuss how you compare with your competitors in terms of pricing. If you plan to price your product or service lower than your competition you will need to discuss how you will be able to do that and yet be profitable. (Remember that discussion we had about not competing on price—keep it in mind). If you will be significantly higher than competition, discuss how you will be able to obtain market share at that price and the impact on your revenue forecast. Also include a discussion on how this pricing will relate to producing profits. Will you be able to garner and keep market share with this pricing? When establishing a price make sure that you carefully calculate costs so that you do not have to increase prices due to inaccurate calculations. An appropriate price is critical as it is a key factor in your ability to penetrate the market and also to keep the market position. Obviously it is most important because you need an amount that will guarantee sufficient revenue. Take time to review standard industry practices in regards to pricing (check trade associations for this information).

EXAMPLE: PRICING

Survey results indicate that the target market would be willing to pay $2.68 per magazine and would be willing to subscribe if the subscription cost less per issue than buying the publication at the newsstand. The magazine cost $1.30 per magazine to produce. In order to raise the price to a more even number but yet keeping it under $3.00 as competitors with similar community magazines have done, a per issue price of $2.75 was determined to be best suited for the community and management. Plus, there is a certain psychological effect of shelling out that extra coin for a purchase. Studies have shown that when many newspapers increased their price from 25 cents to 50 cents, the psychological effect of paying the extra coin-not justifiable to those who had the day before paid only one quarter for it-caused significant drops in circulation. So, in further justification for the $2.75, if a person gives a clerk $3.00 for the magazine, they'll still get change back.

Comment: This is a good description of the determination of pricing. They also need to indicate how this relates to producing profits.

EXAMPLE: PRICING

The school bus market demands low pricing because of bidding specification pricing. Bus Builders is and will continue to be competitive in the parts market while offering the best service and largest inventory and selection. Bus Builders does not always choose to compete on the basis of lowest price. Bus Builders is able to do this because they are the only retailer of Thomas Bus parts in Florida. The commercial products have two tiers, and Bus Builders concentrates on higher profit and lower volume.

Comment: They are not clear on their pricing strategy or how this strategy will relate to producing profits and their ability to penetrate and maintain their market position.

EXAMPLE: PRICING

Retail prices for baby strollers average around $80 for the conventional stroller and $175 for all-terrain strollers. Our stroller will carry a wholesale price of $100 with a suggested retail price of approximately $130, providing the retailer with a 30% mark-up. This will position our price in the upper range of the conventional stroller and the lower range of the all-terrain stroller. However, it will offer the benefits of both market segments.

Comment: Including information regarding their costs would have been beneficial in understanding the appropriateness of their price determination.

POSITIONING

Carefully consider how you want your product or service to be perceived by not only the consumers in the market but also the competitors. To position your product or service you need to consider the need that your product fills for the consumer and what is special about your product or service. Also consider the position of your competitors. Look at what your product or service offers in relation to your competitors and promote it as the unique benefit.

ADVERTISING AND PROMOTION

For advertising to be effective, it needs to be geared for your target market. Think about the media that would reach your target market. What radio stations do they listen to, what magazines do they read? (Demographic information is available from the stations themselves). Also, take a look at what your competitors are doing.

All methods of advertising should be described in this section as well as any promotional tools or methods that you will employ. Indicate what percent of sales that the advertising expense will be and indicate when these costs will be incurred.

EXAMPLE: ADVERTISING AND PROMOTION

ProFit currently allocates 4% of sales to advertising. In the future, the company will allocate 5-6% of sales to advertising. The financial projections show $10,000 being spent in 1998 to "jump start" the business. The financial projections also show $5,000 per year being spent on advertising in years 1999 and beyond. It is assumed that the incentive bonus discussed above will encourage the trainers to actively promote the business by word of mouth.

ProFit currently advertises by word of mouth, brochure mail-outs, doctor's office referrals and a newspaper advertisement in the health section of the Daily Sentinel every Monday. These advertising mediums will be expanded and recurrent to maximize exposure to its target audience. See Appendix C for further details.

Comment: Provides a good explanation of their advertising and promotion plans.

EXAMPLE: ADVERTISING AND PROMOTION

Sport Fan's will utilize guerilla marketing tactics for the bulk of its advertising. To attract guests for a first visit to the restaurant, Sport Fan's must create an interest in the concept prior to opening. To establish initial interest, advertisements will be placed in the CollegeView and SpringTimes magazine a month prior to opening. One week prior to opening, coupons will be printed as part of a full-page ad in each magazine. Guerilla marketing will also be used once the restaurant is open. For example, flyers will be put on vehicles and handed to potential customers as they leave the local bars and nightclubs. Sport Fan's will aggressively promote being one of the only places where students will be able to go and hang out during the early morning hours. Sport Fan's will also continue to advertise in the CollegeView and SpringTimes magazine since both papers are directly targeted toward the same audience as the restaurant. Lastly, Sport Fan's will concentrate on name and brand recognition. The Sport Fan's logo will be placed on several promotional items. Drinks will be served in reusable plastic cups stamped with the logo while T-shirts will be sold displaying the logo and various slogans that characterize the Sport Fan's experience.

Our marketing budget will initially be five percent of projected sales for Year One. Sport Fan's will rely more and more heavily on word-of-mouth and repeat customers for business. Therefore, the company feels it can decrease the budget by one percent each consecutive year until the marketing budget equals one percent of sales. Sport Fan's believes this amount will be sufficient for all subsequent years.

Comment: They have given a good explanation of their advertising and promotion plan. Hopefully they will build the customer base that will enable them to get customers based on referrals and spend less on direct advertising.

EXAMPLE: ADVERTISING AND PROMOTION

With initial funding available for advertising and promotion very limited, barter advertising and trade will be key for the first two years. If, for example, WTXC-TV promised Central City Magazine 10 thirty second newscasts during the first month after a new publication is released, in return, the magazine could give the news station a comparably priced advertisement in the magazine. Another aspect of promotion is community involvement. The company is so dependent upon advertising and readership for its success that it must give back to the community. We plan to do this by donating past editions to schools to help children learn more about their community and sponsor community programs that benefit the local library and spelling bees to encourage education.

Comment: Creative way to advertise without incurring costs.

PRODUCING A REVENUE FORECAST

Obtaining accurate marketing information is so critical because it becomes the basis for the revenue forecast. Use a survey to obtain the data regarding the number of persons that would purchase your product/service. In the following example data from Simmons Study of Media and Markets and a survey was used to determine the market potential. After obtaining the market potential for your business for the targeted market, you need to determine the number of competitors and what share of the potential market you can expect to obtain. Be realistic as you are not going to garner 10% right away. This amount must be multiplied by the average annual expenditure on this product or service. This becomes your revenue forecast. This is a critical figure in developing your pro forma financial statements. It is important to remember that your revenue forecast should come from the data obtained in your market research.

EXAMPLE: MANANA'S SALES FORECAST

246,400	MSA Population
20.1%	Ratio of People aged 18-24
49,527	
29%	Individuals with income < $15,000
14,363	Consumers with appropriate age and income
97%	Consumers that will frequent a closer location
13,932	Appropriate customers dining out
x 9.2	Average visits monthly per consumer
128,175	*potential restaurant visits per month*
x 9	Month in a two semester school year
1,153,575	*Potential dinners sold per 9 months*
x $12.45	Avg. amount of money spent on dinner
$14,362,055	**Sales Forecast Tallahassee MSA**

Comment: Very well defined and easily understood in terms of how the sales forecast was determined.

CHAPTER SUMMARY

The marketing plan is a critical component of the business plan. Within this section you will need to determine your target market and develop a profile of your customer, and review existing data and conduct surveys to determine your market potential. You will also need to analyze your competition which requires a careful evaluation of their strengths and weaknesses in order to determine your competitive advantage. The marketing strategy to get your product or service to the customer is developed based on the market analysis and competitive analysis.

CHAPTER APPLICATION

- ➤ Complete the Marketing Plan Worksheet.
- ➤ Choose a new product or service and determine the best target market for the product or service.
- ➤ Visit a local small business owner and ask the manager to describe the company's marketing strategy.

RESOURCES

Statistical Abstract of the United States, U.S. Bureau of the Census
This resource has comparative data on consumer expenditures. It contains statistics on social and economic conditions in the U.S.

Gale Encyclopedia of Business and Professional Associations
A guide to more than 8,000 businesses, trade, and professional associations. Almost any industry or product group will have one or more associations that gather and disseminate information about it.

U.S. Department of Commerce City & County Databook.
Provides statistical information on population, education, employment, income, & retail sales.

Dun & Bradstreet Directories
List companies by product classification, alphabetically, & geographically.

Study of Media and Markets, Simmons Research Bureau
Provides market research information. Data is broken out by various demographic and economic factors.

The Bibliography of Marketing Research Methods, Lexington Books
This is a very detailed and comprehensive listing of books and journals on how to do research in marketing.

Data Sources for Business and Market Analysis, 4th ed. Scarecrow Press

Presents and describes marketing data and statistical sources from US government, foreign government and organizations, universities, research institutions and trade associations. Also includes business services, advertising media, directories and mailing lists, information centers, and research aids.

County Business Patterns, US Bureau of the Census

It gives the number of establishments, payroll, and employees in aggregate for each industry.

ABI/Inform

This computer database indexes and summarizes articles from over 800 academic journals on business, management, accounting, information sciences, etc.

General Business File

This infotrac searchbank sources covers over 300 business periodicals, the Wall Street Journal, and the business section of the New York Times in addition to 50 local business publications.

American Statistics Index

Indexes and locates statistics from federal agencies on a wide spectrum of subjects including products, industries, states, countries, demographic data and more.

WEB RESOURCES

Business Resource Center

www.morebusiness.com

This site has sample marketing plans for your review. (click on Business plans, then click on Sample Marketing Plan

U.S. Department of Commerce

http://home.doc.gov

This site has a considerable amount of data that would be useful for market research.

Thomas Register

http://www.thomasregister.com

This site has information about manufacturers of industrial products and services, and companies.

Understanding Your Market

http://www.sbaonline.sba.gov

This section of the Small Business Administration web site will help you to better understand your customer.

American Demographics/Marketing Tools
http://www.marketingtools.com
If you need help in determining how to target your marketing this site will be of benefit.

U.S. Bureau of the Census
http://www.census.gov
Provides demographic information valuable in identifying and analyzing trades.

Securities and Exchange Commission
http://www.sec.gov
Provides resources for searching a specific industry.

American Marketing Association
http://www.ama.org
Provides resources on issues related to marketing.

MISTAKES TO AVOID

- ➢ Minimizing the impact of competitors or thinking that you have no real competition.
- ➢ Failing to define your competitive advantage over your competitors.
- ➢ Failing to identify all competitors both direct and indirect.
- ➢ Failing to conduct market research to build a strategy.
- ➢ Failing to include important statistics and growth trends for the industry that your business is in.
- ➢ Believing you can capture all of a small portion of a market that is too widely defined.
- ➢ Failing to have a clearly defined pricing strategy.
- ➢ Failing to define target customer characteristics.
- ➢ Assuming every potential customer will buy from you.
- ➢ Trying to reach too many markets at once.

MARKETING PLAN WORKSHEET

CUSTOMERS

Who are my customers? (age, income level, sex, lifestyle, buying habits)

_____

_____

Where do my customers live, work, and shop?_____

_____

_____

INDUSTRY TRENDS

Describe the current status of your industry_____

_____

_____

What is the total sales volume of your industry in dollars/units?_____

_____

Name the major industry players, their market share, and how well they are doing._____

_____

How do you compare to them?_____

_____

Where is your industry headed in the next five to ten years?_____

_____

Are there any trends in technology that will affect your industry?

_____

_____

Any barriers to entry?_____

_____

Have there been any recent demographic trends that have affected the industry?_____

_____

How will your share of the market shift with changes in the industry?

_____

_____

DEFINING THE MARKET

What is the projected size of my market?_____

_____

What are the needs of my customers?_____
_____

How can I meet the needs of my customers?_____
_____

What is unique about my business?_____
_____
_____

COMPETITION

Name, location of competitors_____
_____
_____
_____

What are their products and how are they distributed?_____
_____
_____
_____

What is their share of the market?_____
_____
_____

What are their strengths and weaknesses?_____
_____
_____

How are their products priced?_____
_____
_____

How is their business currently performing?_____
_____
_____

SAMPLE BUSINESS PLAN: WARM 'N SAFE BOTTLE COMPANY

THE INDUSTRY

The baby bottle industry in the United States is comprised of several major
manufacturers, namely Playtex, Evenflo, Gerber, Munchkin, NUK, Chubs and
Ansa. See Appendix A. The current baby bottle market in the United States is

estimated at $154 million. Of this amount, reusable baby bottles hold 552 percent, $80 million of the market, while the remaining 48 percent is held by disposables. Disposables are defined as baby bottles that are designed for bottle liners and the liners are discarded after each use. The disposable market had grown to a peak of 53 percent of the baby bottle market in the United States, but had shown a steady decline as a percent of the total market over recent years. The Warm 'n Safe bottle will initially be designed as a reusable bottle. However, the Company will evaluate the possibility of entering the disposable market at a later date.

MARKET RESEARCH AND ANALSIS
CUSTOMERS

The average customer for a baby bottle product is a female in her late twenties who is, or will be again, employed outside the home. The median family income of the typical baby bottle customer is 36,120. Because the majority of customers of baby bottles work outside the home, time and convenience is heating bottle accurately are of the essence.

MARKET SIZE AND TRENDS

After peaking at a post-baby-boom of 4.16 million in 1990, the number of births in the United States is expected to stabilize at approximately 4 million and remain at that level through the turn of the century. The current baby bottle market in the United States is approximately $154 million, or 73 million units a year. Currently, reusable bottles constitute 52 percent of the baby bottle market, or 38.6 million units a year. Reusable bottles have increased their market share over disposable bottles by an average of 2 percent a year over the last years. The trend of reusable bottles capturing a larger share of the baby bottle market is expected to continue over the net several years.

COMPETITION AND COMPETITIVE ADVANTAGES

Although there are several major competitors in the baby bottle industry, none of these are currently marketing a product that indicators the temperature of the liquid in the bottle. The Warm 'n Safe bottle provides this key feature with only a minimal increase in manufacturing cost over standard bottles.

Only one other company has attempted to market a temperature sensitive baby bottle. Ansa Bottling manufactured such a product under the trade name Heat Sensitive and later Comfort Temp. This product was being produced and marketed when the current owners, according to John Iodise, President of Ansa Bottling, purchased the company.

The Bottle Ansa designed neglected one major fact of baby bottle usage; sometimes bottles are heated from the outside in (boiling water) and sometimes from the inside out (microwave). Their design simply used the bottle's surface plastic to indicate the temperature. An opaque blue or pink plastic would turn white when the contents were too hot. This neglected the fact that microwaves heat from the center so only after the bottle was shaken would it provide an accurate indication. Due to its inaccurate operation, it was withdrawn from the market. Despite their disappointing results, Ansa's efforts confirmed that based on market surveys, there is market for a bottle with a temperature sensor. In addition, Iodise felt their lack of success was the result of a design flaw and not a lack of market. The Warm 'n Safe bottle overcomes this shortcoming in its design of the temperature indicator device.

ESTIMATED MARKET SHARE AND SALE

According to market information provided by Richard Henry, Vice President of Sales for Munchkin Bottling Company, a leading manufacturer of specialty baby bottles, a manufacturer introducing "just another decorated bottle" without any key features or benefits over current bottles could be expected to capture one to two percent of the total market in the first year of operations. This market share would probably remain at two percent during subsequent years.

Munchkin's market data also indicates that if a company produced a product with significant features or graphics as compared to existing decorated bottles, the company could expect to attain six percent of the market in the first year. That share could grow at 30 percent per year over subsequent years. To achieve these results, however, the product would have to be unique and special.

To present conservative projected pro financial statements, Warm 'n Safe has assumed that the Company will earn two percent and four percent of the total reusable market in the first and second year of operations. A growth rate of 30 percent per year was assumed for years three through five.

ONGOING MARKET EVALUATION

The Company expects to refine the appearance and marketing of the Warm 'n Safe bottle to meet changing demographics of our customers. The Company will install a 1-800 telephone for customers to call with problems or suggestions. In addition, the Company expects to conduct marketing focus groups on a periodic basis t receive input on new graphic and design changes.

ECONOMICS OF THE BUSINESS

The innovative Warm 'n Safe bottle costs $.35 per unit more to produce than a standard baby bottle. The new feature, however, will allow the Company, and retailers, to market the product at prices comparable to other premium bottles currently available.   At a suggested retail of $3.99, a cost to the retailer of $2.19, and a cost to manufacture and deliver the product of $.92, projected gross margins for Warm 'n Safe and the retailer are 58 percent and 45 percent, respectively.

Initially, the Company will produce a clear, quality plastic bottle to enable the customer to see the difference in the Warm 'n Safe product and other bottles. A decorated bottle would obscure the feature that the Company has developed and result in the appearance of "just another baby bottle." Once the Company and its bottle have achieved recognition and acceptance in the marketplace, Warm 'n Safe will then consider adding graphics to the product which results in little additional cost but is perceived as value added by the consumer.

Continued profit potential and durability exist as births in the United States continue at approximately four million annually. In addition, these four million births comprise only two percent of the world's births. Warm 'n Safe plans to secure patents in all countries where there is a market for the product once final approval of the United States patent is obtained and full production begins.

Fixed costs for the Company will be low as the product will be manufactured by currently existing plastics manufacturers and shipped directly to the retailer. The main fixed costs will be for office and limited warehousing space. Warm 'n Safe will initially employ three personnel to manage and operate a small office to service the needs of consumers and retailers as well as staff a small warehousing operation to fill small or emergency orders. The use of brokers and sales representatives will significantly reduce the amount of fixed labor cost to the Company.

Warm 'n Safe will not recognize any revenues until stage four of the Overall Schedule shown in Section IX of the business plan. Once full-scale production and distribution begins in January 1997, however, the Company will generate positive cash flow from operations within the first year. Pro forma financial statements contained in Section XI of the Plan present management's worst, best and most likely case projections of the results of operations through year five.

Funding for the start up period in the amount of $200,000 will be drawn in three stages to limit investor risk. Only after specified milestones have been met will additional funds be requested and the next stage started. The initial draw of $66,000 will be required thirteen months prior to full production (year one of the Plan) to fund the design, manufacture and testing of the spring and cap molds. Draw two in the amount of $57,000 will be required six months prior to full production to complete bottle and stem molds. And draw three of $77,000 will be required three months prior to full production to fund an initial production run to produce initial inventory.

MARKETING PLAN

OVERALL MARKETING STRATEGY

The overall marketing strategy for the Company is to offer our baby bottle as "safe, convenient and worry-free". Our unique temperature-reading indicator will give bottle a strategic competitive advantage over other baby bottles on the market. After final development and testing of the product, we will secure the services of a master broker who will concentrate on selling our product in the United States in the retail channels that sell baby bottles. After significant penetration in the United States market, the Company will aggressively purse patents and distribution in foreign countries.

PRICING

Retail pricing for reusable bottles averages $3.99 for premium bottles and $2.99 for standard bottles. Premium bottles are equipped with a heavier plastic material than standard bottles and may also include a silicone nipple versus a rubber nipple and color graphics on the bottle. The Warm 'n Safe bottle will be equipped with heavier plastic and the silicone nipple. Those features, along with our temperature indicating device, will allow us to retail our bottle at premium prices, or a suggested retail of $3.99. Our cost to retailers will be at $2.19, freight included, which allows the retailer to earn a 45 percent gross margin, comparable to the margin on other baby bottle products.

SALES TACTICS

The Company expects that the unique attribute of its bottle will encourage consumers to purchase the product. We will design and develop packaging that emphasizes the temperature indicator on the Warm 'n Safe bottle and market the bottle as "safe, convenient and worry-free". Initially, the Company will distribute the product as a floor shipper in as many retail accounts as possible to expose the consumer to our product as quickly as possible. To help achieve this objective, the Company will offer price discounts to retailers who purchase these shippers. To avoid the costs of recurring, training and employing a full-time sales force, the Company will select a master broker to set up an established, experienced sales force comprised of other sales representatives. The master broker will establish sales territories within the United States for each sales representative and add additional sales representatives as the need arises. The master broker will be compensated ten percent of gross sales and five percent of the sales from the broker's sales representatives. In addition, the sales representatives will earn five percent of the sales from the broker's sales representatives. In addition, the sales representatives will earn five percent on their sales. These sales costs have been included in the projected income statements.

WARRANTY POLICIES

The company will offer a money-back guarantee to any customer who is not satisfied with the performance of its products. To assist its customers, Warm 'n Safe will provide a 1-800 number on all packaging. In addition, the Company will guarantee to retailers reimbursement for any returned bottles.

ADVERTISING AND PROMOTION

The Company expects to advertise on a regional, then national basis, in the United States after the first year of sales. Advertising during the first year of sales will be five percent of sales and include point-of-sale materials to place on or near the product in the retail store. For years two and three through five of the plan, the Company projects that advertising expenditures will by four percent and three percent of sales, respectively. The Company expects to use the services of an outside advertising agency to assist in spending advertising dollars as effectively as possible.

DISTRIBUTION

Shipping of the Warm 'n Safe product will be primarily from the manufacturer to the retailer, which will require the Company to provide only minimal warehouse space. Only minimal inventory will be maintained on hand at the Company's warehouse facilities for emergency shipments. This process will eliminate the need for the Company to finance large amounts of on-hand inventory. In addition, the process will keep shipping costs to a minimum.

CHAPTER 8
MANAGEMENT TEAM

This chapter will discuss the importance of the management team and the key areas to address in this section of the business plan, including the management team itself, organizational structure, the board of directors, and ownership.

IMPORTANCE OF THE MANAGEMENT TEAM

This is one of the key sections of the business plan and one that is often read early in the business plan review process by potential investors of the business. Oftentimes this section is read or positioned after the Executive Summary. It is important to ask if the idea for the business is great, but it is more important to ask the question, " How capable is the management team to run a business?" In fact, venture capitalists are known to say that they invest in management not in the business idea itself. Many entrepreneurs think that if they have a great idea, investors will invest. This is just not the case. Why? The reason is that many good business ideas have failed because the businesses lacked experienced, competent management. However, this is not to say that a good idea is not important but rather it takes a good idea with good management as well. Therefore selection of this team is critical to the long-term success of your business and will be a key point of evaluation by investors.

> A good
> idea ≠
> interested
> investors

It is important to select a team that will complement you in terms of skills and experience. Avoid the common tendency to choose individuals similar to you. Rather make your selection based on the needs of your particular venture. Determine who is best suited to meet those needs and will complement other members of the management team.

AREAS TO ADDRESS IN THIS SECTION

What needs to be included in this section? Information about the management team, the organizational structure, information about the ownership, and the board of directors.

However, prior to assessing the management team, a business owner needs to begin with an assessment of himself in terms of his own strengths and weaknesses, and skills and experience in relation to the requirements of the company. How will your strengths help you to successfully run the business and how will you compensate for your areas of weakness? Once this has been done you can determine what other positions need to be filled and the expertise that is required for them.

> Important:
>
> Skills +
> Experience
>
> are needed to
> start and run
> a business

One of the common errors that entrepreneurs make is that they start businesses for the wrong reason. A person who is great at developing web sites or cooking things, think that they will be great at running their own business. We have seen entrepreneurs do this over and over again with terrible results. One of the first things that a prospective entrepreneur needs to do is to take a careful assessment of their own skills. It takes organizational, financial, and management skills to run a business.

It is really surprising that individuals want a pilot of an airplane to have lots of experience and they want their family doctor to be very experienced, yet they think they do not need experience to run a business. You need skills and experience to run a business. Starting your business without these skills is going to put you in a very precarious situation.

However, all is not lost. If you do not have these skills and experience, you can get them (e.g. obtain work in a similar industry). We worked with a person who wanted to start a landscape business and recommended that he work for a year in a landscaping business and he heeded our advice. During the year, he started to rethink if he really had all the skills and motivation necessary to run his own business. He decided that being an entrepreneur was not the best use of his skills and abilities.

THE MANAGEMENT TEAM

Include all individuals who will play a significant role in the venture as well as those that will lend credibility to the business such as a board of directors, key advisors, and key management personnel who will be added. You may also want to include a key employee that has a skill that is critical to the business. You need to describe the responsibilities and expectations of each of the key persons involved in the business and what they will contribute to the business, their compatibility to each other and the business, along with the title of their position.

Make sure that the major areas such as marketing, operations, and finance are covered. It is not necessary to have a person for each area but that each area has someone that is responsible for it. Include a brief background of the key persons, their position, including the primary duties of this position, and discuss their educational background, experience, and any special training, skills, or abilities, and accomplishments. Include detailed information about their backgrounds that will be valuable to the business venture. For example, if your sales manager had accomplished five years of twenty percent annual sales gains in his previous position include that information as an investor will think that this person could most likely accomplish the same for your venture. The information that you include in this section should be able to give the reader enough information to make an evaluation of the strength of your management team. More detailed information regarding the management team can be included on their resumes and placed in the Supporting Documents section of the business plan.

Even if a key position has not yet been filled, include a job description for the position, the necessary skills and job experience needed, when you will fill this position, and how you will recruit and hire a person to meet this role. Investors will want to see a well-rounded management team.

If a member of the management team has experienced a business failure include that information as it can show what that the individual has learned from the experience.

EXAMPLE: MANAGEMENT TEAM

The company has been organized as a subchapter S corporation. This has proven to be a wise move as the first four years caused some major financial debt to the corporation. Mr. Michael is currently in the process of filing bankruptcy for the original corporation and establishing another corporate umbrella. The knowledge, skills, and abilities that Mr. Michael has gained through the unsuccessful venture will provide him with excellent examples of procedures to avoid.

Comment: Past failures have proven to be a valuable learning experience.

You will need to mention the compensation package including incentives that you offer members of the management. If you are seeking investment money, this information is important because any investor will want to know the financial stake that your management team has in the business, and other terms of employment. You may have a member of your management team that lacks experience for the position. In this case you would need to explain how you will make up for the deficiencies by obtaining outside assistance either from your advisors (CPA, attorney, consultants) or from experienced Board members. A strong Board of Directors or Board of Advisors can compensate for weak areas in your management team. This should be noted and explained.

EXAMPLE:

> The management team will consist of Margaret Henry as the company's CEO and Thomas Henry as the Vice-president. Tom Watkins and David Smith are heads of Marketing and Sourcing and Jack Davis is the head of Finance. As production increases, additional employees will be hired as needed. The board of directors will include Margaret Henry, Thomas Henry, William Burns, Wilson Smith and Todd Gilbert. Burns is a professor of finance at North State University. Smith is currently a professor of accounting at North State University. Todd Gilbert is currently a corporate attorney in Miami, Florida.

> *Comment: They really need to have a much more thorough explanation of each team member's area of responsibility and experience. At least separate out the Board of Directors in another paragraph and detail the expertise that each would bring to the business and how each complements the management team.*

EXAMPLE: MANAGEMENT TEAM

The *Universal Subs'* management team will consist of two men whose backgrounds include college degrees and restaurant experience. The officers and key employees consist of:

> Larry Russo, CEO/President of Marketing
> Steve Downs, President of Finance

Outside Support consists of:

> Michael Larramore, CPA
> Frank Russo, Information Systems Consultant
> Gladys Allen, Attorney at Law
> Rusty Kilgore, Harry's Subs – Director of Franchising

Stock Allocation

The two founders of Universal Subs, Larry Russo and Steve Downs equally hold all shares of common stock.

OFFICER RESPONSIBILITIES

Larry Russo, CEO/President of Marketing

Develops and maintains the vision of Universal Subs. Oversees marketing, product development, customer service, etc. Seeks business opportunities and funding for new or continuing operations in order to maximize return on investments, and increase productivity. Plans, develops, and establishes policies and objectives of Universal Subs in accordance with Harry's Subs. In addition, will manage marketing plan, advertising, public relations, sales promotion, and merchandising. Will oversee market research and analysis as well as evaluation of competition.

Steve Downs, President of Finance

Manages working capital including receivables, inventory, cash, etc. Performs financial forecasting including capital budget, cash budget, pro forma financial statements, external financing requirements, financial condition requirements. Prepare reports that will outline company's financial position in areas of income, expenses, and earnings, based on past, present, and future earnings.

The responsibilities of the outside management support will be to provide Universal Subs with financial, legal, managerial, and technical guidance.

MANAGEMENT TEAM BACKGROUNDS

Larry Russo, CEO/President of Marketing
Bachelor of Science in Operations Management / Bachelor of Science in Entrepreneurship and Small Business Management

Larry Russo's professional experience includes many different areas. First, Anthony was fortunate enough to work for his that family's business dealt in the field of electrical contracting. Larry was given such responsibilities as supervisor of job sites, which included meeting deadlines and overseeing electricians. Larry learned every aspect of the 23 year-old business and was given the opportunity to eventually take over the family business, but felt the desire to build his own business from the ground up.

Then, Larry went to college and sought employment at Domino's Pizza for 3 ½ years as a driver and associate shift manager. This allowed him to gain valuable experience in the food industry involving management, distribution, production, personnel training, communication, and customer service. In addition to this, Larry acquired knowledge of the Tallahassee food market, customer trends, seasonal forecasting, as well as area demographics. Anthony is the one that came up with the idea for Harry's Subs in Summerville after frequenting Winter Brook, Florida, to visit family. After repeated visits to Harry's Subs, it was then that Larry realized that Summerville, Florida, was neglected of a delicious, consistent, friendly, high quality, submarine sandwich shop

Larry brings to Universal Subs an immense array of entrepreneurial skills, proven small business management skills, knowledge of Tallahassee demographics, and experience in the food industry.

Steve Downs, President of Finance
Bachelor of Science in Accounting / Bachelor of Science in Finance

Steve Downs professional experience includes many areas of restaurant management, operations and customer service. Steve worked for Bobby Rubbino's Inc. (a national restaurant chain) for two and one half years. While at Bobby Rubbino's, Steve gained valuable experience in ordering and maintaining inventory levels. He was also responsible for employee scheduling and preparing payroll. Bobby Rubbino's also provided Steve with an opportunity to develop an important understanding of customer relations. With his understanding of customer relations Steve moved on to become an assistant manager at Charlie's Crab Valet Service. It is here that Steve learned the great importance of communication and customer satisfaction. From here Steve went on to South State University where he earned his Bachelors degree in both accounting and finance. Through his studies Steve learned financial statement preparation and analysis, as well as various aspects of business and tax law. Steve also undertook extensive studies in business management and marketing. Steve is currently enrolled to sit of the Certified Public Accountant's exam on May 8, 1996. Steve brings to Universal Sub's an impressive understanding of restaurant operation and business management as well as a vast array of necessary financial skills (*See Appendix C-2*).

The force of Universal Subs' management team has the combination of management, financial, marketing, and entrepreneurial skills. Although the management team is young and does not have experience in owning their own business, they hope to offset this with their experience, hard work, aggression, and desire to be successful.

Comment:
This is a very thorough section as it includes complete descriptions of each of the members of management and their areas of responsibility. It also describes outside support persons and stock allocation.

EXAMPLE: MANAGEMENT SECTION OF A MANUFACTURING BUSINESS

The management team will be composed of three executives. These managers will be responsible for handling the day-to-day problems that may arise. They will also be involved in determining the tactical and strategic direction that the company will go in. The management team will use its own talents and capabilities to make the day-to-day decisions that will need to be made. If the need arises where the three managers are unable to reach a decision due to the lack of knowledge they will look to the board of directors for assistance.

Comment:
The question is who are these three key management people, what are their positions, their key area of responsibilities, and their capabilities? Contrast this management section with the following management section in which the key members of the management team are described, their key functions in the business are identified and experience that is relevant to the business is noted.

The management team will consist of John Green as the President, CEO. His duties will center on the day-to-day operations of the company and the sales and marketing functions. He graduated from Rhodes College in 1999 with a Bachelor's Degree in general business administration. He is currently an MBA Student at North State University with a concentration in Entrepreneurial Management.

126

The Vice President in charge of sales and marketing will be Jack Green. Mr. Green was an employee of Wal-Mart for twenty years where he rose to the rank of Executive Vice President in charge of the jewelry division. Mr. Green has over thirty years in the retail business and was an integral part in Wal-Mart's growth from 25 stores to the number one retail company in the world. He retired in 1989 and moved to Florida. Two years later he invented, patented, and began marketing WaterWear sunglasses. Along with his partner, Mr. Green is the owner of Nations Eyewear a company out of Fullerstown, Florida, with annual sales in excess of $30 million.

Robert Johnson will be the Vice President in charge of programming and technical solutions. Robert Johnson is the owner and founder of SmartNet in Summerville, FL. Along with his partner, the company has over ten years of internet consulting and marketing services. SmartNet developed the web site for the Florida Bar Association as well as numerous other web-based applications for profit and non-profit organizations.

INFORMATION ABOUT OWNERSHIP

Include the names, the percentage of ownership and form of ownership, type of common stock, and extent of involvement with the business. Including information about who controls your company will help the reader get a better understanding of who will be making decisions in the business. Lenders in particular will be interested in this information since they will require a sizeable stake in the business in return for the funds that they are investing.

EXAMPLE: OWNERSHIP

Our management team consists of three people. Their backgrounds consist primarily of college degrees in Business Administration.

Officers and Key Employees	Age	Stock
Paul Brown, President / CEO	[23]	[33 1/3]
Vice President Finance		
George Miller, President of Marketing	[23]	[33 1/3]
Cameron Adams, President of Administration	[23]	[33 1/3]
Manana's Corporate Franchise Support	[**]	[0]
Wyatt Thomas, Corporate Attorney	[56]	[0]
Harold James, Controller	[21]	[0]

Of the six members who make up the corporate staff, there are three founders who hold the following positions:

⇒   Paul Brown, President / CEO

⇒   George Miller, Director of Marketing

⇒   Cameron Adams, Director of Administrations

Each founder has been provided with 33 1/3% of the original stock issue.

Comment: This plan indicates the amount of stock ownership. The type of stock should also be indicated.

EXAMPLE: OWNERSHIP

James Michael has always managed the company. This management structure will continue to be in effect during the turnaround phase of the business. His mother will continue to handle the daily operations of the business when he is not available. Once the business has successfully completed the turnaround phase, Mr. Michael hopes to establish a training procedure program.

Comment:
Although this business was structured as a subchapter S corporation, no mention is made of the percentage of ownership of the involved parties nor the type of common stock.

EXAMPLE: COMPENSATION AND OWNERSHIP

Dr. Holden	—Salary $90,000 per year, no benefits. Ownership 45%
Mr. Pauley	—Salary $25,000 per year, no benefits. Ownership 6%
Mr. Robertson	—Salary $25,000 per year, no benefits. Ownership <1%
Earlier investors	—25% of the company
Investor(s) in this round of funding	—25% of the Company

Comment: They have identified involved parties and percent of ownership (note that ownership is >100%). Overall they have been thorough in this section. It would be beneficial to have more detailed information on their experience and how it related to the business.

ORGANIZATIONAL CHART
The purpose of the chart is to indicate key persons involved in the business and to show their areas of responsibility. Include an organizational chart that includes descriptions of the functions of each position and how it relates to the other positions. Include a narrative description of the chart. In the beginning there is probably only a few persons involved and they probably have to wear many hats.

Nonetheless, it is important to identify the areas of responsibility of these individuals because the company will grow and this will warrant more structure in the organization. Undefined areas of responsibility and decision making can become a source of contention particularly in a partnership.

EXAMPLE: ORGANIZATIONAL CHART

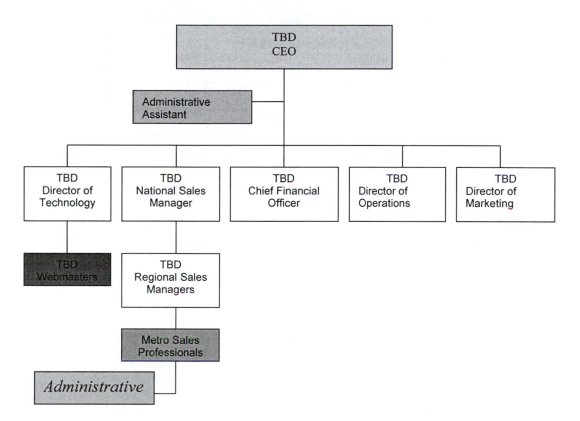

BOARD OF DIRECTORS

List members of the Board and their value to your business. Indicate their corporate affiliations and their areas of experience, education, training, and any special contributions they will make to the business. If you have not selected a board, take the time to detail the skills of the persons that you would like to have on the board for your business. It is not unusual for a small business to use the skills of their board of directors to provide the expertise that they could not afford to have on their management team. If this is the situation of your business you should emphasize the board's knowledge and experience.

When selecting your board seek individuals that complement your skills. You may want to begin by listing your own skills and then list the skills required for your business. Select board members on the basis of these skills and their related. Resist the temptation to fill the board with friends, rather select on the basis of what they can contribute to your business. If you have not selected a board yet, list the skills and experience that you would seek for your board.

EXAMPLE: MANAGEMENT SECTION DESCRIBING THE BOARD OF DIRECTORS

To insure that the business become successful a board of directors was put in place. The board of directors will be composed of five members. Mr. Matthew Carlson is a CPA that has degrees in Finance and Accounting from Florida State University. He is currently working as an accountant for the Centerplex in Summerville. Prof. James Doe currently a Professor of Management at North State University, will serve on the board as the management consultant. Dr. Wilson will occupy one of the seats of the board. He has a degree in Physical Chemistry from Northwestern University and has developed the product MagicFilm that currently has a patent pending.

Comment: Although only three seats on the board have been filled at this time, this section gives the reader a clear idea of the background of these members. This section could be improved by adding more detail about the contribution the members bring to the business.

EXAMPLE: MANAGEMENT SECTION DESCRIBING THE BOARD OF DIRECTORS

The Board of Directors is currently comprised of the following members: the two founders, the Chairman of the Board, the Chief Executive Officer, the Director of Operations, the Director of Technology, and the Accounting Manager. In addition, directors of the venture capital firm that provides the company with funding will sit of the board. Directors will not be paid any fee or compensation for acting as such, although the Chairman may be reimbursed for reasonable expenses incurred when attending Board meetings.

Comment: Unfortunately none of these positions have been filled (except for the two founders) so we can only make assumptions about the skills, expertise, and experience that they will bring to the company. It would be better not to mention these persons at this point. Additionally, they have too many company members on the board and defeat the purpose of the use of the board to bring different perspectives to the business. Also, they should pay board members for their participation.

EXAMPLE: BOARD OF DIRECTORS

Carmen Black - Corporate Attorney- will serve as legal and financial advisor
Byron Jones - successful entrepreneur and owner of Jackson Fabricators, will serve as Management and Business Consultant
George Godfrey - Majority owner of the Godfrey Guitar Company - will serve as chairperson based on his extensive expertise in manufacturing and guitars.

Comment: This is a very limited board. It would be beneficial to know more about the type of business that Mr. Jones was involved in and Ms. Black's areas of expertise.

PROFESSIONAL SUPPORT SERVICES

If you have established working relationships with an accountant, attorney, insurance agency, or other services, describe each service and what experience and contacts they will bring to your business. Indicate their education and where they received their degrees. Check with peers in your industry for their recommendations of quality support service providers. If potential lenders or investors look at your plan, this will be an indicator to them that you have put into place the support that you will need for the business. A good idea is to try to find a firm with strong credentials that is just starting out as they are more likely to take you on and you get the benefit of top-notch services. Plus you can mention this in your business plan.

EXAMPLE: PROFESSIONAL SUPPORT SERVICES

Outside Services
Robert Cox —CPA, accounting, taxes, financial strategies
Finch, Goldman, & Rose of Santa Cruz —Legal Counsel, contracts, acquisitions, possible IPO
Insurance—to be determined—risk management, workmen's compensation, disability, liability
Banker—same as investor(s)

Comment: More information regarding the experience of these advisors would be of value. It is not clear whether the description regarding the advisor is the area in which they will be assisting the business or if this is their area of expertise in their respective fields.

CHAPTER SUMMARY

This is one of the key sections of the business plan as the success of your business is dependent upon the strength of the management team. It is important to carefully select this team in terms of the experience and skills that they bring to the business and to seek individuals that complement each other in these areas. An organizational chart can be developed to clearly define areas of responsibility and the persons responsible for them. A board of directors should be established as they can provide the expertise that you cannot afford to have on the management team. Professional support service providers can also add credibility to your business and relationships with them should be developed early on in the business.

MISTAKES TO AVOID

> - Selecting a team with similar skills and experience rather than one that complements each other.
> - Having undefined areas of responsibility.
> - Delay or avoid setting up a board of directors.
> - Place friends or family in positions for which they are not qualified.
> - Failing to identify outside advisors.
> - Attaining key personnel by giving away too much ownership or too high compensation.

CHAPTER APPLICATION

1. Complete the Management Worksheet of the business plan.
2. Meet with owner of a growing company and ask how they determined management compensation and how much to pay self.
3. Meet with entrepreneurs of a growing company and determine extent of the management team, their strengths, and their use of a Board of Directors, and outside advisors
4. Review the following management section of the business plan for XYZ Company:

- Have they included the key elements for this section?
- How could it be improved?

If you were a potential investor, what would be your evaluation of the capabilities of this team?

Management Plan of XYZ Company

Form of Business Operation:

A sole proprietorship being jointly owned by Sidney Carr
and Mary Carr.
Board of Directors:
Chairman - Sidney Carr, owner/research manager
Mary Carr, owner/operations manager
Advisory Board:
Chairman - Sidney Carr, owner/research manager
Mary Carr, owner/operations manager
Attorney- as needed
CPA- as needed
Insurance- as needed

RESOURCES

Ernst & Young
www.ey.com/
This Ernst & Young site contains articles that will assist you in determining how
to best utilize a Board of Directors.

EntreWorld
http://www.entreworld.org
This site has information on starting and growing a business

Institute of Management and Administration Business Pages
http://www.ioma.com/
Articles on compensation and industry resources.

Advanced Consulting Group
http://www.advgroup.com
Contains articles to assess entrepreneur with management concerns.

Canada's Business and Consumer
http://strategis.ic.gc.ca/SSG/cw03240e.html
Information on establishing a Board of Directors

MANAGEMENT WORKSHEET

Management Team:
List the key members of your management team.

_____
_____
_____
_____
_____

 Identify their position and detail their areas of responsibility.

_____

_____

_____

Give background information on each, including education, skills, abilities and experience they bring to this business. Describe their successes and their areas of strengths._____
_____

Identify key management that you plan to add to your team (include position and anticipated date of addition).
_____
_____
_____

What style of management will be used?
_____
_____

Ownership:
What is the ownership interest of each involved. Include stock options.
_____
_____

Explain the compensation package of each, include salary, benefits, bonuses and other incentives.
_____
_____
_____
_____
_____

Organizational Structure:
How will the company be organized? Note key management and their positions._____
_____

Prepare an organizational chart of the management
structure._____

_____

Board of Directors:
If you have selected a board of directors, list them, their experience, and the value
they will bring to the company._____

_____

_____

Professional Support Services:
Identify professional support resources that are currently working with your
business, their qualifications, and how they will assist your company. Include
your attorney, accountant, consultants, etc.

_____

_____

_____

_____

_____

SAMPLE PLAN: WARM 'N SAFE BOTTLE COMPANY

MANAGEMENT TEAM

The management team will be built in stages. Initially, Ryan Addison will be the only employee at Warm 'n Safe Bottle Company. His diverse expertise in engineering and manufacturing will be sufficient for all tasks in the early start up stages of the Company. Addison will hold the position of President and Chief Executive Officer. Dan Mays will be brought on board as the Director of Marketing as the Company enters stage four. May's experience in retail will be required once the Company begins its initial production phase. Kevin Harper will join the Company as Director of Finance at the beginning of year two. Harper's experience in accounting and finance for a major convenience store chain will provide the required financial support as the Company expands and accounting issues become more complex. Alex Farmer will also join the Company at the beginning of year two as Director of Manufacturing.

Financial compensation for the management team can be found in Section XI of the Plan. In addition, each of these employees, the board members and other professional advisors will be compensated through the issuance of stock of the company. The following table outlines proposed distribution of stock:

	Initial	Year 2	Year 4
Investor	20%		
Board Members	6%		
Attorneys	2%		
Ryan Addison	22%		
Dan Mays	2%	2%	3%
Scott Tilden	2%	2%	
Kevin Harper	2%	2%	
Alicia Whitney	2%	2%	
Alex Farmer	1%	2%	1%
Un-issued Stock	41%	31%	27%

Un-issued stock will be reserved for future financing needs, as incentives for attracting new key personal and other needs as agreed upon by the board of directors. In the event that the Company is sold, un-issued stock will be divided among the employee owner according to their percentage of the employee ownership.

The board of Directors will consist of Addison, Dan Mays, Bennett Marshall, Ph.D., and the investor. Dr. Marshall is currently a professor of finance at West State University. Professional advisors to the board will consist of Lester Gordon, Esq., Doug Kessler of Star Commerce Bank and Anita Downs, CPA.

CHAPTER 9
PRODUCTION

In this section we will consider the different aspects of production including production processes, <u>outsourcing</u>, and research and development.

When writing this section, you will want to include information that will provide answers to questions that investors may have with sufficient detail without becoming too tedious with explanations because an investor will not provide money for a venture that they do not clearly understand. There is a tendency among entrepreneurs to want to get too detailed in the actual production process in this section when it is really more important to focus on what is critical to the process and what it is about the process that will set you apart from your competition. This is particularly true if the business plan is written for the purpose of acquiring funding. However, if the plan will be used solely for planning internal operations, the plan should be very detailed and thorough.

PRODUCTION PROCESSES

You will need to spend a great deal of time discussing the process in detail for your use internally, describing the process from raw material to the finished product. Include lead time, the technology required for the process, where inventory will be stored, and how the product will be distributed. For external use of the business plan you can have less detail but include more information regarding how you will market this product.

In this section, address not only the materials needed to produce the product but the personnel and the capital equipment required for the process. These factors are critical. Include information on production rates (the time and the number of persons it takes to produce your product) and the capacity of the facility. Detail the various stages of production and evaluate them as to efficiency with the goal of reducing time and costs while maintaining quality. Include a flow chart of the manufacturing processes. If your production process includes any new technologies include information on that and explain any advantages or disadvantages of your production process. Discuss whether you will outsource all or part of the production process. We will discuss the option of outsourcing in greater detail later in this chapter.

You will want to establish quality control procedures for the manufacturing process. If you plan to sell your products internationally you will need to get your products certified to meet international quality control standards. Additional information regarding these standards is provided in the Resources section of this chapter.

It is necessary to determine the cost of goods sold. For a manufacturing company this is the cost of producing the product. In order to determine this number you will need include material, labor, and overhead that is directly related to the production of the product. You may want to consider the use of variable labor if your business often special orders or if there is seasonal work as this will reduce your overall labor costs.

You will also need to determine your operating expenses. These are the expenses that are necessary to run your business. This will be discussed in more detail in the financial section of this book.

EXAMPLE: PRODUCTION PROCESSES

Harbour Master will manufacture its boats and its trailers. Motors will be provided through contract agreements with several different companies. Harbour Master's manufacturing philosophy is "Pay attention to the details, and keep the process simple." The remainder of this section is devoted to describing the manufacturing process for the boats and the trailers.

- The CAD software renders drawings of the flat metal components that must be cut to shape for manufacture.
- Computer Numerically Controlled(CNC) machines are fed the instructions for cutting the metal components and the plasma cutting torches cut the components.
- During the initial stages of operation, plasma cutting may be outsourced. Later Harbour Master will purchase its own equipment.
- Cut component metal is then sent to a bending fixture where the bottom, sides, and transom are bent to the required shape for the boat being manufactured.
- The shaped metal us then tack welded to hold it in place for the final welding process.
- A computer controlled robotic welding is used to complete the welding of the hull. The machine uses a guide that follows the joint of the metal component to ensure a consistent and quality weld.
- A latitudinal rib and longitudinal stringer are then welded on the interior to further strengthen the hull.
- Two-part polyurethane foam is then added to the interior of the hull to provide flotation, greater strength, and sound deadening.
- The floor of the boat is then placed on top of the expanded foam and welded or glued into place.
- Gunnels for the side of the boat are cut by the CNC plasma cutter and welded over the sides of the hull.
- Rub rails constructed of extruded aluminum are then welded directly to the sides of the hull.

- The boat is then flipped upside down.
- The aft 2/3 and center of the hull is then cut out and a metal tunnel component welded in its place to create a tunnel system.
- Longitudinal strengthening and directional elements are welded to the bottom of the hull.
- The boat is then flipped right straight up.
- The transom and interior welding are then complete for the boat.
- Check and grind welds to smooth them.
- Apply paint and decals for the boat according to model.
- Install purchased hardware, carpeting, and electrical.
- Place boat in a trailer, mount engine and other associated control components.

Comment: They have been very thorough in their description of the manufacturing process. In a previous section they outlined the manufacturing equipment required, but they need to include lead time for the process.

EXAMPLE: PRODUCTION COSTS

Estimated production costs for 10,000 units

Materials

Square steel tubing $118,000	
20,000 12 inch clamps @ $3.50 each	$ 70,000
20,000 swivel castors @ $2.00 each	$ 40,000
20,000 locking castors @ $2.50 each	$ 50,000
10,000 cardboard boxes 200# white @ $3.75 each	$ 37,500
Material Subtotal	$315,500

15% overrun[1]	$ 47,325
Subtotal	$362,825

Labor Costs
Based on five $9/hr workers----45/hr. x 8/hr/day = 360 day
360/day x 5/day/week = 1800/week x 20 weeks = 36,000
Plus 75% for benefits, 27,000

Subtotal $63,000

Total $425,825

Cost per unit $ 42.58

_____

[1] This 15% overrun handles concerns like damages and worker's compensation

Comment: They need to indicate capital equipment costs and capacity of facility.

SUPPLIERS

It is important that you indicate that you not only have adequate sources of supply but that these sources are reliable. Obviously price is an important consideration but also be concerned about getting quality supplies that are delivered on time. Indicate backup sources of supply as well. You do not want to be solely dependent upon one source since you may experience a problem at some point in time. Detail the contracts that you have with the suppliers. This is important since you rely on them to provide you with the needed materials.

CAPITAL EQUIPMENT

Typically manufacturing is a very capital intensive process and you will need to examine costs and availability of each piece of needed equipment. Discuss where and how you will be able to purchase the equipment and the depreciation schedule for each. Include not only equipment needed to manufacture the product but transportation vehicles and office equipment. Note if any of the equipment needs to be replaced and the maintenance involved for each piece. Trade associations can direct you to sources of equipment. Also Thomas Register is a source of not only equipment suppliers but also of suppliers and distributors.

EXAMPLE: CAPITAL EQUIPMENT

Computer Aided Design (CAD) computer design system $74,000
Computer Numerically Controlled (CNC) Plasma Cutter $89,000
Metal Bending Fixture $45,000

Computer-controlled Robotic Welding Machine $600,000
MIG Welding Machines $175,000
TIG Welding Machines $50,000
Foam Insulation Machine/Sprayer $25,000
Rhino Lining Machine $26,000
Iron worker $36,000

Comment: Need to discuss where and how they will be able to purchase the equipment, and include transportation vehicles, and office equipment.

PERSONNEL

You will need to determine the number of personnel needed and the skills required to start and run the business. You will not need to address the management that is required and their areas of responsibility as this has been done in the Management section of the business plan. However, you will need to examine the pool of available labor in the area of the proposed facility. It is critical that there is a sufficient pool of labor in the vicinity as even the best facility cannot operate without adequate personnel. Determine how you will train and evaluate employees and include this information in this section.

If the plan is for a new business you can get an estimate of the personnel required by reviewing the operations of your competitors. If you have previous experience in this industry you will already have a good idea of what it will take to manufacture the product. If you are an existing business evaluate your current production process to determine if it can be improved so that costs can be better controlled and quality can be improved.

FACILITY

Manufacturing requires a facility and you will need to provide information on the building and the land. Include information on your space requirements, whether the facility is adequate for production, and if your location is near sources of labor. Also note what methods of transportation are available to move your product and to obtain supplies. Again a good location near transportation, labor, and suppliers is important so that you can deliver your product efficiently in terms of cost and time. You may want to include a layout of the facility in the Supporting Documents section of the business plan. Costs of the facility should be included and indicate whether you plan to purchase the land and building or whether you will lease it. If you will lease the facility, you will want to give the terms of the lease including the length of the lease, restrictions, and the rate charged. If you will have to make any improvements to the facility you will need to include that as well. If you are an existing business discuss the adequacy of your current facility and whether it is adequate to handle growth. Mention any advantages of the location and your plans if you outgrow the facility.

EXAMPLE: FACILITY

Since the production of the "Metal Works" will be subcontracted, all production and operating facilities will be owned by Cliff Brannon. With a 7000 square foot facility in Winter Brook, Florida, Brannon will begin part-time production with five employees. Brannon has the equipment needed to efficiently produce this product. Due to the high unemployment rate in Winter Brook, he will not have difficulty in hiring labor. He has the optional space to hire more employees depending in the success of the test market. There is also the option to contract more facilities in area that are close to retail distributors depending on the success of the test market.

Comment: They should note what methods of transportation that are available to move their product and obtain supplies. Cost of the facility should be included.

EXAMPLE: FACILITY

The manufacturing facility will be located in Lynn Haven, FL. This location will provide needed space for initial production and expansion to a larger location will be determined as our projected sales levels are met over the next five years. The company already owns the current manufacturing facility. An efficient production process hinges on proper layout of the manufacturing facility (Appendix F)

Comment: Information is not given regarding the size of this location, costs of the facility, nor whether it is near sources of labor or transportation. However, layout of the plant is given in the company's appendix.

OUTSOURCING

Include details of your plans if you are planning on outsourcing production. You will need to address alternate sources of product if your subcontractor has problems or is not able to fulfill the supply needs of your business. Compare outsourcing production of your product or at least outsourcing various components of the product. Eliminating facility maintenance, equipment, and the workforce necessary to produce the product may be advantageous to the business.

You will want to thoroughly consider the option of outsourcing and look at not only the cost benefits but also the time savings as well. Setting up a production process cannot only be very costly for equipment and personnel but also is very demanding of the entrepreneur's time. This may mean that there is less time to focus on marketing the product. This is true even of a relatively simple product. Discuss the advantages of outsourcing in this section.

EXAMPLE: OUTSOURCING

The Weed Waster will be manufactured in the United States by a company in North Florida or South Georgia region. The company feels that in order to keep an eye on quality control the facilities should be located close to the company's headquarters. The company chosen to manufacture Easy Weed will be given full control of purchasing the material for the construction of the product as long as the materials chosen do not jeopardize the quality of the Weed Waster.

All distribution to retail stores will be from the manufacturer so a company with the ability to receive and load truck quickly will be desired. Locating the facility in the United States should ensure that any order taken can be delivered in about a week barring a truck strike.

The company will be located in the Northern Florida region because of its low warehouse costs and it is a convenient place for the management staff to live. The operation will be run initially with one office person and the three managers. The company will grow as needed. The company does not see the need to relocate any time in the near future.

Comment: They may want to consider alternate outsourcing options in the situation that this one does not work out as well as expected.

EXAMPLE: OUTSOURCING

Our products are going to be outsourced to several firms, however, we are going to maintain an office in Summersville, Florida, to store and ship the inventory. The inventory will be packaged and shipped by a labor force made up of part-time employees. Our salaries and wage expense is based upon $6 per hour and the average employee can complete 20 packages per hour. The facility and storage will cost approximately $2000 per monthly including electricity. We have made an arrangement with UPS to pick up the packages from the warehouse. We will minimize inventory through the use of just-in-time inventory. Also, the shipping time to the customer is going to be 4-6 weeks, but the shipping time from our suppliers to us is only 2-3 weeks. This allows buffer for unexpected sales.

Comment: They have addressed key areas in the production process for this t-shirt business.

EXAMPLE: OUTSOURCING

In house manufacturing was considered, however, the decision was made to outsource to another company. Epitome Inventions Holding Corporation built the original prototype and will, due their competitive price and terms, manufacture PatientLite. The price quoted by Epitome includes packaging and shipping. The initial manufacturing price is $160 per unit, decreasing to about $100 with volume beyond 1,000 units.

Comment: Cost benefits are considered but no mention is made of the time savings if any. Discuss the advantages of the decision to outsource.

RESEARCH AND DEVELOPMENT

You need to determine to what extent your industry is driven by technology as this will indicate the importance of R & D in your business. If you are in an industry that is continually innovating product then research and development is critical to the survival and long term success of your business. For example, this is true of the computer industry where it is necessary to have excellent R & D organization to remain competitive. Failure to continually be innovative could mean the difference between survival and failure. Even if your business sells a traditional product like bread you will need to develop new products as the concerns of your customer changes. The point is that research and development must be given high consideration in any type of business. What you will need to consider is not only the extent that your industry is driven by technology but also your future commitment to technology.

Include any new products or services currently in development in this section. Discuss the research staff that will be needed to maintain the necessary level of innovation to remain competitive in your industry. Also determine the equipment and supplies needed for research and development and include in this section.

EXAMPLE: RESEARCH AND DEVELOPMENT

After the development and production of version one of the Golf Pro product, Golf Product International will analyze the demand for the product and determine if the demand exists for Golf Products International to develop a new version of the Golf Pro. If this is the case, future additions to the Golf Pro product could include scoring of the round, tips section, and the speed of the club head as it passes.
The cost of manufacturing the completed Golf Pro product is as follows:

Wafer board	.42
Circuitry	.58
Battery	1.00
Sleeve	.50
Manufacturing	8.00
Packaging/distribution	3.00
Total	$13.50

These figures were developed based on small unit purchases of parts required. As the demand for parts increases, economies of scale should provide for a decrease in manufacturing cost as the demand for the production unit increases. An overall schedule for the development and distribution of the Golf Pro product is included as a separate section within the business plan.

Comment: This addresses not only the need for future development but includes costs of production at the current levels.

EXAMPLE: RESEARCH AND DEVELOPMENT

Much of the effort at Easy Sprout during the past three year period has been spent on research and product/process development. The sprout jar and products have been tested for ability to be manufactured and are currently ready to market.

Comment: Much of the research and development has been to bring product to market. They do not indicate whether additional research will be done to develop additional products nor do they indicate how critical this is to their industry.

PRODUCTION PROCESSES FOR SERVICE AND RETAIL BUSINESSES

If you have a service or retail business you may be thinking that you do not have to address operations processes since you are not involved in manufacturing. Unfortunately this is not true. Obviously service and retail businesses have different operations requirements from manufacturers but those requirements still need to be addressed in the business plan. Compared to a manufacturer, your operational plans will be relatively simple. Basically they consist of purchasing products for sale, the shipping of these products, and the sale of them. Nonetheless you need to consider this process as it requires securing a facility, locating personnel, selecting suppliers, and purchasing some equipment (this depends on the nature of your business). Let's take a closer look at the components of this process.

> Retail and service businesses: Sorry, but you **do not** get to skip this chapter

The location of your business is particularly critical for retail and service businesses and often is a factor in whether the business will succeed or not. When discussing the location for a retail business include information on traffic patterns, facility costs, and demographic data. The information that you obtained in the marketing section of the business plan will be useful, particularly the demographics of the area and anticipated growth patterns.

Another important consideration is the personnel required for your business. Personnel is an important component in a service and retail business as customer service is a key to success. Estimate the number of staff required for your operation and determine whether sufficient skilled personnel can be found in the area.

Retailers will need to identify their sources of suppliers since having reliable and reasonably priced suppliers are key components of their operations. Not only will you want to give sources of supplies but provide details on any supply agreements.

If you need equipment for your business you will need to list any required equipment. Indicate whether you will purchase or lease the equipment and indicate the costs involved.

CHAPTER SUMMARY

This section considered the production process and the factors that need to be addresses including suppliers, capital equipment, personnel, and the facility itself. Any plans to outsource the production process should be detailed along with research and development projects.

CHAPTER APPLICATIONS

> ➤ Complete the Production Worksheet

> ➤ Interview the owner of a firm that outsource their production processes and determine why this was the appropriate choice for this business.

> ➤ Review the Thomas Register and determine the product category for your business, the number of companies included, and the number of different product categories that are included.

> ➤ Analyze the following Production Section of the Business Plan and make suggestions for its improvement.

EXAMPLE

DentuLab Inc. subcontracts the manufacturing of all components. These components are then shipped to the facility in Summersville, Florida, where the remaining 25% of the assembly is completed. The components are then tested, labeled, and packaged for shipping. Presently there is no assembly line in place. One person performs all four of the previously mentioned tasks.

Currently demand for the product is slow. Slow demand allow DentuLab to give each unit individual attention. At the present time, DentuLab is not able to handle a high volume of orders without creating a backlog.

This plant has the capacity to assemble approximately 200 units per month. It is believed that the plants production capabilities could be increased by another 200 units if the facility was redesigned. All components are presently assembled manually although there are plans to introduce automated devices as demand increases.

MISTAKES TO AVOID

➢ Failure to outline the manufacturing process in its entirety.
➢ Lack of information on distribution and selling of the product.
➢ Failure to list all equipment requirements and not planning long term equipment changes.
➢ Lack of contingency plan to meet production and staffing.
➢ Lack of backup suppliers

RESOURCES

Thomas Register
http://www.thomasregister.com
Source of suppliers, distributors, and equipment manufacturers.
Trade associations can help find persons to assist with manufacturing design and sources to find equipment.

American Society for Quality
http://www.asq.org
Information on standards and certification. Includes ISO 9000 international certification for a small manufacturing company, and FAQ's on certification.

International Organization for Standardization
http://www.iso.ch
Information on standardized procedures.

PRODUCTION WORKSHEET

Production Processes:
Briefly describe your production process, its stages, and any new technologies used._____
_____

List the materials that are required for production ._____
_____

What are the lead time requirements?_____
_____

Given your current capacity, how many units can be produced in a month?
_____

Are you operating at capacity? If so, how will you accommodate growth?
_____

What is the cost to produce one unit? Breakeven point?_____
_____

Do you have any production advantages?_____
_____

What safety procedures are in place, what is your record?_____
_____

How will you manage inventory?_____
_____

What are your operating competitive advantages (techniques, experience, direct costs)_____

Detail any environmental concerns for production of the product such as pollution and disposal of waste, etc._____
_____

What are your location requirements? (include information on proximity to suppliers, labor, and transportation)_____
_____

Have you implemented quality control measures ?_____
_____

Facility:
Describe the manufacturing facility and condition._____

Note any renovations that are needed._____
_____
_____

What are your space requirements?_____
_____

Suppliers:
List your major suppliers of raw materials and terms of contract with them or
anticipated contractual relationships with suppliers._____
_____

What are the names of alternate suppliers?_____
_____

Capital Equipment:
Is the capital equipment leased or purchased?_____
_____

What are your capital equipment requirements?_____
_____

What equipment do you currently have? What do anticipate purchasing in the
near future?_____
_____

Personnel:
How many employees do you have (distinguish between full and part time)?
_____

If you have shifts, how long are they and how many do you have?_____
_____

Do you have a well trained work force? What are the training
needs/requirements?_____

Research and Development:
Have you planned any future development of products? If so, what will this
involve in terms of capital requirements, facilities, personnel?

How much money do you spend on R & D?_____
_____

What is your company's commitment to R & D?_____
_____

Is your industry driven by technology?_____
_____

Outsourcing:

Will the product be outsourced? If so, what portion will be contracted out (initially and in three years)?_____

What costs will be involved in outsourcing? Include any inventory costs, shipping costs. _____

What are the names of alternate sources of subcontractors that could supply your business? How do they compare in terms of costs and quality? _____
_____

If you outsource any or all of your production, name and describe the company and what component they produce and the cost._____
_____

SAMPLE PLAN: WARM 'N SAFE BOTTLE COMPANY MANUFACTURING AND OPERATIONS

The Warm 'n Safe baby bottle during the initial four years will most likely be manufactured in the Far East, where most bottles for the United States market are produced today. The component manufacture will be contracted only through manufacturers identified as quality injection molders. Firms experienced in providing service worldwide will also perform the assembly, packaging and shipping.

Alternative suppliers have been identified in the United States, although manufacturing costs are expected to be higher. These sources would have the advantage of shorter delivery time due to its closer proximity. The United States manufacturers will be kept as a secondary source in case supply problems occur. Since the investment castings (molds) will belong to the Company, injection molding can actually take place anywhere worldwide where injection-molding capabilities exist.

Manufacturing will occur year round. When manufacturing reaches sufficient levels, bulk purchasing of plastic will be performed during seasonal price drops. This should lead to a materials cost savings of at least five percent.

Operations during the initial years will be based in Northwest Florida. This area, having both an international port and airport, will be sufficient during the early years. The area also provides a location base with low labor and warehouse costs. The initial warehouse space selected has ample space for growth and is available at fixed, long-term, low rates. The initial staff will consist of only three permanent employees to operate the office and warehouse. Other employees with needed expertise will join the Company in year two of operations. When sufficient qualities justify the relocation of warehousing, a more central nationwide location will be selected.

Initially distribution will occur only in the United States. However, since only two percent of the births worldwide occur in the United States, an incredible potential for future expansion exists. The Company plans to seek foreign patent protection within one year of obtaining its United States patent. To date, no conflicting patents have been identified on the worldwide cross search though the United States Patent Office.

CHAPTER 10
FINANCIAL PLAN

In this section you will take a look at the financial statements and documents that you will need to have in your business plan. They include the income statement (sometimes referred to as the profit and loss statement), the balance sheet, the cash flow statement and the breakeven analysis. This section is critical as these statements provide the key information regarding the future profitability and funding needed for your business.

> Hopefully you will have more profit than losses

UNDERSTANDING FINANCIAL STATEMENTS

Financial statements have a high value to you as a business owner. They are the life-blood of your business! How can they be used? They can be used to evaluate a business, measure performance over time, and also to determine the start-up funding requirements of a business.

The key to developing financial statements is having a good accounting system in place. It is worth spending money to have a good accounting system such as QuickBooks in place. Many businesses start and fail due to financial problems so getting your accounting system in place is worth the time and effort. Once your business is operational these statements should be used systematically. That means reviewing them on a regular basis so that the data is of value to you as you make business decisions and plan your profits.

> These statements are absolutely essential!

HISTORICAL ACCOUNTING STATEMENTS

Historical statements show the past performance of your business. You can use this information as a measuring tool to compare past performance with the present and with the future (projected). Only include the statements for the past three years. What statements should you include? These statements are the income statements, the balance sheets, and the cash budget. Let's take a look at each of these statements.

> Without planning-- could be hysterical statements

INCOME STATEMENT

Sometimes called a Profit and Loss (P & L), the income statement gives the amount of profit that is generated by a company over a given time period (monthly, quarterly, annually). It provides information regarding the following areas of business: revenue, cost of goods sold, operating expenses, financing costs (interest paid to creditors), payment of taxes, and profit. Terminology for each element often varies with the nature of the business and with the person who compiles the report, but the concept that revenue less expenses equal profit remains the same.

Let's look at the income statement for Benson & Co. as an example (Exhibit 10.1). The business sold 10,000 items at $52 each and it cost them $32.50 to manufacture the product. The company paid administration costs of $42,000 to maintain its operation along with $13,000 in interest and taxes at a rate of 30%. A convenient starting point is to establish the level of sales: $520,000 worth of goods was sold (10,000 x $52). Next it is useful to establish the cost of these sales: they cost $325,000 (10,000 x $32.50). The difference between the sales and the cost of these sales ($195,000) is known as the gross profit. Gross profit reports how much money the items themselves have generated. If the business was run from home and had no other administrative costs and had no interest to pay, it obviously would have cleared $195,000. In order to calculate profit, though, it is also essential to deduct the other expense items listed. If administration costs of $142,000 are deducted from the gross profit of $195,000, the net operating income of the business, regardless of the way it was financed, is $53,000. The net operating income is also known as the operating income of the earnings before interest and tax (EBIT). If the $13,000 paid in interest is deducted from the operating income, a figure of $40,000 can be reported as being earned during the period before any allowance for paying tax. The figure is known as the earnings before tax (or EBT). If income tax is to be paid at a rate of 30%, then the firm will eventually have to pay 30% of $40,000 as taxes (i.e., $12,000), and this will leave the business with $28,000 as the net income or net profit.

> You must work through this example— NO skipping

Exhibit 10.1

			INCOME STATEMENT FOR THE YEAR		
Sales revenue				$ 520,000	
Cost of goods sold				$(325,000)	
Gross profit				$ 195,000	
Operating expenses	$ 130,000				
Depreciation Expense	$ 12,000				
				$(142,000)	
Net operating income				$ 53,000	
Interest expense				$ (13,000)	
Earnings before tax				$ 40,000	
Income tax expense				$ (12,000)	
Net income				$ 28,000	

COMPONENTS OF THE INCOME STATEMENT

In order to better understand the income statement, you will need to have a clear understanding of its components.

SALES REVENUE
Revenue is the stream of benefits accruing to the firm from the sales of products or service **(operating revenue)**. **Non-operating revenue** can be derived from interest earned or some other non-operations-related items, such as depreciation recovered on the sale of an asset.

You must become familiar with these terms

COST OF GOODS SOLD
The stock of goods on hand ready for processing or sale is known as **inventory**. **The cost of goods sold (COGS)** is the inventory cost associated with a particular sale. Cost of goods sold includes the cost of raw materials and certain costs of processing (depending on the accounting methodology used). The estimation of cost of goods sold is based on the following relationship:

$$\text{beginning inventory} + \text{purchases} - \text{ending inventory} = \text{cost of goods sold}$$

For example, if the firm purchases $45,000 during the period and its beginning inventory was $5,000 and its ending inventory is $10,000, then its cost of goods sold for the period is $40,000.

GROSS PROFIT
Gross profit margin or **gross margin** describes the relationship between gross profit and sales. In the case of Benson & Co. (Exhibit 10.1), the corporation earned a gross profit equal to 37.5 percent of its sales revenue. The gross margin is calculated as:

$$\text{gross margin} = \frac{\$195,000 \text{ gross profit}}{\$520,000 \text{ sales revenue}} = 37.5\%$$

OPERATING EXPENSES
Operating expenses are those costs incurred by the firm in its operations. These include rent, payroll, utilities, and other costs of running the business. In the case of closely held businesses, there is often a problem with the intermingling of the business and personal expenditures. Excessive "perks" and the personal use of business assets do not constitute realistic operating expenses and their inclusion in the financial report distorts reality. Higher operating expenses lead to lower profitability.

Items of expense, often exhibited separately under the general heading of operating expenses, include:

- *Salaries and wages.* These will include all wages and benefits *paid* to the owners and the employees of the business.
- *Travel and entertainment.* These expenses must be business related.
- *Utilities.* The cost of telephone, water, and electricity should only be included insofar as they represent expenses related to genuine business activity.
- *Vehicle expenses.* Regarding costs relating to the repairs, maintenance, and running costs of vehicles, personally related costs must be removed from business expenses.
- *Advertising.* The lack of advertising expense may be one indication that a small firm is having financial problems. This is because advertising is a key element in some types of firms' ability to attract new and continuing sales, and yet it is an easy expense to defer in order to access immediate liquidity.

DEPRECIATION EXPENSE

Depreciation is the name given to the cost allowance applied to use of a firm's long-term assets. The cost of such an asset is paid at the time the asset is first purchased and it would be economically irrational to offset this cost entirely against revenues in the period that the asset was purchased. Instead, the asset is gradually "written off" by the depreciation mechanism.

GENERALLY ACCEPTED ACCOUNTING PRINCIPLES (GAAP) suggest that firms apportion an equal amount of the cost of the asset to each year of its use. In other words, if an asset costs $5,000 and has a life expectancy of five years, then $1,000 will be allocated to each of the first five years of its life, and will be added to the expenses of the firm each year. This is known as **straight-line depreciation**. The other type of depreciation is **accelerated depreciation**. This type of depreciation accelerates annual depreciation. Common types of accelerated depreciation are sum-of-the-years or double-declining balance methods. With these techniques the depreciation charge in the earlier years is much higher than under straight-line depreciation.

NET OPERATING INCOME

The net operating income is the difference between the revenues of the business and the expenses, with the exception of interest and taxes. As stated earlier in this chapter, this figure is also widely known as earnings before interest and taxes, or EBIT. It is a figure that is critically important in the analysis of performance, as shall be seen throughout this book, because it signals whether or not the owners of the business should be borrowing to invest in the business.

INTEREST

Interest is always separated from other operating expenses because it arises from the way in which the business is financed, rather than the way in which the business is operated. Revenue is a financial charge against the revenues of the firm rather than a charge associated with the firm's operating activities. Interest is a cost associated with the way in which the firm's assets have been financed and does not have anything to do with the value of the assets themselves.

EARNINGS BEFORE TAXES

This figure is the difference between the adjusted revenues of the business and the associated expenses. The figure reported as earnings before taxes forms the basis for the determination of any income taxes relating to the firm for the period.

INCOME TAX

In the case of many small businesses, especially sole proprietorships and partnerships, the taxation figure may not be evident. This is because the income for the particular business under consideration may be combined with other personal and business income of the owner before the owner's taxation is computed. In the instance of these two ownership systems, the business itself does not pay income tax; only the owner pays income tax. In the instance of the corporation, however, the firm itself does pay income tax, and this figure should be evident.

NET INCOME

The net income of the business is the earnings after payment of taxation in the case of the corporation (in the case of the proprietorship or partnership there will be no such figure). If the business is structured as a corporation, these profits either can be paid out to the owners of the corporation by way of a **dividend** or they can be retained by the business, in which case they are known as **retained earnings**.

DIVIDENDS

The amount of net income of the corporation paid our to its owners is called dividends. As explained earlier, small firms that are organized as sole proprietorships, partnerships, and sub-chapter S corporations do not pay dividends; instead, all net income flows to the owners as income.

Many small corporate businesses likewise will never pay a dividend. This is not for any legal reason (as is the case with the sole proprietorship) but because many such businesses rely on retained earnings to fund their growth, and secondly because dividends (on which tax has already been paid) are taxed (again) in the hands of the shareholder. Thus, the owner-manager of the small business, given the choice of withdrawing money as either wages or dividends will generally use the former mechanism. For example, assume that the corporate tax rate is 40 percent, the owner pays personal tax at a rate of 20 percent, and the corporation earns $1000,000 before taxes and prior to paying its owner any money. If the corporation pays $100,000 ($40,000 paid in corporate taxes leaves $60,000 for the owner's salary, which, in turn, is taxed $12,000 at the personal rate) and then distributes the balance as a dividend, the total tax paid will equal $52,000, whereas if the $100,000 is taken by the owner as wages, the total tax paid would only equal $20,000. The former circumstance would leave the owner with $48,000 available for personal consumption, the latter with $80,000. However, the Internal Revenue Service frequently reviews corporate returns to insure that income is not being paid in wages that should be taxed as corporate income.

In summary, the dividend policy of the small corporation is inextricably intertwined with other mechanisms, such as the payment of wages, in an attempt to minimize taxation.

EVALUATING THE INCOME STATEMENT

When evaluating the income statement look at trends over time, see what is happening in terms of your gross profit and net profit. Try to understand what is happening to cause the results that you are seeing (for example, prices are low or COGS is high). Note the amount of interest that is paid and evaluate executive compensation. Focus on the growth and stability of revenue and pay specific attention to operating expenses. Compare the figures for your business to industry averages.

BALANCE SHEET

The balance sheet is basically a statement that describes the financial condition of the business at a certain point in time (usually the end of the fiscal year). It reports what the business owns (the assets of the business), to whom the business owes money (the liabilities of the business) and how much the owners have contributed (amount of equity in the business). Regardless of the size of your business the categories are the same the only difference is in the detail.

EXHIBIT 10.2						
			BALANCE SHEET AS OF DECEMBER 31, 2001			
Current assets:			*Current liabilities:*			
Cash		$ 2,000	Accounts payable			$ 30,0
Accounts receivable		$ 60,000	Accrued expenses			$ 17,0
Inventory		$ 80,000	Notes payable			$ 20,0
Prepaid expenses		$ 10,000	Income tax payable			$ 3,0
Current assets		$ 152,000	Current liabilities			$ 70,0
Long-term assets:			*Long-term liabilities:*			
Equipment	$120,000		Bank loan @ 13% interest			$ 80,0
Depreciation	$ (12,000)					
Net fixed assets		$ 108,000	Owners' equity:			
			Paid-in capital		$ 82,000	
			Retained earnings		$ 28,000	
			Total owners' equity			$ 110,0
Total assets		$ 260,000	Total liabilities & owners' equity			$ 260,0

LAYOUT OF THE BALANCE SHEET

Exhibit 10.2 reflects the financial position of Benson & Co. at the end of its first year of operations and depicts the following scenario: The Bensons' contributed $82,000 to start the business and selected the corporate form of ownership. They borrowed $80,000 on a long-term basis from their bank. This loan was secured by a mortgage of their family dwelling plus a debenture over the assets of the corporation plus the personal covenants (i.e., guarantees) of Mr. and Mrs. Benson. The money was used to buy $120,000 of manufacturing equipment, which generated a profit of $28,000 after allowing for $12,000 depreciation. The Bensons' withdrew nothing for their personal use during the period and lived on the rent paid to them by their older children, who were still living at home. At the end of the year there was $2,000 in the bank, accounts receivable were $60,000, and there was $80,000 in inventory on hand. During the year, the business prepaid $10,000 of next year's expenses. Trade creditors were owed $30,000 and the taxation authorities were owed $3,000. The business had accrued $17,000 in expenses and owed the bank $20,000 in short-term borrowing.

One side of the balance sheet lists assets. On the other side it lists the claims on those assets. These claims comprise external liabilities and owners' equity. These two sides must equal.

COMPONENTS OF THE BALANCE SHEET

Let's review the components of the balance sheet in more detail.

ASSETS
An asset is something that is owned. Accountants usually divide assets into two groups: those that are of a permanent nature, such as real estate, or plant and machinery, and those that are of a more temporary nature, such as cash or inventory (trading goods) on hand. These two groupings are known as **fixed assets** and **current (or short-term) assets**, respectively. Sometimes it is difficult to decide into which of these groups certain assets fall. To a certain extent, it depends on the nature of the business -- what is a permanent asset to one business may well be a temporary asset to another.

LIABILITIES
A liability is something owed; it is a claim against assets. As with assets, some liabilities are more permanent than others. A mortgage borrowed against real estate is usually regarded as a permanent, or long-term, liability, as is a debenture or bond secured against the assets of a business. On the other hand, monthly trade credit, or accounts payable, is a good example of a more temporary obligation. More permanent forms of liability are usually grouped together as **long-term**

liabilities and more temporary liabilities (less than a year) are usually grouped as **current liabilities**.

There are two groups of people with claims against the assets of a business. One is people who are not involved with the ownership of the business, but who have advanced credit in some form to the business. The other is people who are involved with the ownership of the business. The former group includes mortgages, bankers, and those who advance trade credit for supplies to the business. The latter group comprises the owners of the business. They have contributed money to the business and so are owed this money by the business; they are shown in a balance sheet as part of its long-term financing. These two groups of claims are thus divided into the **debt** and equity components of the liabilities of the business, the debt being owed to "outsiders," the equity being owed to the owners.

EQUITY

Equity is also known as **owners' equity**, **capital**, or **net worth**, and it can arise in two ways. First, equity can arise directly from the capital contributions of the owners of the business. In the case of a non-corporate ownership form, this may occur where the owners personally contribute to the assets of a business. In the case of the corporate ownership form, equity occurs when the owners of the firm buy the shares that the corporate form of business issues. This does not necessarily mean that if an individual buys shares on the stock exchange then that person is contributing to the capital of a business; in that case the person is merely buying someone else's record of contribution -- the transaction does not affect the total claims on the business at all.

Don't be confused by the different terms

The second way in which equity can arise is through the retention of profits by the business. Profits are amounts generated above expenses and belong to the owners of a business. Where these (or part of these) are paid out to the owners, they are known as dividends in the case of a corporation or drawings in the case of a non-corporate ownership form, such as a sole proprietorship or partnership. If only part of the profit of a business is paid out to its owners, then the undistributed balance (known as retained earnings) can be regarded as a further contribution to the equity of the business by its owners.

One point that should be made clear at this stage is that the balance sheet of a business shows the amount that has been contributed to the business by the owners. This is not necessarily the same as the value of that contribution. In other words, cost is not necessarily value. Financial reports do not directly provide the value of equity, instead they show the recorded historical contributions to equity.

CURRENT ASSETS

The current assets of a business are assets of a short-term nature that will be collected during the next accounting period. The major types of current assets include cash, accounts receivable, inventory, marketable securities, and prepaid expenses.

Cash The cash item shown in the balance sheet reflects cash in the bank as well as any petty cash held by the business at balance date.

Accounts Receivable Whenever a business sells goods or services on credit, the purchaser's obligation to the business is recorded as **accounts receivable**. The balance in accounts receivable at any time reflects the amount that people owe the business as a result of its sales.

If customers do not pay their accounts on time, then the business will have less cash coming in. This has two side-effects: first, interest is foregone on the money "advanced," and, second, the cash needs of the business must be funded from other sources, such as borrowing, and this costs the firm interest. However, a trade-off needs to be made by the owners of the business between refusing to advance credit to potential customers (and losing the profit that would have been made on those sales) and carrying the cost of the receivables.

Inventory The **inventory** account displays the book value of inventory on hand at balance date. There are three different types of inventory: raw materials, work in process, and finished goods. The valuation of inventory is a specialized process much debated by accountants. Different methods of valuation will provide different amounts to be reported in the balance sheet, and because the cost of goods sold is closely related to the valuation of raw materials inventory, it will also affect the profit reported by any accrual accounting system.

Marketable Securities One of the problems with cash is that it earns no interest. If a business has large amounts of cash on hand at a particular time, it makes sense for that business to invest that money temporarily in readily negotiable securities. These are known as **marketable securities**. Marketable securities range from temporary investments in government or corporate debt to certificates of deposit with a bank. The prime requirement of marketable securities is that they should be easily negotiable back into cash; in other words, they need to be **near cash**. The most common investments of this type for small businesses in the United States include Treasury bills, bank certificates of deposit, and money-market mutual funs.

Prepaid Expenses Prepaid expenses include all of those payments that have been made in one period that actually cover part of a subsequent period as well. Payment of fire insurance is a good example. In this case, assume that the balance date is December 31 and an insurance payment of $1,000 is paid on July 1. Obviously, one-half of the premium "belongs" to the current year while the other half "belongs" to the next year. Including the total premium in this year's expenses would overstate the costs of running the business this year. Prepaid expenses are a bit like longer term assets, but instead of depreciating them over a number of future periods, in the case of long-term assets, they are generally expensed in the subsequent period. Nevertheless, in some extreme cases, prepaid expenses may have an effect far longer than the subsequent period. For example, a front-end loan fee paid for a loan that has a five-year duration would be classed as a prepaid expense but should be amortized over the term of the loan, i.e., written off in a similar manner to straight-line depreciation.

FIXED ASSETS

These assets often are not itemized in the balance sheet, which only reports a summary of all assets. The value of the assets reported is usually a book value, which is calculated by deducting the accumulated depreciation figure from the historical cost of the assets. Accumulated depreciation in turn is computed as all of the depreciation recorded for the assets up to the current balance date.

For example, assume that an asset was purchased three years ago for $10,000 and is being depreciated over five years with straight-line depreciation. Its book value today would be $4,000, as shown in Exhibit 10.3.

Exhibit 10.3			COMPUTATION OF BOOK VALUES	
Year	Historical cost	Annual depreciation	Accumulated depreciation	Book value
1	$ 10,000	$ 2,000	$ 2,000	$ 8,000
2		$ 2,000	$ 4,000	$ 6,000
3		$ 2,000	$ 6,000	$ 4,000

CURRENT LIABILITIES

The current liabilities of the business refer to liabilities that are due to be paid during the next accounting period. This usually means that all liabilities due during the next year, including those portions of any long-term debt that will fall due for payment during the next year will fall into this category. The major subgroups of current liabilities include accounts payable and accrued expenses.

Accounts Payable Accounts payable result from credit purchases by the business. Delaying the payment of accounts payable is one way to create liquidity for a business and it may be costless in the short term (although the firm's reputation maybe at stake in the longer term if a formal arrangement to defer payment is not made with the creditor). However, in many cases, discounts are available for prompt payment, and these can be very expensive to ignore.

Because the owner of the small business usually finds funding business activities difficult and trade credit is one way of funding those activities, the availability and use of trade credit is critical to the success of the business. As a principle, the payment of trade credit should be slowed down as much as possible (once the discount for prompt payment is lost, the only way to reduce the cost of such borrowing is to lengthen the period over which the money is borrowed) while the collection of accounts receivable should be sped up as much as possible.

Accrued Expenses Accrued expenses is a summary account that records all of those expenses that are due at balance date but for which no invoice has yet been received. These expenses usually comprise those items for which invoices are received on a less-than-monthly basis and may include such items as holiday pay, property taxes (or rates), electricity, interest, and taxation accrued. They can total a significant amount for a business that is labor intensive and that has debt financing that is serviced, for example, on a quarterly basis.

Notes Payable **Notes payable** are securities resulting from the formal short-term borrowing activities of the business. They are often not due for full repayment during the subsequent accounting period, but will be relatively short term in nature. Notes payable are often used to finance inventory purchases.

Short-Term Bank Debt There are two ways in which funding can be advanced from a bank. The first is an advance of the total loan approved. This is usually secured by a personally guaranteed note in the case of a small business. The second way is for the bank to offer a **line of credit** similar to personal credit cards. The business uses the line of credit as needed by drawing against it.

Long-Term Liabilities

The long-term liabilities of a business include all of those debts that are not due for a relatively long period of time. The most common form of this financing activity in the case of the small business is the **mortgage** over real estate. Because most small businesses are unable to issue **bonds** or **debentures** in the public market, the lender usually takes collateral security over not only business assets, such as land, buildings, plant, machinery, and other chattels like inventories, but also over the personal assets of the proprietors of the business, such as their homes.

OWNERS' EQUITY

Owners' equity records the financial contributions to the business of its owners. These contributions can be in the form of contributions from outside the business itself or from profits generated by the business that its owners elect not to pay out to themselves (in dividends), but rather to reinvest in the business to fund its future activities. Retained earnings are all of the accumulated earnings in a business that has not been paid out since its inception.

One of the major differences between the smaller business and its larger counterparts is that all of the contributions of the owners to the business may not be reflected in the balance sheet. Initially, many of the assets of the small business may have been "donated" by the owners to the business, and therefore have never been captured by the formal accounting process. Secondly, the contribution of time in the development of a small business is rarely recognized in the recorded equity of such a business. In other words, the accounting reports may understate the correct asset and equity positions of small businesses.

The way in which the equity of the small business is reported in the balance sheet will depend on the ownership structure of the business. Chapter 3 explained how small businesses range in ownership structure from sole proprietorships through partnerships and sub-chapter S corporations to corporations. To exemplify the different ways in which such businesses would display the equity portions of their balance sheets, assume that there has been an initial contribution by the owner or owners of the business of $50,000 and that the business has earned and retained $10,000 in its first year of operations. Equity for a sole proprietorship, a partnership, and a corporation would be shown as in Exhibits 10.4, 10.5, 10.6 respectively.

Exhibit 10.4

			EQUITY: THE SOLE PROPRIETOR		
Contributed equity			$ 50,000		
Retained earnings			$ 10,000		
Total equity			$ 60,000		

Exhibit 10.5

			EQUITY: THE PARTNERSHIP		
Contributed equity -- Ms. Velasquez		$ 30,000			
Retained earnings		$ 6,000			
Ending equity				$ 36,000	
Contributed equity -- Mr. Kourt		$ 20,000			
Retained earnings		$ 4,000			
Ending equity				$ 24,000	
Total equity				$ 60,000	

Exhibit 10.6								
						EQUITY: THE CORPORATION		
		Paid-in capital			$50,000			
		Retained earnings			$10,000			
		Total equity			$60,000			

Notice that, regardless of the form of ownership, the amount of equity reported is the same: $60,000 and, in the case of the partnership, the contribution of each partner is reported. But, in the case of the corporation, the relative shareholdings of the owners are not reported in the balance sheet.

EVALUATING THE BALANCE SHEET

The worksheet at the end of the chapter will provide an opportunity for you to begin developing your balance sheet and includes an explanation of the sections of the balance sheet. You will want to calculate some basic ratios and compare these ratios over time. You will also want to compare them with industry averages. Focus on the current assets and how they are financed. Pay a lot of attention to the amount of debt that the business has incurred. Compare AP with sales terms and evaluate how long it takes the firm to pay its payables. Also determine if the firm is getting a reasonable rate of return on the assets it has employed.

PROJECTED (PRO FORMA) STATEMENTS

These are the statements showing the anticipated performance of your business for the next three to five years. They are often referred to as pro forma statements. These statements include the income statement, balance sheet, and cash flow statement (cash budget). They should be done on a monthly basis for the first year, quarterly for the second and annually thereafter. If financing is required these statements should reflect the effect and the amount of the financing.

> Now you have to figure out your future finances

The income statement shows the projected revenue and expenses. This is where the information obtained in the marketing section is utilized. The sales forecast that was developed based on market potential of your targeted market is utilized to determine revenue. The sales forecast is the basis for all else that follows. From this, cost of goods sold can be calculated based on this activity level. Other expenses may be estimate by compiling estimates based on previous years costs if you are an existing business or by estimating them as a certain percentage of sales. However these cost estimates are obtained, it must be recognized that past costs or historical costs are relevant to the proforma income statement only if they are costs expected to continue in the future. For example, if raw materials and labor costs are expected to increase in the future, these increased cost figures are the ones that must be used to estimate costs of goods sold for the proforma income statement.

Gross profit is calculated by subtracting estimated costs of goods sold from sales revenue, and EBT are calculated by subtracting operating expenses from gross profit. Selling expenses could include such items as sales representative's salaries and commissions, transportation costs, sales office salaries, postage and stationery expense, advertising expenditures, and travel costs. Administrative expenses could include administrative officers' salaries, clerical salaries, insurance premiums, depreciation (office equipment, etc.), and supplies. Some of these expenses, such as sales commissions, will vary as sales vary; that is, they are considered variable expenses. Other expenses, such as depreciation of office equipment, are fixed; they do not change as sales or output change. However, both variable and fixed expenses can change from one year to the next, and these new costs must be included in the estimates of operating expenses. For example, if sales commissions are to be increased by 2% of sales and officers' salaries will be raised by 6% of their current levels, then these additional costs must be included in the estimation of operating expenses.

After all revenue and expenses have been estimated to arrive at EBT, EAT must be determined. The various municipal, state and federal taxes must be estimated and subtracted from earnings before taxes to arrive at earnings after taxes.

The procedure as outlined can be combined with the sales forecast to illustrate the construction of monthly pro forma income statements for January, February, and March (you will construct monthly for the whole year). The assumptions required to construct these income statements are as follows.

1. The most likely sales levels for each month are $150,000, $210,000, $210,000 and $300,000 in January, February, March, and April, respectively. This was based on market research which showed a MSA population of   with 20% of the population aged 18-24 (target market); of that 30 % are consumers with the appropriate income. Average visits per month per consumer is 9. The average amount spent by consumer per visit is $20. This equals $210,000. However, the first month of sales is expected to be   % below this figure.
2. Cost of goods sold is 80% of sales; material purchases are made one month in advance of sales.
3. Operating expenses are estimated at

Table 10-7

				January	February	March
Salaries				$ 30,000	$ 40,000	$ 40,000
Rent				$ 2,000	$ 2,000	$ 2,000
Depreciation				$ 2,500	$ 2,500	$ 2,500
Quarterly interest at 6% on $500,000 (accrued)				$ 2,500	$ 2,500	$ 2,500

4. The corporate tax rate is 40%

Table   10-8   contains the monthly and quarterly pro forma income statement for the first quarter.

> These monthly pro forma income statements are an explicit statement of management's expectations of revenues, costs, and earnings during the planning period. Given the assumptions and/or decisions used to construct these statements, a loss is expected each month during the first quarter. The purpose of the pro forma income statement is to indicate expected profitability and allow management sufficient time to control or influence these results by seeking alternatives that could change revenues and/or costs and ultimately its profitability. While management may or may not be able to change its plans and influence these expected losses, it would also want to have an estimate of the cash or liquidity position of the firm over the same time period because that is another important facet of the firm's operation. Such an estimate or plan is provided by the cash budget.

Table 10-8   Three Months and First Quarter, Pro Forma Income Statement

		January	February	March	Quarter
Net Sales		$ 150,000	$ 210,000	$ 210,000	$ 570,000
Cost of goods sold		$ 120,000	$ 168,000	$ 168,000	$ 456,000
Gross earnings		$ 30,000	$ 42,000	$ 42,000	$ 114,000
Operating Expenses					
Salaries		$ 30,000	$ 40,000	$ 40,000	$ 110,000
Rent		$ 2,000	$ 2,000	$ 2,000	$ 6,000
Depreciation		$ 2,500	$ 2,500	$ 2,500	$ 7,500
Interest		$ 2,500	$ 2,500	$ 2,500	$ 7,500
Earnings before taxes (loss)		$ (7,000)	$ (5,000)	$ (5,000)	$ (17,000)
Taxes (credit)		$ (2,800)	$ (2,000)	$ (2,000)	$ (6,800)
Earnings after taxes (loss)		$ (4,200)	$ (3,000)	$ (3,000)	$ (10,200)

THE CASH BUDGET

Oftentimes, business owners think that if they have a positive net income on the income statement it means that the business has cash.   This is not necessarily true. The reason for this is that sales revenue is often not received when it is earned and expenses are not paid when they incur. This creates a difference between profits and cash flow. The reason for this is that the income statement is based on accrual based accounting that matches expenses with revenues when they occur.   It records income when it is earned whether or not the income has been received in cash and records expenses when they are incurred even if the money has not be actually paid out. The cash budget will help the business owner to understand how and when cash flows through the business.

> You are not done yet…just one more statement

The key information (the projected sales and expenditures) developed for the income statement will be utilized for the cash budget. What this statement will do is indicate if additional financing is required and when it is needed. It will be up to you to determine what type of financing will be obtained (discussed in a later section) and how it is to be repaid.

The cash budget is a key financial statement as it will provide information as to when cash will be coming into the business, where it will come from and how it will be used. It is a very critical budgeting tool for the business.   Why is this so important? Well a business that cannot pay its bills cannot stay in business for very long even though it may be showing a profit on its income statement. The key thing about the cash budget to remember is that your cash inflows must be at least equal to or greater than your cash outflows.   If you are seeking a loan the cash budget will enable the bank to determine the ability of the business to generate sufficient cash to repay the loan. This statement should be created on a monthly basis for a start-up company.   An existing business should prepare at least an annual statement.

Forecasting cash sales (if any) and credit sales is probably the most difficult aspect of preparing a cash forecast because of all the factors that impinge upon sales performance: pricing policy, credit-granting policy, credit terms given, competition, the business cycle, government legislation, defaults, etc. Experience has shown that errors in the estimation of sales, and subsequently receivables, can be considerable. Nevertheless, the best effort should be made, whether through historical ratios or projection of trends.

Expenditures can usually be estimated with a far greater degree of accuracy than is the case for sales. However, for those firms that purchase inventories in a fluctuating market, say raw materials, accurate forecasting can also be a problem. There is a good argument for suggesting that all small businesses should evaluate different scenarios. It is not uncommon to find three scenarios per forecast produced: optimistic, expected or most likely, and pessimistic. "What-if" situations are examined, say, the pessimistic solution is viewed and the cash requirement is then based upon that projection. Should the expected situation be used and it falls short of reality such that additional financing is required, then the same problems and difficulties as before arise. Showing all three scenarios to the bank at least indicates the *most* cash that *may* be required.

Clearly, the damage arising from the need to seek financing for short-term, unanticipated shortfalls in cash cannot be overemphasized. Even if the financing body, usually the bank, grants a temporary facility, the mere fact that the business has needed it does not engender confidence in the management of the business. Sometimes there may be a very good reason, but too often such borrowing is the result of poor forecasting, Other things being equal, notifying the bank in advance that a loan is required at some point in the near future gives the bank more confidence in the business and in its management.

CONSTRUCTING THE CASH BUDGET

How do you actually construct the cash budget? First, the business owner must identify the sources and uses of cash. They need to know where all funds will be obtained. Additionally, they need to know how the firm plans to expend these funds.

Second, not only must the owner identify the sources and uses of cash, but you also need to know the total amount of these planned receipts and disbursements. If you can accurately estimate the total receipts and disbursements over a given time period, you will be able to identify the cash shortages or surpluses expected in that period. As a business owner you are interested in both shortages as well as surpluses. If you expect a shortage, you can plan for it and find the best, least cost, source of funds to meet the shortage. Worse yet, if an extremely tight money market exists, they can recognize that sources of funds may dry up and alert other managers to the possible necessity of a cutback in operations. Cash, above a minimum operating amount, should not be left idle, since by doing so the firm forgoes interest revenue and thus causes net earnings to be less than they would be otherwise. If you can accurately estimate the amount of surplus cash, you can make plans to invest these idle funds in highly liquid, risk-free, interest-bearing assets such as U. S. government securities.

Third, the business owner must know when to expect surpluses and shortages if they are to invest idle funds or search out sources of funds to meet shortages. Consequently, business owners are interested in the timing of cash shortages and surpluses. The mechanism of the cash budget aids the business owner in explicitly recognizing and planning for (1) sources and uses of cash, (2) cash shortages and surpluses, and (3) the timing of cash flows.

Although any one of a number of formats may be adopted for the cash budget, the persons constructing and/or utilizing the cash budget must be fully aware of its tentative nature. In constructing the cash budget, many conditions and operating decisions pertinent to cash flows are assumed. Conditions and decisions may change, however, requiring adjustment in the cash budget. If the cash budget is not carefully monitored for possible changes as new information becomes available, it will fail to provide the up-to-date information required for optimum use of cash.

To construct the cash budget for the XYZ Company, the assumptions on which the income statement were made must be reviewed. These assumptions were

1. The levels of sales in January, February, and March are estimated at $150,000, 210,000, and $210,000, respectively.
2. Cost of goods sold is 80% of sales, with material purchases made one month in advance of sales.
3. Operating expenses requiring cash are estimated at

Table 10.9					January		February		March	
Salaries					$	30,000	$	40,000	$	40,000
Rent					$	2,000	$	2,000	$	2,000
Depreciation					$	2,500	$	2,500	$	2,500
Quarterly interest at 6% on $500,000					$	-	$	-	$	7,500

4. The corporate tax rate is 40%.

In addition, the following information pertaining to, and decisions affecting, cash movement is assumed:

5. Sales are 75% credit and 25% cash.
6. Credit sales are collected as follows:
   60% collected within the first month following sale.
   30% collected within second month following sale.
   10% collected within the third month following sale.
7. Total sales in October, November, and December were $300,000, $350,000, and $400,000, respectively.
8. Raw materials that are purchased one month in advance of sale are paid for in the month purchased. However, starting in March, purchases will be paid for the month following purchase.
9. Wages and rent are paid in the month incurred.
10. Interest on the long-term debt is paid quarterly; a quarterly dividend on common stock of $2,000 is to be paid in March.
11. The minimum cash balance required is $100,000, and this is the cash balance at the beginning of January.
12. The firm expects to sell common stock in March with net proceeds of $500,000.

13. A new piece of equipment is to be purchased for $600,000 and paid for in March.
14. Long-term debt is to be reduced by $100,000 in March.

Since considerable detail is required to construct a cash budget, it may be helpful to use a worksheet to compile certain subsections before constructing the complete cash budget. Table 10.10 contains a worksheet designed to facilitate the determination of collections on accounts receivable.

The first entry in Table 10.10 is sales. Sales for the last three months of the previous year are actual values, whereas sales for January, February, and March are expected sales. Assumption 5 allows actual and expected sales to be divided into credit and cash sales. Assumption 6 provides the necessary information to compute collections on accounts receivable. Computations of collections for the latter part of the year are not really required, since we are interested in developing monthly cash budgets for the first 3 months of the coming year, but are included to facilitate understanding of the computation process. In October, credit sales were $225,000 (75% of $300,000). In November, December, and January, collections of 60%,

Table 10.10 Worksheet: Collections on Accounts Receivable							
		Oct.	Nov.	Dec.	Jan.	Feb.	Mar.
Sales		$300,000	$350,000	$400,000	$150,000	$210,000	$210,000
Cash sales		$ 75,000	$ 87,500	$100,000	$ 37,500	$ 52,500	$ 52,500
Credit sales		$225,000	$262,500	$300,000	$112,500	$157,500	$157,500
Collections	60%		$135,000	$157,500	$180,000	$ 67,500	$ 94,500
	30%			$ 67,500	$ 78,750	$ 90,000	$ 33,750
	10%				$ 22,500	$ 26,250	$ 30,000
Collections on accounts receivable					$281,250	$183,750	$158,250

30%, and 10%, respectively, are made. Reading diagonally, down the table, the corresponding dollar amounts of $135,000, $67,500, and $22,500 are collected in these 3 months. The calculations of collections for the remaining months are obtained in the same manner. Collections on accounts receivable in each of the first 3 months of the coming year are obtained by summing the collections on the preceding months' sales.

Table 10-11 A Cash Budget		January		February		March	
Beginning cash balance		$ 100,000		$ 100,000		$ 100,000	
Receipts: Cash sales		$ 37,500		$ 52,500		$ 52,500	
Collections		$ 281,250		$ 183,750		$ 158,250	
Other		$ -		$ -		$ 500,000	
Total cash available		$ 418,750		$ 336,250		$ 810,750	
Uses: Purchases		$ 168,000		$ 168,000		$ -	
Salaries		$ 30,000		$ 40,000		$ 40,000	
Rent		$ 2,000		$ 2,000		$ 2,000	
Interest and dividends		$ -		$ -		$ 9,500	
Other		$ -		$ -		$ 700,000	
Total Disbursements		$ 200,000		$ 210,000		$ 751,500	
Cash available end of period		$ 218,750		$ 126,250		$ 59,250	
Less: Minimum Cash Balance		$ 100,000		$ 100,000		$ 100,000	
Surplus (shortage)		$ 118,750		$ 26,250		$ (40,750)	
Investment (borrowing)		$ 118,750		$ 26,250		$ (40,750)	

The cash budget can now be constructed using the other assumptions and operating plans specified as it appears in Table 10-9. Total cash available each month is the summation of the cash balances at the beginning of the month, cash sales, collections on accounts receivable, and other sources. Other sources for March contain the entry of $500,000 from the sale of common stock only. Total monthly disbursements are the summation of all cash uses. The use of cash for purchases in March is zero because management, while still making material purchases a month in advance of sales, decides to buy on 30-day credit terms. Because interest on debt and common stock dividends are paid quarterly, March is the only month in which there is an entry. The other entry in March for cash uses reflects the $100,000 reduction of debt principal and the $600,000 asset purchase. After the management requirement of a minimum cash balance of $100,000 is met, there are surpluses of $118,750 and $26,250 in January and February that can be invested in highly liquid, risk free, interest-bearing U. S. government securities. In March, a deficit of $40,750 exists after meeting the minimum cash requirement. The firm has the option of selling $40,750 of the $118,750 invested in U. S. government securities from its January investment, or it may borrow $40,750 in March. It is also possible the management may choose to abandon its minimum cash balance requirement temporarily. All these options are available, and the construction of the cash budget allows management sufficient time to consider the alternatives.

Because there are various types of cash budgets in practice and the amount of detail also varies considerably, it should be helpful to point out that the overriding concept in the construction of a cash budget, regardless of format and detail, is

Beginning cash balance + cash inflows = cash outflows-ending cash balance

Keeping this concept in mind will aid understanding the cash budget regardless of the format used.

EVALUATING CASH BUDGETS

Short-term forecasting may also be applied to check the accuracy of the longer-term forecast and to assist in the planning of repayment of short- and long-term debt and the in the acquisition of capital assets. As noted above, seasonal businesses are particularly at risk from external vagaries and, while the cash budget may suffer a greater risk of being inaccurate, it is very important that such businesses undertake the exercise. If the purchase of inventories does not correlate with receipt of cash arising from their subsequent sale, the business will find itself in difficulties from which it may not be able to extricate itself.

The cash forecast also guides the firm in a growth situation. It will guide its credit-granting policies and influence the decision on cash discounts given and received. The compilation and use of cash forecasts will certainly significantly reduce the likelihood of a firm running into insurmountable problems through overextending.

THE PRO FORMA BALANCE SHEET

Whereas the cash budget indicates liquidity and pro forma income statement profitability, the pro forma balance sheet illustrates the expected overall impact of plans and operations on assets and liabilities. Once the pro forma income statement and cash budget are competed, the pro forma balance sheet naturally follows. The pro forma balance sheet should be constructed for each month. This statement can easily be generated with accounting software. However the balance sheet in Table 10.12 is constructed for the end of the first quarter.

Table 10.12 An Actual and Pro Forma Balance Sheet		
	December Actual	March Pro Forma
Assets		
Cash	$ 100,000	$ 100,000
Marketable securities	$ 30,000	$ 175,000
Prepaid taxes	$ - - -	$ 6,800
Accounts receivable	$ 427,500	$ 231,750
Inventory	$ 280,000	$ 400,000
Total current assets	$ 837,500	$ 913,550
Plant, property, and equipment	$ 350,000	$ 950,000
Less: Accumulated depreciation	$ 90,000	$ 97,500
Net fixed assets	$ 260,000	$ 852,500
Total Assets	$ 1,097,500	$ 1,766,050
Liabilities and Equity		
Accounts payable	$ - - -	$ 240,000
Notes payable	$ 130,000	$ 170,750
Total current liabilities	$ 130,000	$ 410,750
Bonds payable	$ 500,000	$ 400,000
Total liabilities	$ 630,000	$ 810,750
Common stock $5 oar value	$ 200,000	$ 700,000
Retained earnings	$ 267,500	$ 255,300
Total Liabilities and equity	$ 1,097,500	$ 1,766,050

Typically, the construction of a pro forma balance sheet requires information from three sources. First, actual asset and liability levels from the last period of operations are required. Table 10.12 contains the actual December balance sheet and the pro forma balance sheet ending in March. Second, taxes and changes in retained earnings through net income (or loss) and dividend payments must be obtained from the pro forma income statement. Third, data from the cash budget are required.

The minimum cash balance, investments in marketable securities, total borrowing, and value of the new fixed asset can be obtained from the cash budget and added to the respective amounts from the December actual balance sheet to obtain the expected values in March. The $6,800 in prepaid taxes reflects first quarter losses and is carried as an asset because it can be used in later quarters to offset the tax liability of future earnings. Accounts payable is determined by the March purchases for April sales that will not be paid for until April. Debt entries are obtained from the changes in debt that are part of the cash budget. The increase in accumulated depreciation of $7500 is from the pro forma income statements.

The change in the common stock is also available from the cash budget. The accounts receivable, retained earning and inventory entries are somewhat more involved. The accounts receivable entry is found from the relationship of beginning accounts receivable + credit sales = collections + ending accounts receivable:

December accounts receivable			$ 427,500
Plus: Credit sales for the quarter			$ 427,500
Total			$ 855,000
Less: Collections for the quarter			$ 623,250
Equals: Accounts receivable in March			$ 231,750

A similar procedure is used to find the March ending inventory inasmuch as beginning inventory + purchases = cost of goods sold + ending inventory:

In addition, ending retained earnings can be obtained in a similar manner:

December ending inventory			$ 280,000
Plus: Purchases during the quarter			$ 576,000
Equals: Total available			$ 856,000
Less: Cost of goods sold for the quarter			$ 456,000
Equals: Ending inventory in March			$ 400,000

December retained earnings			$ 267,500
Less: Dividend			$ 2,000
Loss for the quarter			$ 10,200
Equals: Retained earnings in March			$ 255,300

The balance sheet needs to be developed at start up and annually. What information will you obtain? Basically the assets that are necessary to support the level of operations (from the income statement). It will indicate how these assets will be financed. This statement will be evaluated through ratio analysis by investors to determine if your inventory turnover and debt to equity ratios are within the parameters that are needed to justify your projected future financing.

175

ASSUMPTION STATEMENTS

Include a set of assumption statements as a basis for the proforma statements. They are basically an explanation of the figures in the projections.   The accuracy of these assumptions is critical as your financial projections are based upon them and the statements are only as accurate as the information upon which they are based. The critical elements are the sales forecast (which is based upon the market potential) and the calculated expenses. How do you develop accurate statements? You will need to do market research and develop your sales forecasts based upon that information (see Defining the Market in the Marketing section). It is best to be realistic with these figures and base them upon factual information. There is industry specific data that is available to assist in projecting sales and expenses including Robert Morris Associates Annual Statement Studies and Financial Research Associates. This is basically a compilation of average financial statements for companies of various sizes in many different industries.

Since they are projected statements they will only be as accurate as the information that you base them upon. If you are an existing business you will have a previous record to use as a basis to develop these statements. However, if you are a start-up you do not have a basis upon which to build the statements. What should you do to develop them?   Develop a written list of assumptions upon which to base your projections. It is very critical that you have accurate market research to develop sales projections.

Some plans include a worst case, most likely, and best case scenarios. When developing pro forma statements it is best to be factual and lean toward the conservative side and project out for three years. You can check the projected statements against the actual (monthly) and modify them---this becomes a management tool for you.

EXAMPLE:

The following are projected statements for a business (Lake Side Café). Note that they have done a good job with identifying the assumptions upon which the statements are based.

Most Likely Case					
	Lake Side Café				
	Pro Forma Income Statements				
	1998	1999	2000	2001	2002

Total Sales [1]	$ 42,000	$ 46,200	$ 53,130	$ 53,130	$ 53,130
Cost of Goods Sold:					
Coffee/Cocoa [2]	$ 4,200	$ 4,620	$ 5,313	$ 5,313	$ 5,313
Juices/Waters/Sodas [3]	$ 420	$ 462	$ 531	$ 531	$ 531
Paper/Products [4]	$ 84	$ 92	$ 106	$ 106	$ 106
Pastries/Candies [5]	$ 2,940	$ 3,234	$ 3,719	$ 3,719	$ 3,719
TOTAL COGS	$ 7,644	$ 8,408	$ 9,670	$ 9,670	$ 9,670
Total COGS as % of Sales	18%	18%	18%	18%	18%
GROSS MARGIN	$ 34,356	$ 37,792	$ 43,460	$ 43,460	$ 43,460
Gross Margin as % of Sales	82%	82%	82%	82%	82%
Operating Expenses:					
Misc. Business Expenses [6]	$ 1,680	$ 1,848	$ 2,125	$ 2,125	$ 2,125
Cleaning & Shop Supplies [7]	$ 2,000	$ 2,000	$ 2,000	$ 2,000	$ 2,000
Insurance Expense [8]	$ 805	$ 805	$ 805	$ 805	$ 805
Advertising Expense [9]	$ 2,100	$ 2,310	$ 2,657	$ 2,657	$ 2,657
Rent Expense [10]	$ 2,250	$ 3,600	$ 3,600	$ 3,600	$ 3,600
Utilities/Phone Expense [11]	$ 2,280	$ 2,280	$ 2,280	$ 2,280	$ 2,280
Equipment Purchases [12]	$ 600	$ 300	$ 100	$ 100	$ 100
Equipment Depreciation [13]	$ 800	$ 800	$ 800	$ 800	$ 800
Loan Payment [14]	$ 5,480	$ -	$ -	$ -	$ -
Salaries Payable [15]	$ -	$ 4,944	$ 4,944	$ 4,944	$ 4,944
Sales Tax [16]	$ 2,940	$ 3,234	$ 3,719	$ 3,719	$ 3,719
TOTAL OPERATING EXPENSES	$ 20,935	$ 22,121	$ 23,030	$ 23,030	$ 23,030
Total Operating Expenses As % of Sales	50%	48%	43%	43%	43%
NET INCOME (LOSS)	$ 13,421	$ 15,671	$ 20,431	$ 20,431	$ 20,431
Net Income (Loss) as % of Sales	32%	34%	38%	38%	38%
Federal Income Taxes [17]	$ 2,013.15	$ 2,350.59	$ 3,064.58	$ 3,064.58	$ 3,064.58
INCOME (loss) AFTER TAXES	$ 11,408	$ 13,320	$ 17,366	$ 17,366	$ 17,386
Income (Loss) after Taxes as % of Sales	27%	29%	33%	33%	33%

[1] Based on monthly sales of $3,500 per month for year 1; increasing 10% year 2; and 15% year 3 remaining constant through year 5.

[2] Based on coffee purchases equal to 10% of Total Sales.

[3] Based on beverage purchases equal to 1% of Total Sales.

[4] Based on paper product purchases equal to 2% of Total Sales.

[5] Based on pastry purchases equal to 7% of Total Sales.

[6] Based on expenses during first 6 months in business equal to 4% of Total Sales.

[7] Based on expenses during first 6 months in business.

[8] Based on annual insurance rate of $749 and workers' compensation of $55.00.

[9] Based on advertising expenses equal to 5% of Total Sales.

[10] Based on $250 rent per month: 3 months pre-paid in year 1; $300/ month in years 2-5.

[11] Based on $150 utility/ $40 phone expenses during first 6 months in business.

[12] Based on estimated equipment needs.

[13] Based on straight-line depreciation over five years of the expected life of the equipment.

[14] Based on loan repayment in year 1.

[15] Based on 960 hours/year for one employee earning $5.15 - minimum wage.

[16] Based on 7% sales tax

[17] Based on 15% federal income tax rate.

		Pro Forma Balance Sheet							
	Dec. 31, 1998		Dec. 31, 1999		Dec. 31, 2000		Dec. 31 2001		Dec. 31, 2002
Assets:									
Cash	$	6,711	$	8,655	$	12,535	$	12,535	$ 12,535
Equipment [2]	$	4,600	$	4,900	$	5,000	$	5,000	$ 5,000
Inventory [3]	$	300	$	400	$	500	$	500	$ 500
Total Assets:	$	11,611	$	13,955	$	18,035	$	18,035	$ 18,035
Liabilities:									
Sales Tax Payable [4]	$	203	$	223	$	257	$	257	$ 257
Salaries Payable [5]	$	-	$	412	$	412	$	412	$ 412
Total Liabilities	$	203	$	635	$	669	$	669	$ 669
Stockholder's Equity:									
Retained Earnings	$	11,406	$	13,320	$	17,366	$	17,366	$ 17,366
Total Liabilities & SE:	$	11,611	$	13,955	$	18,035	$	18,035	$ 18,035

[2] Based on purchase of equipment of $600 year 1; $300 year 2; $100 years 3-5.
[3] Based on increase in COGS.
[4] Based on 7% sales tax.
[5] Based on salaries paid once a month; $5.15/hour for 80 hours/month.

EXAMPLE: ASSUMPTION STATEMENTS

Explanation of Key Assumptions Used in the Financial Statements

1. Project market sales to continue to increase at an average of approximately 15% per annum to a total of 1,100,737.
2. Achieve a .02% market share by year five that will lead to a sales volume of 2200 in year five.
3. Salaries begin at 19,000 and will increase at a rate of 20% of sales. George's salary will be $11,000 in year one, and Cindy's salary will be $8,000.
4. Advertising quarterly in the "Music Trade" magazine @ $550 an advertisement beginning in year one.
5. Advertising quarterly in "Guitar Player" magazine @ $3000 an advertisement beginning in year three.
6. Accounts Receivable will be calculated as 15% of sales.

7. Income tax rate of 40%.

Comment: Limited assumptions. The market share seems unrealistic and the growth rate stated does not match with the numbers on the income statement. Need to separate assumptions for the income statement and the balance sheet.

EXAMPLE: SORORITY SWIMWEAR PRO FORMA INCOME STATEMENT ASSUMPTIONS

Sales and Marketing

To present a conservative view of pro forma results, the assumption was made that the market share will be captured only from 18-24 year old women that attend the largest 75 colleges. In actuality, the vast markets available by all women in the U.S. and the desirability of our product will result in greater sales than in these pro forma financials.

Simmons Study: 25.2% of all women 18-24 years old purchased at least one bathing   suit within the last 12 months. Through our survey, over 75% of 18-24 college women purchased bathing suits within the last 12 months.

Assumption: We assume a very conservative 12% of the college market can be reached by our company. These 12% will pay an extremely competitive price of only $45.00 (years 1-2), $49.00 (years 3-5).

Our target market is as follows:

Year 1 -- Largest universities in the state of Florida (73,380 potential customers)
Year 2 -- Largest universities in the Southeastern U. S. (202,596 potential customers)
Year 3 -- Largest universities in the entire Eastern U.S. (533,749 potential customers)
Year 4 -- Largest universities in Eastern and Midwest (901,369 potential customers)
Year 5 -- All major colleges and universities in the U. S. (1,030,470 potential customers)

Cost of Goods Sold

	Year 1-2	Year 3-5
Manufacturing (outsourced)	$10.50	$13.50
Shipping	$1.90	$1.90

Salaries and Wages

	Year 1	Year 2-3	Year 4-5
Sam Jensen - President and CEO	$35,000	$55,000	$75,000
Tom Lawson - VP of Marketing	$24,000	$45,000	$65,000
Josh Heren - VP of Operation	$24,000	$45,000	$65,000
Lisa Noble - Designer	$20,000	$32,000	$40,500

Office Manager	$18,000	$30,000	$38,500
Secretary/Clerk	$15,000	$21,000	$26,500

Sales Agents will be paid 10% of their sales and 5% of their rep sales. There will be one sales   rep per targeted school.   Head sales agent is independent and pays all expenses. Sales reps are expected to sell 75% of product while head sales agent is expected to sell 25% directly to retailers. The head sales agent is also responsible for setting up sales force.

Payroll Taxes and Insurance

OASDI 6.2% to 61,200 per employee
Medicaid   1.45% no limit
FUTA   .8% to 7,000 per employee
FL SUI 2.5% to 7,000 per employee
Work. Comp.   1.02% of payroll expense
Health Insurance is 3, 500 per family per year and is paid by the employer.

Royalties to the universities are 8%.

Advertising is estimated to be 7% if sales per year. This includes color brochures and classifieds.

Equipment and Supplies are expected to be .35% of sales per year. This does not include start up equipment.

Rent is based on $1.10 per square foot per month x 1,200 square feet x 12 months. This estimate is based on current rental charges in the Tampa area.

Utilities costs are based on $.67 per square foot per month x 1, 200 square feet x 12 months. This estimate is based on current utility charges in the Tampa areas.

Telephone expense is estimated to be $6,000 the first year and expected 5% increase each year thereafter. This includes all charges and a !-800 number.

Insurance expense is estimated to be 1.15% of sales.

Bad Debts are estimated to be 3.5% of sales.

Travel expense is estimated at 1.5% of sales. This includes all travel expenses for employees on salary. Sales agents and reps are independent.

Miscellaneous expense is estimated to be .2% of sales.

Pro Forma Balance Sheet Assumptions

Accounts Receivable assumes sales are constant and the balance is December's sales less an allowance for bad debts of 3.5%.

Inventory will consist of all orders sent back. These bathing suits will be sold at wholesale and will be 2% of sales.

Common Stock assumes 100,000 shares are authorized 25,000 are issued, par value $1.00. Shares left over will be used for future financing. A three year term loan will be taken out at 18% with an additional matching line of credit for extra orders.

Equipment consists of $5,000 worth of office supplies.

Accounts Payable assumes sales are constant and the balance is December's cost of goods sold.

Comment: They have been thorough in developing their assumptions, but the market growth rate seems excessively high.

Sorority Swimwear Designs, Inc.
Pro Forma Balance Sheet

	Start Up Period	Year 1	Year 2	Year 3	Year 4	Year 5
ASSETS						
Current Assets						
Cash	$ 5,035	$ 22,330	$ 379,577	$ 1,098,338	$ 2,377,640	$ 3,889,302
Accounts Receivable	0	$ 31,737	$ 87,625	$ 251,373	$ 424,507	$ 485,308
Inventory	$ 40,000	$ 7,925	$ 21,880	$ 62,768	$ 106,000	$ 121,183
Total Current Assets	45,035	$ 61,992	$ 489,082	$ 1,412,479	$ 2,908,147	$ 4,495,793
Long Term Assets						
Equipment & Supplies	$ 5,000	$ 5,000	$ 5,000	$ 5,000	$ 5,000	$ 5,000
Less Allowances	$ 500	$ 500	$ 500	$ 500	$ 500	$ 500
Total Long Term Assets	$ 4,500	$ 4,500	$ 4,500	$ 4,500	$ 4,500	$ 4,500
TOTAL ASSETS	$ 49,535	$ 66,492	$ 493,582	$ 1,416,979	$ 2,912,647	$ 4,500,293
LIABILITIES						
Current Liabilities						
Accounts Payable (includes salaries, unearned rent)	$ 4,645	$ 32,782	$ 68,754	$ 159,823	$ 259,849	$ 292,372
Long term debt	$ 90,000	$ 65,183	$ 35,543	0	0	0
TOTAL LIABILITIES	$ 96,645	$ 97,965	$ 104,297	$ 159,823	$ 259,849	$ 292,372
STOCKHOLDERS' EQUITY						

	Start Up Period	Year 1	Year 2	Year 3	Year 4	Year 5
Common Stock	$ 25,000	$ 25,000	$ 25,000	$ 25,000	$ 25,000	$ 25,000
Retained Earnings	$ (70,110)	$ (56,473)	$ 364,285	$ 1,232,156	$ 2,627,798	$ 4,182,921
Total Stockholders' Equity	$ (45,110)	$ (31,473)	$ 389,285	$ 1,257,156	$ 2,652,798	$ 4,207,921
TOTAL LIAB. & EQUITY	$ 49,535	$ 66,492	$ 493,582	$ 1,416,979	$ 2,912,647	$ 4,500,293

Pro Forma Cash Flows

	Start Up Period	Year 1	Year 2	Year 3	Year 4	Year 5
Cash flows from operating activities						
Net income per income statement:	$ (69,965)	$ (13,798)	$ 380,827	$ 783,799	$ 1,388,012	$ 1,635,982
Add: Depreciation	0	$ 500	$ 500	$ 500	$ 500	$ 500
Deduct: Increase in inventory	$ 40,000	$ (32,075)	$ 21,880	$ 62,768	$ 106,000	$ 121,183
Increase in prepaid expenses	0	$ 1,000	$ 1,200	$ 1,550	$ 1,780	$ 1,987
Decrease in accounts payable	0	$ 500	$ 1,000	$ 1,220	$ 1,430	$ 1,650
Net cash flows --- operating	$ (109,965)	$ 17,277	$ 357,247	$ 718,761	$ 1,279,302	$ 1,511,662
Cash flows from investing activities:						
Cash from stock issue	$ 25,000	0	0	0	0	0
Net cash flows -- investing	$ 25,000	0	0	0	0	0
Cash flow from financing activities						
Cash paid for dividends	$ 90,000	0	0	0	0	0
Net cash flows - financing	$ 90,000					
Increase in cash	$ 5,035	$ 17,277	$ 357,247	$ 718,761	$ 1,279,302	$ 1,511,662
Beginning cash	0	$ 5,053	$ 22,330	$ 379,577	$ 1,098,338	$ 2,377,640

Ending cash	$ 5,035	$ 22,330	$ 379,577	$ 1,098,338	$ 2,377,640	$ 3,889,302

Sorority Swimwear Designs, Inc.
Pro Forma Income Statement

	Start Up Period	Year 1	Year 2	Year 3	Year 4	Year 5
Sales						
Direct	0	$396,252	$ 1,094,018	$ 3,138,444	$ 5,300,049	$ 6,059,164
Retail	0	$ 15,000	$ 42,500	$ 122,500	$ 162,500	$ 187,500
Internet	0		$ 11,250	$ 38,000	$ 81,000	$ 114,750
Total Sales	0	$ 411,252	$ 1,147,768	$ 3,298,944	$ 5,543,549	$ 6,361,414
Cost of Goods Sold	0	$ 109,189	$ 301,462	$ 986,368	$ 1,665,729	$ 1,904,308
Royalties (8%)	0	$ 18,811	$ 52,523	$ 139,500	$ 232,928	$ 267,413
Gross Profit	0	$ 283,252	$ 793,783	$ 2,173,076	$ 3,644,892	$ 4,189,693
Sales, G & A Expenses						
Head Sales Agent	0	$ 10,648	$ 29,401	$ 84,345	$ 142,438	$ 162,839
All Sales Reps	0	$ 14,859	$ 41,025	$ 117,691	$ 198,751	$ 227,218
Total	0	$ 25,507	$ 70,426	$ 202,036	$ 341,189	$ 390,057
Salaries and Wages	$ 24,000	$ 136,000	$ 228,000	$ 228,000	$ 310,500	$ 310,500
Payroll Taxes	$ 2,628	$ 11,790	$ 18,828	$ 18,828	$ 25,139	$ 25,139
Workers' Comp. Ins.	$ 244	$ 1,387	$ 2,325	$ 2,325	$ 3,167	$ 3,167
Health Insurance	$ 3,500	$ 21,000	$ 21,000	$ 21,000	$ 21,000	$ 21,000
Advertising	$ 4,875	$ 28,788	$ 80,344	$ 230,926	$ 388,048	$ 445,299
Office Supplies	$ 5,000	$ 1,439	$ 4,017	$ 11,546	$ 19,402	$ 22,265
Rent	0	$ 18,576	$ 18,576	$ 18,576	$ 18,576	$ 18,576
Utilities	0	$ 9,648	$ 9,648	$ 9,648	$ 9,648	$ 9,648
Telephone	$ 2,500	$ 6,000	$ 6,300	$ 6,615	$ 6,945	$ 7,293
Insurance	0	$ 6,169	$ 17,217	$ 49,484	$ 83,153	$ 95,421
Bad Debts	0	$ 14,394	$ 40,172	$ 115,463	$ 194,024	$ 222,649
Travel Expense	$ 12,000	$ 6,169	$ 17,217	$ 49,484	$ 83,153	$ 95,421
Miscellaneous Expense	$ 1,000	$ 823	$ 1,148	$ 3,299	$ 5,544	$ 6,361
Total S, G & A Expense	$ 55,747	$ 287,689	$ 535,217	$ 967,231	$ 1,509,489	$ 1,672,797
Interest Expense	$ 14,218	$ 9,361	$ 3,555			
Total Expense	$ 69,965	$ 297,050	$ 538,772	$ 967,231	$ 1,509,489	$ 1,672,797

Income Before Taxes	$ (69,965)	$ (13,798)	$ 587,305	$ 1,205,845	$ 2,135,403	$ 2,516,896
Taxes	0	0	$ 206,478	$ 422,046	$ 747,391	$ 880,914
Net Income (Loss)	$ (69,965)	$ (13,798)	$ 380,827	$ 783,799	$ 1,388,012	$ 1,635,982

BREAKEVEN ANALYSIS

Breakeven Analysis can be a very important tool for the entrepreneur as it can be beneficial in making the decision whether to pursue the business idea or if an existing business whether to add a new product or service to the mix. Basically it is a calculation that determines how much product must be sold to breakeven. (Here we go into some simple math so hang on). The breakeven point is the dollars of revenue or units of sales that will be necessary to cover both the fixed and variable expenses.

Variable Costs: These are costs that vary directly with sales (examples include variable labor costs, costs of goods sold, sales commissions)
Fixed Costs: These are costs that remain constant regardless of the sales volume and must be met regardless of whether you make any sales or not. (examples include interest charges, rent, insurance, office and administrative costs.)

In order to find the breakeven point, we need to find where
$$TR = VC + FC$$
Where, TR = Total Revenue,
VC = Variable Costs, and
At the point where TR = VC + FC this is the breakeven point and this can be shown in
FC = Fixed Costs. the graph below (first equations and now graphs!):

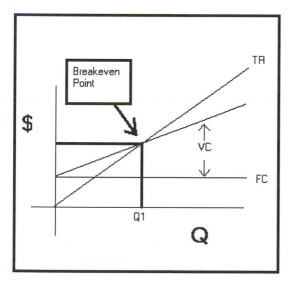

$ = Sales volume in dollars
Q = The number of inputs sold

TR = Total Revenue
TC = Total Costs [VC + FC]
FC = Fixed Costs
VC = Variable Costs

The breakeven point can be derived from the formula shown below:
$$TR = VC + FC$$
$$P(Q) = V(Q) + FC$$
Where   P = Price per unit
              V = Variable Cost per unit

Furthermore, we can then solve for Q:
$$P(Q) = V(Q) + FC$$
$$P(Q) - V(Q) = FC$$
$$Q(P-V) = FC$$
Therefore, $Q = FC/(P-V)$

The breakeven value can be ascertained by solving for Q. The simplest way to demonstrate this is by doing a problem.

- Suppose a firm is going to introduce a new product which they hope to wholesale at $12. Their fixed costs are expected to be $50,000 (rent, utilities, etc.) and the variable coat of their product is expected to be $2 per unit, which is composed mainly of labor expenses.

    The breakeven point is:

    $Q = \$50,000 / (\$12-\$2)$

    $Q = 5000$ units

Okay, so what does this mean? It means that if we expect have sales higher than 5000 units, we will make a profit. So if we are considering the project, we would need to be darn sure that our sales are going to exceed this number, before we do a full-blown business plan or make sure that we will have sales that are considered above this.

EXAMPLE:

Brumo's Deli
Break-Even Analysis

Assumptions: Advertising, Insurance and Operating Supplies increase as shown in Breakdown.

Fixed Cost Breakdown:

	Year 1	Year 2	Year 3	Year 4	Year 5
Rent	$36,000	36,000	36,000	36,000	36,000
Utilities	6,500	6,500	6,500	6,500	6,500
Telephone	1,000	1,000	1,000	1,000	1,000
Advertising	33,864	35,218	36,626	38,092	39,616
Insurance	6,500	6,500	6,700	6,700	6,800
Operating Supplies	1,000	1,000	1,250	1,250	1,500
Operating Permits	1,700	1,700	1,700	1,700	1,700
Salary	88,000	88,000	88,000	88,000	88,000
Total Fixed Costs:	$174,564	$178,192	$179,674	$179,242	$181,116

Break-Even=Fixed Cost/Contribution Margin

628901/967540=.65   174,564/.64=$268,560

Break-Even Year 1 = $268,560

664123/1006245=.66   178,192/.66=$269,987

Break-Even Year 2 = $269,987

690687/1046494=.66   179,674/.66=$270,718

Break-Even Year 3 = $270,718

718314/1088353=.66   179,242/.66=$271,578

Break-Even Year 4 = $271,578

748047/1131887=.66   181,116/.66=$274,418

Break-Even Year 5 = $274,418

Comment: They have indicated the costs used to calculate the breakeven levels and have done so for the five years of projections.

EXAMPLE: JENN'S FITNESS PROFESSIONALS

Break-even Analysis				
Best Case				
	Total Expenses	Revenue per session	Break-even number of sessions	Sessions per Trainer
1997	4,058	15.00	271	135.27
1998	46,416	15.00	3,094	618.88
1999	56,674	15.00	3,778	472.28
2000	8,550	15.00	570	57.00
2001	85,550	15.00	5,703	475.28
2002	106,613	15.00	7,108	507.68

*Break-even is determined by dividing the total expenses by the revenue Jenn's Fitness receives from each session to determine the number of sessions needed to break-even.

Best Case

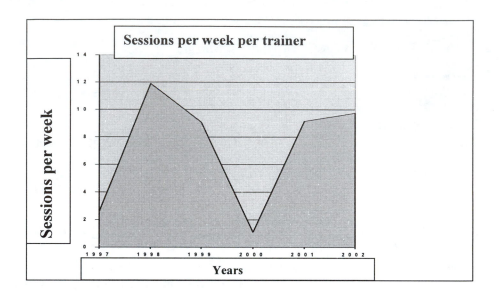

Break-even Analysis				
Most Likely Case				
	Total Expenses	Revenue per session	Break-even number of sessions	Sessions per Trainer
1997	4,058	15.00	271	90
1998	40,416	15.00	2,694	539
1999	49,674	15.00	3,312	414
2000	65,019	15.00	4,335	434
2001	61,450	15.00	4,097	341
2002	64,887	15.00	4,326	309
*Break-even is determined by dividing the total expenses by the revenue Jenn's Fitness receives from each session to determine the number of sessions needed to break-even.				

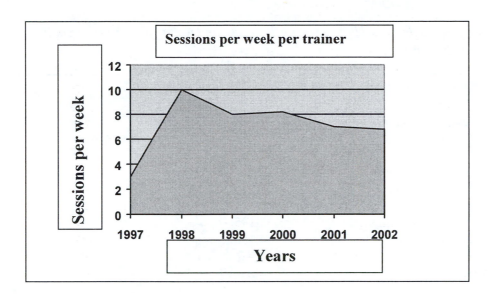

Break-even Analysis				
Worst Case				
	Total Expenses	Revenue per session	Break-even number of sessions	Sessions per Trainer
1997	4,058	15.00	271	135.27
1998	31,416	15.00	2,094	418.88
1999	25,174	15.00	1,678	209.78
2000	29,019	15.00	1,935	193.46
2001	52,550	15.00	3,503	291.94
2002	87,113	15.00	5,808	414.82
*Break-even is determined by dividing the total expenses by the revenue Jenn's Fitness receives from each session to determine the number of sessions needed to break-even.				

They have determined breakeven for best case and worst case and even put into graph format.

EXAMPLE: BREAKEVEN ANALYSIS FOR MORRISON LIFT

Outside Manufacturing

Total Units sold	250
Total sales	77,500
Total variable costs	53,125
Contribution	24,375
Contribution margin ratio	.3145
Total fixed costs	54,150
Sales price/unit	310
Variable cost/unit	212.50
Breakeven sales	172,360
Breakeven units	556

Assumptions:
Units sold and total sales based on first year projections
Breakeven in sales is derived by TFC/CMR
Breakeven in units is derived by: TFC/(Sales price/unit-variable costs/unit)

Comment: It would be helpful to note that this is for year one and that they will not attain breakeven level but will do so in the subsequent years.

EXAMPLE: BREAKEVEN POINT FOR KENYA PLAINS

The unit selling price is $8. The variable costs include labor, materials, and overhead. It is estimated that cost of goods will be $2.72, labor will be Hourly rate / time taken to cook and handle the food which is about 10 minutes per plate. Cooks are paid at a rate of $10. Overhead will include only electricity that will be used in the kitchen. All the equipment we use conserve energy, and thus work well with minimal voltage. It is estimated that overhead is about 1% of unit selling price which comes out to .80 cents.
Total fixed costs include lease payments and taxes on licenses. Which come up to a total of $45,000 in the first two years

Unit Selling Price is		$8.00
Variable Cost is:	Cost of Food and Drink	$2.72
	Cost of Labor	$1.60
	Variable Overhead	$0.08

	Total Variable Costs	$4.40
	Unit Contribution Margin	$3.60

Total Fixed Costs are $45,000

Break even point = Fixed Costs / Unit Contribution Margin = 12,500 units or (12,500*8) = $100,000.

Comment: The analysis is only as valid as the assumptions it is based upon— some concern for the accuracy of the basis of the assumptions.

ASCERTAINING THE AMOUNT OF FUNDS NEEDED

If you are seeking funding you will need to clearly indicate the type of funding that you are seeking and the amount required. You will need to give a complete breakdown of how the funds will be used and when they will be required. If your business has previously received funding, this amount should be stated and any stock that was issued. If your business has plans to seek additional funding in the future, indicate the stages in which it will be required. How do you actually determine the amount needed? You should start by figuring out the capital needed to purchase tangible assets for your business such as equipment, inventory, land, buildings. You will need to get cost estimates for these assets and then you will need to calculate anticipated costs of each for your business. If you need working capital that amount will be indicated by the cash flow statement. Make sure that there is consistency between the numbers that you come up with here and those in the financial statements. Pay particular attention to the balance sheet since it shows sources of capital and where it is used in the business.

ASCERTAINING THE TYPE OF FINANCING NEEDED

One of the main things that an entrepreneurs needs to assess in their business plan is the type of financing they need. While most stating entrepreneurs need equity (or long-term funds) frequently they only need debt for a short period of time. If the funds are only needed for less than two years, debt is preferred as it is cheaper. Additionally, if you issue equity, then you have those shares with your company for an infinite time period.

You can tell the type of financing you need by looking at the pro forma balance sheets under the funds needed. If this account shows:

Year		1	2	3	4	5
Funds Needed	50	0	0	0	0	

Debt is needed here as the funds are needed for only short term. Normally it is easier to get financing with debt than with equity but debt does pose a risk if the firm cannot pay the debt service.

If you see funds needed as below then the firm definitely needs equity.

Year		1	2	3	4	5
Funds Needed	60	60	60	60	60	

The decision of whether to use debt or equity, must rest on both the risk of using debt and the time period of funds needed.

CHARTS AND GRAPHS NEEDED

Graphs of future profits do not impress sophisticated investors. Using graphs of spreadsheets or business plan software it is easy to generate graphs. Most people are able to do that. Realize that if all it took were a few graphs everyone would obtain financing. The assumptions are more important. You have to convince investors that sales will actually increase in the future and a graph does not do this. However, do not conclude that you should not include them, the point is that they give a visual perspective to the numbers but it is the basis for the numbers that is the critical thing.

Example:

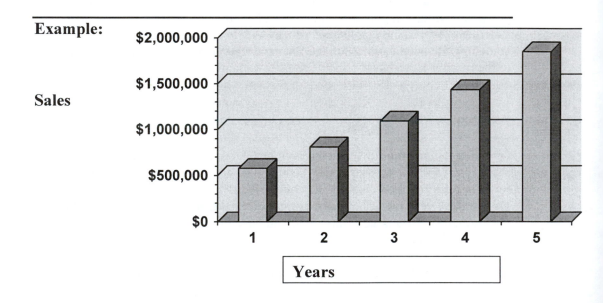

RESOURCES

Financial Research Associates
Provides industry ratios to use for developing and analyzing financial statements.

Industry Norms & Key Business Ratios (Dun & Bradstreet)
Provides balance sheet figures for companies in over 800 different lines of business as defined by SIC numbers.

RMA Annual Statement Studies (Robert Morris Associates)
Industry norms and ratios for each SIC code. Provides a compilation of average financial statements for companies of various sizes in many different industries.

Entrepreneurial Edge
Provides a wealth of information on Financial Management which includes modules on developing each of the statements.
www.lowe.org

Toolkit
www.toolkit.cch.com
Provides information and modules for developing financial statements. Click on Managing your Business Finances.

InterSoft Solutions Finance Hub
http://financehub.com/
Information and list to sites about VC, financing issues, and legal.

Preparing a Cash Flow Forecast
http://www.small business.ca/workshop/cashflow.html
Assists with process of preparing a cash flow forecast.

SBA
http://www.business.gov/
Information on financing and expanding your business.

MISTAKES TO AVOID

➢ Failing to develop assumptions for your statements.

➢ Inconsistencies between the financial statements.

➢ Overestimating the revenue and profit projections and underestimating operating expenses.

> ➢ Exceptionally high salaries for a new company.

> ➢ No information showing that the owners have made a significant financial investment in the business.

> ➢ The return on investment is not consistent with what investors are earning in similar ventures.

CHAPTER APPLICATIONS

> ➢ Complete Financial Worksheet
> ➢ Interview an entrepreneur in the same industry and determine how he/she developed the pro forma statements
> ➢ Interview a banker to determine lending policy for small businesses and the types of financing offered
> ➢ Interview an entrepreneur of a growing company about his financial strategy for growth.
> ➢ Complete Assignment 10.1

ASSIGNMENT 10.1							
In early 1999, Dave's second year of business, his banker suggests that they meet and examine							
progress again. She asks Dave to calculate the business' profit for its first year and to provide a							
statement of assets and liabilities as of December 31, 1998. At this stage Dave hasn't actually							
prepared his accounts for the year, but Sandy, the firm's accountant produced the following figures:							
	Operating expenses				$	80,000	
	Income-tax expenses				$	3,414	
	Cost of goods sold				$	125,000	
	Sales revenue				$	250,000	
	Personal drawings (wages to Dave)				$	20,000	
	Interest expense				$	4,720	
	Cash				$	111	
	Bank short-term loan				$	7,000	
	Bank long-term loan				$	50,000	
	Vehicle (cost)				$	24,000	
	Depreciation expense on vehicle				$	4,800	
	Plant & equipment (cost)				$	41,000	
	Inventory				$	23,438	
	Accrued liabilities				$	9,000	
	Depreciation expense on equipment & plant				$	4,100	
	Accounts receivable				$	31,250	
	Accounts payable				$	11,250	
	Prepaid expenses				$	5,000	
	Paid-up capital				$	30,000	
	Income tax payable				$	683	

Dave is always in a hurry because the business is booming. He decides that he is a specialist in assembly and not in accounting., and he asks you to prepare the statements for his banker.

Required:

1. Prepare the income statement and balance sheet for Dave's Bikes & Co. for the banker.

Year Ending _____

Revenue

   Gross Sales

      Less Returns and Allowances

   Net Sales

   Cost of Goods Sold

   Gross Profit

Operating Expenses

   Selling

      Salaries and Wages

      Payroll Taxes

      Commissions

      Advertising

      Other

   Total Selling Expenses

General and Administrative

      Salaries and Wages

      Payroll Taxes

      Employee Benefits

      Insurance

      Depreciation

      Automobile Expense

      Dues and Subscriptions

      Legal and Accounting

      Office Supplies

      Telephone

      Utilities

      Rent

      Taxes and Licenses

      Other

   Total General and Administrative

Total Operating Expenses

Operating Profit (Loss)

Net Income (Loss) Before Taxes

Income Taxes

Net Income (Loss)

Cash Flow Information (Monthly)

Month:	1	2	3	4	5	6	7	8	9	10	11	12
Beginning Cash Balance												
Cash Receipts												
Cash Sales												
Collect Accounts Receivable												
Loans from Banks												
Other Receipts												
Total Cash Receipts												
Cash Disbursements												
Purchases												
Salaries												
Payroll Taxes/Fringe Benefits												
Rent												
Utilities												
Interest												
Other												
Purchase Capital Equipment												
Loan-Principal Repayment												
Owner's Withdrawals												
Total Cash Disbursed												
Net Cash Flow												
Ending Cash Balance												

Balance Sheet Information

ASSETS

    Current Assets

        Cash   _____

        Accounts Receivable   _____

        Inventory   _____

        Prepaid Expenses   _____

        Total Current Assets   _____

    Fixed Assets

        Equipment   _____

        Land   _____

        Buildings   _____

        Vehicles   _____

        Furniture   _____

    Less accumulated depreciation   _____

        Total Net Fixed Assets   _____

LIABILITIES

    Current Liabilities

        Accounts Payable   _____

        Notes Payable   _____

        Interest Payable   _____

        Taxes Payable   _____

        Accruals   _____

    Total Current Liabilities   _____

    Long Term Debt   _____

EQUITY

        Shareholder's Equity   _____

        Retained Earnings   _____

        Total Stockholders Equity   _____

Total Liabilities and Stockholder's Equity   _____

FINANCIAL WORKSHEET

Are the assumptions based on a most likely scenario?_____

What are your start-up costs?_____

What are your profit margins?_____

If you are a startup business does the projected sales suggest you should enter the market?_____

Calculate the breakeven point for this business._____

Detail the terms of investment in this business and potential returns to the investors._____

_____

Income Statement and Balance Sheet Worksheet

Explain the assumptions for the income statement. Include assumptions regarding revenues and your operating expenses. Be specific._____

_____

Explain your startup costs._____

What capital expenditures will you have? What is the depreciation schedule?_____

What are your interest rates on debt owed? State the principal reduction on each._____

Discuss your payment terms for inventory purchases._____

_____

Cash Flow Worksheet

Determine if the firm has sufficient cash and how stable are the firm's cash flows?_____

How well do the cash inflow match the outflows?_____

Does the firm have an adequate buffer of cash?_____

ASSUMPTIONS WORKSHEET

Income:

What is the forecasted annual revenue amount?_____

What percent of sales are COGS?_____

List operating expenses:_____

Balance Sheet:

Property and Equipment purchased?_____
Depreciation schedule?_____

Cash Flow:

Accounts Receivable collected (determine collection period)_____
Accounts Payable (determine time frame paid)_____
Notes Payable?_____
Additional Funding?_____

WARM 'N SAFE BOTTLE COMPANY: THE FINANCIAL DATA

According to market information provided by Ron Vickson, Vice President of Sales for Little Guys Bottling Company, a leading manufacturer of specialty baby bottles, a manufacturer introducing just another decorated bottle without any key features or benefits over current bottles be expected to capture one to two percent of the total market in the first year of operations. This market share would probably remain at two percent during subsequent years. This assumption is the basis for the worst-case scenario presented in the projected financial statements for Warm 'n Safe Bottle Company.

Munchkin's market data also indicates that if a company produced a product with significant features or graphics as compared to existing decorated bottles, the company could expect to attain four percent of the market in the first year. That share could grow at 30 Percent per year over subsequent years. To achieve these results, however, the product would have to be unique and special. These are the assumptions that Warm 'n Safe has used to project the Company's best-case scenario financial results.

To present conservative projected pro forma financial statements, Warm 'n Safe has assumed that the Company will earn only two percent per year is assumed for years three through five. Based on the above projected market share percentages, the current U.S. reusable bottle market of approximately 38.6 million units and a selling price of $2.19 for the Warm n'Safe bottle. Projected sales were calculated for all three scenarios. Based on industry practices of retailing premium bottles at $3.99, Warm n'Safe established its cost at $2.19 to provide a 45 percent gross margin to the retailer.

The most likely case scenario pro forma financial statements are, in management's opinion, a conservative, yet realists, projection of Warm 'n Safe's first five years of production. These statements reflect positive cash flow in the first year of full production (year one of the Plan). The Company will also generate a profit after taxes in the first year of operation. Under this scenario, the Company will generate cash and grow in value sufficiently to allow Company to purchase an investor's ownership and allow the investor to realize a 50 percent return investment by the end of year five.

PRO FORMA INCOME STATEMENT ASSUMPTIONS
SALES

To present a conservative view of pro forma results, the assumption was made that market share will be captured only from existing U.S. reusable market. In actuality, however, worldwide patents, the vast markets available outside the U.S. and the desirability of the product will result in greater sales than used in these financials.

To convert dollar bottle market to units for projection purposes:

Calculations	Dollar Sales	Units	Average Selling Price
U.S. bottle mkt	154,000,000		
U.S. reusable 175,000+32,430,000 mkt	80,000,000	38,605,000	2.076,
U.S. premium 20,000,000/ reusable mkt ((2.99+3.49)/2)	20,000,000	6,175,000	3.24
U.S. standard 60,000,000/ reusable mkt ((1.80+1.90)/2)	60,000,000	32,430,000	1.85

Warm 'n Safe's pricing structure allows retailers 45% gross margin based on a suggested
retail of $3.99, while providing Warm 'n Safe a 58.0% gross margin.

Cost of Goods Sold

Bottle including silicone nipple, standard ring & disk, shipping	$0.57
Warm 'n Safe Modifications	0.35
Cost of Warm 'n Safe bottle	0.92

Master Broker engaged to set up established, experienced sales force. Master broker is paid 10% of his sales and 5% of his reps sales. The reps are each paid 5% of their sales. All pay their expenses and the master broker is anticipated to make 20% of the total projected sales.

Salaries and Wages

	Year 1	Years 2-5
Ryan Addison-President and CEO	60,000	60,000
Dan Mays -VP of Marketing	55,200	55,200
Warehouse Manager	24,000	24,000
Chief Financial Officer		50,000
Manufacturing Director		50,000
Secretary/Clerk		20,000
	139,200	259,200

Payroll Taxes

OASDI	6.20% to 61,200 per employee
Medicaid	1.45% no limit
FUTA	.8% to 7,000 per employee
FL SUI	2.50% to 7,000 per employee

Worker's compensation insurance is based on 1.01% of payroll expense.
Health insurance is based on a rate of $3,600 per family per year and is paid entirely by the Company.
Advertising is estimated at 5% of sales in year 1, 4% in year 2 and 3% in years 3 through five.
Bad Debts are estimated to be 3% of sales.
Depreciation is for office equipment and furniture with a cost of $20,000 and manufacturing equipment with a cost of $111,000 depreciated straight-line over 5 years.

Dues and Subscriptions based on estimated cost of trade journals, etc. to keep abreast of industry trends and activities.

Insurance expense is estimated to be 2.12% of sales and includes product liability and Directors and Officers coverage.

Miscellaneous expense is estimated t be .15% of sales.

Rent is based on .60% per square foot per month * 1,000 square feet * 12 months. This estimate is based on currently available office space in the Panama City business district. An additional $.30 per square foot per month * 10,000 square feet * 12 months is estimated at the same site for inventory storage.

Supplies are based on $.355% of sales.

Travel is estimated at .37% of sales per year for trade shows.

Utilities – Electricity costs are based on $.89 per square foot per month * 1,000 square feet * 12 months. This estimate is based on current utility charges in the Belleville City area. Telephone expense is estimated to be $6,800 per year to include a 1-800 number for consumers and retailers.

Pro Forma Balance Sheets Assumption

Accounts Receivable assumes sales are constant over the year (1/12 each month) and the accounts receivable balance at any balance sheet date is December's sales less an allowance for bad debts of 3%. (1/12 * Annual Sales * .97)

Inventory assumes that although major orders will be shipped direct from manufacturer, equivalent of 1 month's sales will be kept in inventory at Company's office for emergencies. (1/12 * Annual Cost of Goods Sold)

Fixtures and Equipment assumes a $20,000 purchase of office furniture and equipment (PC's) and an $111,000 purchase of manufacturing equipment with depreciation computed on a 5 year straight-line method.

Accounts Payable and Accrued Expenses assumes sales are constant over the year (1/12 each month) and the accounts payable balance at any balance sheet date is December's cost of goods sold.

Common Stock assumes 100,000 shares of stock, par value $.10, are authorized and issued.

Additional Paid in Capital assumes that $30,000 shares of the above stock is issued to an investor at $6.67 per share.

Retained Earnings is the prior year's retained earnings balance plus the current year's net income.

Warm 'n Safe Bottle Company
Pro Forma Income Statements
Most Likely Case

	Start Up Period	Year 1	Year 2	Year 3	Year 4	Year 5
Sales	$0	$1,690,680	$3,381,360	$4,395,768	$5,748,312	$7,438,992
Cost Of Goods	$0	$710,240	$1,420,480	$1,846,624	$2,414,816	$3,125,056
Gross Margin	$0	$980,440	$1,960,880	$2,549,144	$3,333,496	$4,313,936
S, G & A Expenses						
Sales Reps						
Master Rep	$0	$101,441	$202,882	$263,746	$344,899	$446,340
Others	$0	$67,627	$135,254	$175,831	$229,932	$297,560
Total	$0	$169,068	$338,136	$439,577	$574,831	$743,900
Salaries & Wages	$29,000	$139,200	$259,200	$259,200	$259,200	$259,200
Payroll Taxes	$2,681	$11,341.00	$21,214	$21,214	$21,214	$21,214
Worker's Comp Ins	$293	$1,406	$2,618	$2,618	$2,618	$2,618
Health Ins	$2,700	$10,800	$21,600	$21,600	$21,600	$21,600

	Start Up Period	Year 1	Year 2	Year 3	Year 4	Year 5
Advertising	$0	$84,534	$135,254	$131,873	$172,449	$223,170
Bad Debts	$0	$50,720	$101,441	$131,873	$172,449	$223,170
Depreciation	$0	$26,200	$26,200	$26,200	$26,200	$26,200
Dues & Subscriptions	$0	$400	$400	$400	$400	$400
Insurance	$0	$35,842	$71,685	$93,190	$121,864	$157,707
Miscellaneous	$326	$2,536	$5,072	$6,594	$8,622	$11,158
Patents	$5,000	$60,000	$40,000	$0	$0	$0
Rents	$0	$43,200	$43,200	$43,200	$43,200	$43,200
Supplies	$4,000	$5,917	$11,835	$15,385	$20,119	$26,036
Travel	$6,000	$6,256	$12,511	$16,264	$21,269	$27,524
Utilities	$0	$17,480	$18,179	$18,906	$19,662	$20,448
Total S, G & A Expenses	$50,000	$664,900	$1,108,545	$1,228,094	$1,485,697	$1,807,545
Income Before Taxes	($50,000)	$315,540	$852,335	$1,321,050	$1,847,799	$2,506,391
Income Taxes	($19,000)	$119,905	$323,887	$501,999	$702,164	$952,429
Net Income	($31,000)	$195,635	$528,448	$819,051	$1,145,635	$1,553,962

Warm 'n Safe Bottle Company
Pro Forma Balance Sheets
Most Likely Case

Current Assets	Start Up Period	Year 1	Year 2	Year 3	Year 4	Year 5
Cash	$2,000	$130,172	$548,156	$1,311,409	$2,373,914	$3,817,412
Accounts Receivable	$0	$136,663	$273,327	$355,325	$464,655	$601,319
Inventory	$44,000	$59,187	$118,373	$153,885	$201,235	$260,421
Total Current Assets	$46,000	$326,022	$939,856	$1,820,619	$3,039,804	$4,679,152
Property & Equip @ Cost						
Fixtures & Equip	$111,000	$131,000	$131,000	$131,000	$131,000	$131,000
Less Allowances	$0	($26,200)	($52,400)	($78,600)	($104,800)	($131,000)
	$111,000	$104,800	$78,600	$52,400	$26,200	$0

	Total Assets	$157,000	$430,822	$1,018,456	$1,873,019	$3,066,004	$4,679,152
Current Liabilities							
Accrued Expenses		($19,000)	$59,187	$118,373	$153,885	$201,235	$260,421
Long-Term Debt		$0	$0	$0	$0	$0	$0
Stockholder's Equity							
Common Stock		$10,000	$10,000	$10,000	$10,000	$10,000	$10,000
Additional Paid in Capital		$197,000	$197,000	$197,000	$197,000	$197,000	$197,000
Retained Earnings		($31,000)	$164,635	$693,083	$1,512,134	$2,637,769	$4,211,731
Total Stockholder's Equity		$176,000	$371,635	$9,000,083	$1,719,134	$2,864,769	$4,418,731
Total Liabilities & Equity		$157,000	$430,822	$1,018,456	$1,873,019	$3,066,004	$4,679,152

Warm 'n Safe Bottle Company
Pro Forma Cash Flows
Most Likely Case

	Start Up Period	Year 1	Year 2	Year 3	Year 4	Year 5
Net Income	($31,000)	$195,635	$528,448	$819,051	$1,145,635	$1,553,962
Add Items Not Requiring Cash						
Depreciation	$0	$26,200	$26,200	$26,200	$26,200	$26,200
Cash From Operations	($31,000)	$221,835	$554,648	$845,251	$1,171,835	$1,580,162
Sources of Cash						
Issuances of Stock	$207,000	$0	$0	$0	$0	$0
Increase in Accounts Payable	($19,000)	$78,187	$59,186	$35,512	$47,350	$59,186
Total Sources of Cash	$188,000	$78,187	$59,186	$35,512	$47,350	$59,186
Uses of Cash						
Increase in Accounts Receivable	$0	$136,663	$136,664	$81,998	$109,330	$136,664
Increase in Inventory	$44,000	$15,187	$59,186	$35,512	$47,350	$59,186

Increase in Fixed Assets	$111,000	$20,000	$0	$0	$0	$0
Total Uses of Cash	$155,000	$171,850	$195,850	$117,510	$156,680	$195,850
Increase in Cash	$2,000	$128,172	$417,984	$763,253	$1,062,505	$1,443,498
Beginning Cash	$0	$2,000	$130,172	$548,156	$1,311,409	$2,373,914
Ending Cash	$2,000	$130,172	$548,156	$1,311,409	$2,373,914	$3,817,412

Warm 'n Safe Bottle Company
Pro Forma Income Statements Highlights
Worst Case

	Start Up Period	Year 1	Year 2	Year 3	Year 4	Year 5
Sales	$0	$845,340	$1,690,680	$1,690,680	$1,690,680	$1,690,680
Cost of Goods	$0	$355,120	$710,240	$710,240	$710,240	$710,240
Gross Margin	$0	$490,220	$980,440	$980,440	$980,440	$980,440
S, G & A Expenses	$50,000	$487,464	$770,577	$714,397	$715,153	$715,939
Income Before Taxes	($50,000)	$2,756	$209,863	$266,043	$265,287	$264,501
Income Taxes	($19,000)	$1,047	$79,748	$101,096	$100,809	$100,510
Net Income	($31,000)	$1,709	$130,115	$164,947	$164,478	$163,991

Pro Forma Balances Sheet Highlights

	Start Up Period	Year 1	Year 2	Year 3	Year 4	Year 5
Current Assets	$46,000	$102,502	$288,411	$479,558	$670,236	$860,427
Property & Equip, Net	$111,000	$140,800	$78,600	$52,400	$26,200	$0
Total Assets	$157,000	$207,302	$367,011	$531,958	$696,436	$860,427
Current Liabilities	($19,000)	$29,593	$59,187	$59,187	$59,187	$59,187
Stockholder's Equity	$176,000	$177,709	$307,824	$472,771	$637,249	$801,240
Total Liabilities & Equity	$157,000	$207,302	$367,011	$531,958	$696,436	$860,427

Pro Forma Cash Flow Highlights

	Start Up Period	Year 1	Year 2	Year 3	Year 4	Year 5
Cash From Operations	($31,000)	$27,909	$156,315	$191,147	$190,678	$190,191

Total Sources of Cash	$188,000	$48,593	$29,594	$0	$0	$0
Total Uses of Cash	$155,000	$73,925	$97,925	$0	$0	$0
Increase in Cash	$2,000	$2,577	$87,984	$191,147	$190,678	$190,191
Beginning Cash	$0	$2,000	$4,577	$92,561	$283,708	$474,386
Ending Cash	$2,000	$4,577	$92,561	$283,708	$474,386	$664,577

Warm 'n Safe Bottle Company
Pro Forma Income Statements Highlights
Best Case

	Start Up Period	Year 1	Year 2	Year 3	Year 4	Year 5
Sales	$0	$3,381,360	$4,395,768	$5,748,312	$7,438,992	$9,636,876
Cost of Goods	$0	$1,420,480	$1,846,624	$2,414,816	$3,125,056	$4,048,368
Gross Margin	$0	$1,960,880	$2,549,144	$3,333,496	$4,313,936	$5,588,508
S, G & A Expenses	$50,000	$1,019,775	$1,311,325	$1,484,941	$1,806,759	$2,224,922
Income Before Taxes	($50,000)	$941,105	$1,237,819	$1,848,555	$2,507,177	$3,363,586
Income Taxes	($19,000)	$357,620	$470,371	$702,451	$952,727	$1,278,163
Net Income	($31,000)	$583,485	$767,448	$1,146,104	$1,554,450	$2,085,423

Pro Forma Balances Sheet Highlights

	Start Up Period	Year 1	Year 2	Year 3	Year 4	Year 5
Current Assets	$46,000	$773,058	$1,602,218	$2,821,872	$4,461,708	$6,650,274
Property & Equip, Net	$111,000	$104,800	$78,600	$52,400	$26,200	$0
Total Assets	$157,000	$877,858	$1,680,818	$2,874,272	$4,487,908	$6,650,274
Current Liabilities	($19,000)	$118,373	$153,885	$201,235	$260,421	$337,364
Stockholder's Equity	$176,000	$759,485	$1,526,933	$2,673,037	$4,227,487	$6,312,910
Total Liabilities & Equity	$157,000	$877,858	$1,680,818	$2,874,272	$4,487,908	$6,650,274

Pro Forma Cash Flow Highlights

	Start Up Period	Year 1	Year 2	Year 3	Year 4	Year 5
Cash From Operations	($31,000)	$609,685	$793,648	$1,172,304	$1,580,650	$2,111,623

Total Sources of Cash	$188,000	$137,373	$35,512	$47,350	$59,186	$76,943
Total Uses of Cash	$155,000	$367,700	$117,510	$156,680	$195,850	$254,605
Increase in Cash	$2,000	$379,358	$711,650	$1,062,974	$1,443,986	$1,933,961
Beginning Cash	$0	$2,000	$381,358	$1,093,008	$2,155,982	$3,599,968
Ending Cash	$2,000	$381,358	$1,093,008	$2,155,982	$3,599,968	$5,533,929

DESIRED FINANCING

The management team has projected that Warm 'n Safe Bottle Company will need capital of $200,000 to begin operations. These funds will be primarily used to secure patents, fund initial plastic mold manufacture and complete development and testing. Anticipated immediate sales should generate sufficient cash to fund operating activities once actual production begins and no additional funding needs are expected.

In exchange for the seed capital in the amount of $200,000, Warm 'n Safe Company is prepared to surrender 20 percent ownership in the Company. Warm 'n Safe Bottle Company anticipates that an investor willing to provide these funds will require a return on investment of 50 percent per year and be able to liquidate his investment in the Company in five years. At a 50 percent return rate, this investment at the end of five years will be $2,010,000.

Based on most likely case scenario pro forma financial statements and using five times after tax earnings as a basis for valuing Warm 'n Safe Bottle Company, a 20 percent ownership in Warm 'n Safe Bottle Company will be worth approximately $1,554,000 at the end of five years. Assuming ten times after tax earnings as an approximate basis for valuing Warm 'n Safe Bottle Company, a 20 percent ownership in the Company will be worth approximately $3,108,000 at the end of five years.

In the event that Warm 'n Safe Bottle Company is not prepared or desirous of issuing an initial public offering at the end of the five-year period, the financial situation of the Company would allow Warm 'n Safe Bottle Company to purchase the initial investor's stake in the Company at the same rate mentioned above.

CHAPTER 11
OTHER IMPORTANT DATA

In this chapter we will consider other data necessary to the business plan including a time schedule for your business plan and critical risks.

TIME SCHEDULE

In this section you will want to identify key objectives or milestones of the business and when they need to be accomplished. These objectives may include financing objectives such as the initial financing to be secured, a certain profit level to attain, or a debt to retire. Marketing objectives may include a certain level of annual sales to reach, a specific increase in market share, or the market testing of a product. If you are an existing business begin by listing the key objectives that you have reached at this point and when they were attained. Next list those objectives yet to be accomplished and the plans in place to reach them. Identify the persons that will be responsible for their accomplishment. Develop a timeline for the objectives showing when you plan to reach them. Note alternate plans if the objective is not reached. Make sure that your objectives are realistic and can be attained in the timeframes that you set. More often than not, objectives take longer than planned and you will encounter problems and setbacks of some sort so you need to consider this when establishing the timeline for your objectives.

Example: Time Schedule for Start-up

Task Name	Start Date	1997 May	June	July	Aug	Sept	Oct	Nov	Dec
Phase 1									
Establish General Partnership	May-97								
General Partner Contribution Received	May-97								
Secure Office Space in Orlando	May-97								
Subscribe to Publications & Directories	May-97								
Join Professional Organizations	May-97								
Establish Web Site	May-97								
Identify Prospective Investors	May-97								
Attend Meetings, Trade Shows, etc	May-97								
Present Offering to Prospective Investors	May-97								
Review Business Plans Received	May-97								
Meet With Entrepreneurs	Jul-97								
Phase 2									
First Stage Funding Received	Jul-97								
Select Reviewed Plans For Due Diligence	Jul-97								
Negotiate Deal Structure	Sep-97								

Task Name	Start Date	1998 Jan	Feb	March	April	May	June	July	Aug
Phase 3									
Make Investments	Jan-98								
Identify Prospective Investors	Jan-98								
Attend Meetings, Trade Shows, etc	Jan-98								
Present Offering to Prospective Investors	Jan-98								
Review Business Plans Received	Jan-98								
Meet With Entrepreneurs	Jan-98								
Select Reviewed Plans For Due Diligence	Jan-98								
Negotiate Deal Structure	Jan-98								
Make Investments	Jan-98								
Review Portfolio Companies' Performance	Jan-98								
Receive Stage 2 Funding	Jun-98								

Completed Tasks	
On Going Activities	

Comment: They have given a detailed schedule for the start up tasks for this company. This same format can be used for any stage of a business with

---

EXAMPLE: TIME SCHEDULE FOR OPERATIONS

The following operational schedules have been established to consider potential growth. This schedule begins on January 1, 1996

Pessimistic Growth:

Nov. 1996	Hire additional salesperson.
May 1997	Purchase one new rack.
Sep. 1998	Purchase one new rack.
Feb. 1999	Hire additional warehouse person.
Sep. 1999	Purchase one new rack.
Jun. 2000	Purchase one new rack.

Moderate Growth:

Oct. 1996	Hire additional salesperson.
Nov. 1996	Purchase one new rack.
Jun. 1997	Purchase one new rack.
Sep. 1997	Hire additional warehouse person.
Dec. 1997	Purchase one new rack.
May 1998	Purchase one new rack.
Sep. 1998	Purchase one new rack.
Jan. 1999	Purchase one new rack.
	Lease new vehicle.
	Hire delivery person.
Apr. 1999	Purchase one new rack.
Jun. 1999	Purchase one new rack.
Jul. 1999	Warehouse expansion begins.
Sep. 1999	Purchase one new rack.
Oct. 1999	Lease additional vehicle.
	Hire delivery person.
Nov. 1999	Purchase one new rack.
Jan. 2000	Capacity reached.
	Warehouse expansion complete.
	Purchase one new rack.
Feb. 2000	Purchase one new rack.
Apr. 2000	Purchase one new rack.
	Hire new delivery person.
	Lease additional vehicle.
Jun. 2000	Purchase one new rack.
Jul. 2000	Purchase one new rack.

Aug. 2000	Purchase one new rack.
Oct. 2000	Purchase one new rack.

Optimistic Growth:

Sep. 1996	Hire additional salesperson.
Oct. 1996	Purchase one new rack.
Mar. 1997	Purchase one new rack.
May 1997	Lease additional vehicle.
	Hire another delivery person.
Sep. 1997	Purchase one new rack.
Feb. 1998	Purchase one new rack.
Jun. 1998	Purchase one new rack.
Sep. 1998	Purchase one new rack.
Dec. 1998	Purchase one new rack.
Feb. 1999	Purchase one new rack.
Mar. 1999	Begin expansion of warehouse.
May 1999	Purchase one new rack.
	Lease additional vehicle.
	Hire additional delivery person.
Jul. 1999	Purchase one new rack.
Sep. 1999	Purchase one new rack.
Oct. 1999	Capacity reached.
	Expansion of new warehouse complete.
	Purchase one new rack.
Dec. 1999	Purchase one new rack.
Jan. 2000	Purchase one new rack.
Mar. 2000	Purchase one new rack.
Apr. 2000	Hire new delivery person.
	Lease additional vehicle.
	Purchase one new rack.
May 2000	Purchase one new rack.
Jun. 2000	Purchase one new rack.
Aug. 2000	Purchase one new rack.
Sep. 2000	Purchase one new rack.
Oct. 2000	Purchase one new rack.
Nov. 2000	Purchase one new rack.
	Hire Additional delivery person.
	Lease additional vehicle

Comment: They have developed a schedule that portrays three levels of growth. However, they need to indicate persons responsible for their accomplishment. This is a limited time schedule in that it only addresses operations and does not include other critical functions of the business.

CRITICAL RISKS

It is important to list potential problems or risks that the business may encounter in the critical risks section of a business plan. Some of these risks are additional competitors entering the market, inability to reach sales projections, and underestimating costs.

Avoid the misconception that some entrepreneurs have, that a business idea cannot go wrong. Very few entrepreneurial ventures go as planned. Every business has inherent risks and it is to your advantage to identify them up front. Why? It will help you prepare for them or to even avoid their occurrence. Additionally, potential investors are thinking about risks as well. Failure to address risks may cause funding sources to believe that you have either not identified them or choose to ignore them, neither of which will give them much confidence. Actually, it is reassuring to investors to know that you understand the risks because then you are more likely to take action to avoid or minimize the risks. It is important not only to list them but to also address how you will deal with any or all of them should they occur. If it is possible to minimize their impact, identify how that will be done. But always be up front about them.

> Every business has inherent risks **What?** And you thought you had the perfect idea

What types of risks should be identified? There are certain areas that you should consider when thinking about potential risks to the business. These may include sales projections that are not reached, production costs that are high, supply problems, or problems obtaining capital. One very important area is that of competition. What will happen if and when additional competitors enter your market? If you are a new business you will want to consider what existing competitors may do when you enter the market. Consider also that you may not get the market share that you anticipated either because there is no real market need or the market is not ready. If you are a manufacturing firm you will want to consider problems with design of your product or other technology related factors. A common risk that is often overlooked for all new business is underestimating costs and overestimating profits.

If you are an existing business you should identify problems faced in the past and how they were resolved. Discuss what was done to prevent their reoccurrence if possible. For example, you may have experienced difficulty in obtaining an adequate supply of inventory and had to go to another supplier on short notice that did not offer as low terms. This increased your costs and decreased your profitability. However, now you have resolved the situation by establishing terms with several suppliers at costs comparable to your main supplier.

EXAMPLE: CRITICAL RISKS

There are many risks that are inherent in the operations of Metal Works, Inc., and with its product the "HandyGrip". One risk is the lack of business experience on the part of Randy Clark. This will be overcome by the consulting group that Clark has put in place. In the future, Clark will have the option of hiring a manager to deal solely with the operations of Metal Works, Inc., if needed.

There are two main risks that are associated with the manufacturing aspect of Metal Works, Inc. First, because there is only one manufacturer, Brannon's manufacturing, one must be concerned with the possibility of something happening to Brannon's facilities. If this happened, production of the "HandyGrip" would halt, therefore causing delays and lessening the goodwill of the retailers who expect the product. To correct this, Metal Works will contact other manufacturers who are able to produce the "HandyGrip" at a day's notice.

The second risk that is associated with manufacturing is the machine that Brannon has invented to bend the steel tubing. There is only one such machine, and as before, if something were to happen to Brannon facilities the steel bending machine would be lost. Luckily the machine takes one day to make. Therefore, if something were to happen to Brannon's then a new machine could be made for another manufacturing facility and the chance of delay is lessened.

The final risk is the dependence of Metal Works on the "HandyGrip". When developing a company that produces, one must be concerned with the fact that the company's lifecycle may be that of the product's. To avoid this, Metal Works is currently developing accessories that will be manufactured if and when the "HandyGrip" is successful. This will ensure that the company not disappear when the "HandyGrip" disappears.

Comment:
They presented risks from management, manufacturing, and product and did an excellent job in addressing all of them.

EXAMPLE: DATASTORE

The company has an obvious risk with carrying the liability of legal documentation. Most of these files are not replaceable and cannot afford to be tampered with or damaged in anyway. Another critical aspect of this industry revolves around capturing customers. The companies within the industry assess fees for pulling boxes out of the system. Therefore, once a company adopts a customer, it is unlikely for the customer to pay these large exit fees in order to store their documents elsewhere.

Comment: The section identifies various risks but does not indicate how they will address the areas of risk. This is very important. It is not sufficient to just identify risks, you also need to tell how you will deal with them.

EXAMPLE: CRITICAL RISKS

There are a few things that could go wrong with this venture. First there is the issue of market rejection. The market may not be as receptive to the product as we anticipated. To combat this we will take several losses for the first year by throwing frequent "Taste of Africa" functions. These events will be free so that every one can participate. We will also customize the taste of the food to fit customer preferences. Most of our dishes can be made to individual specifications.

Another issue of great concern has to do with the politics and international trade policies. Most of our products will be imported from African countries. If there is a problem in one of the countries we import from, we may not be able to get the product, which means that we will not be able to sell. Consequently, we will have to raise prices just a little higher because we will have to go through numerous middlemen before we get the product. However, when we raise prices we will also increase the value of the meal by either making each serving larger or giving specials to customers.

If none of the solutions above work, we will sell the business. It is important to remember that Serengeti's plan to use investor's money in the third year of operations, after it has established a track record. The 50-seat building is an avenue to test the market's acceptance of our product and to see if we can maintain our competitive advantage. This initial venture requires very little start up costs, such that we may cash out in the event that the business does not realize the necessary profits.

Comment:
Although they mention several critical risks, the manner in which they address them would cause concern to any reader and in particular potential investors. They first mention taking a loss on several marketing functions but this is really a marketing expense. They also say that they may not be able to import product but then imply they can but may have to pay more to go through middlemen. If they pass the cost to the consumer but then give larger meal portions they have increased their costs. Finally, they say if the above solutions don't work, they will sell the business. How do they plan to do that if they cannot get product and are taking losses to market the product?

215

EXAMPLE: CRITICAL RISKS

Morrison's Medical acknowledges several risks associated with PatientLite. These risks are as follows:

- The pending review of the current Medicare/Medicaid agenda could change the depth of coverage provided by government programs for non-critical medical equipment such as patient lifts. This legislation is not likely to pose an initial threat to the success of the PatientLite, although long-term effects are uncertain. Morrison's will continue to monitor the changes of Medicare/Medicaid legislation.

- Mr. Brad Stewart has no prior experience as a CEO, yet, Morrison's Medical believes his experience in management and sales combined with his background in the medical field will prove him capable and competent. Mr. Stewart's skill and enthusiasm will not only substantiate his usefulness throughout the process of bringing a new product to market, but will also exemplify his long-term ability to run Morrison's.

- Established DME companies pose a threat of copying the PatientLite, although Morrison's patents provide protection against patent infringement. More likely, due to the projected success of the PatientLite, a competitor may develop a directly competing product which will erode projected sales figures.

- The PatientLite cannot lift an unconscious person since the user must be able to sit upright. Morrison's Medical does not include this segment in its target market.

Comment: Critical risks are identified but several are not adequately addressed, particularly the lack of experience on the part of Mr. Stewart, possibly they could have a strong Board of Directors to supplement his skills. Also, they do not adequately address what they will do if a competing product erodes projected sales figures.

CHAPTER SUMMARY

It is important to address the critical components of a business plan but equally important to address when the key objectives of the plan will be accomplished by developing a time line. It is also imperative to state what could possibly negatively impact the plans for your company and how you are prepared to deal with those potentialities.

MISTAKES TO AVOID

➢ Thinking that the schedule will not have any deviations.
➢ Not considering alternative plans if objectives are not attained.
➢ Setting unrealistic objectives and timeframes in which to reach them.
➢ Not carefully assessing potential risks of the business.
➢ Not mentioning potential litigation.
➢ Failing to carefully assess potential problem areas.

CHAPTER APPLICATION

➢ Complete the Time Schedule and Critical Risks Worksheet
➢ Evaluate the following business ideas and determine three potential critical risks for each.

With the idea of creating a venture that Jeff and I would both have adequate knowledge of, we decided on the formation of an outdoor sporting goods store. Instead of stocking what the normal sporting goods store does, we decided to develop a niche in the industry. Our niche is that we specialize only in outdoor sporting equipment for extreme sports such as roller-blading, rock climbing, hiking, and mountain biking. We are also including water sports such as white-water rafting, kayaking, and wake-boarding. Having this niche, we can provide the customer with the newest in extreme gear and establish ourselves with the customer as a reputable store.

Our business start-up plan involves the purchase of a piece of land in which to build our infrastructure. We are aiming at a layout that is similar to Sam's Warehouse, yet nearly half the size. With such a layout, we will be able to move equipment around with small machines. Because we plan to build our business from the ground up, this will extend the length of time in which it will take to establish our business. We have estimated a startup time of around five to six months. This will give us ample time to build, order and arrange inventory, and train staff members.

The Pet Place provides a service much like a child day care center only for dogs instead of children. Just as you would a child, dog owners would drop off their precious puppies on their way to work and retrieve them in the evening on their way home. While at the day care, the dogs would have the freedom to run and play in an atmosphere complete with the comforts of home including furniture, toys, and social interaction. Dogs have the freedom to choose between indoor fun and supervised outdoor play.

RESOURCES

Biz Planit
http://www.bizplanit.com/vplan/risk/basics.htm
Information regarding the areas to address in a Critical Risks section

Inc. Magazine
http://www.inc.com
Popular magazine for entrepreneurial businesses. This site has a large archive of articles on varied business topics. Under Advice, has a specific area for writing a business plan.

Entrepreneurial Edge
http://edge.lowe.org
Great resource for businesses getting started.

TIME SCHEDULE AND CRITICAL RISKS WORKSHEET

Time Schedule:

Identify objectives in terms of the market, obtaining financing, setting up operations, etc._____

When will each objective be accomplished and who is the person responsible?_____
_____
_____

Set up a timeline with this information in terms of priority._____
_____

What needs to happen to reach each of the objectives?_____
_____
_____

Critical Risks:

Identify problems or risks that your business is facing or may face and the probability of their occurrence._____
_____
_____

What will you do to avoid facing these potential problem/risks._____
_____
_____
_____

If they do occur how will you deal with them?_____
_____
_____

What can be done to minimize their effect on your business?_____
_____
_____

Sample Plan: Warm 'n Safe Bottle
CRITICAL RISKS

The only critical point remaining for the manufacture of the Warm 'n Safe bottle involves the change from a cold rolled spring to an injection-molded spring. The dynamics of all solids are such that upon heating they expand, therefore the principle that leads to the spring's growth should not falter. Plastics have been used years in dishwashers, microwaves and for food storage as they are safe and dependable.

The property of thermal expansion simply has not been tested on a tested on an injection-molded spring. At least there is no published data, which can be found. Plastic containers are used for heating in microwaves and time and time again return to the original size without distortion. The repeated heating and cooling has not shown to have a degradable effect on food storage containers through thousands of cycles. Therefore, this principle of repeatability should transfer to the spring. Since testing of a spring heated and cooling in various liquids has not been performed, a risk exists.

In light of the fact that over five hundred plastics are presently widely used, a suitable substitute able to resolve an unexpected problem would be likely. Due to the simplicity of the design, the ability to engineer a spring with repeatable characteristics should not be insurmountable.
In the event the injection molded spring fails and an alternative solution not found the exposure to the investor has been limited.

CHAPTER 12
EXECUTIVE SUMMARY

The purpose of the Executive Summary is to provide an overview of the business plan and to generate interest in the business as an opportunity. Basically it should highlight the key sections of the business plan including information about the product or service, market potential, production, the management team, profit potential and financing needed.

The Executive Summary should be concise (less than two pages), yet give the reader a clear idea of the business. This section is written last since it is a brief summary of the other sections. However, it is the first section read by investors and other interested parties so it needs to be well written to generate interest in the rest of the plan. If it is not, it is highly unlikely that the rest of the plan will be read. You will need to accentuate the positive aspects of your business. Make it as compelling as possible and keep in mind to whom you are directing the plan.

> This is the make it or break it section

It is important to note that in this section as well as for the rest of the business plan that not only interest be generated but that it be substantiated with data and not consist of fluff or hype. There have been many business plans written that go on and on about how great the venture concept is while having minimal support to indicate that. Even if there was support, hype is a turnoff to a reader—just give them the facts in an interesting format. Although the business plan can be used as a selling tool it does not have to sound like a commercial.

What should you include in this section: the company's current status, its products or services, benefits to the customers, the financial forecasts, amount of financing needed, and how investors will benefit. Tell investors exactly how they will be repaid their investment whether through operations, refinancing, or selling stock to others.

Include the following sections in the Executive Summary:

> ➤ **Description of the Product or Service**
> Describe the product in a manner that enables the reader to have a clear understanding of its features.

> ➤ **Market**
> Include information about the target market, market potential, the competition, and your marketing strategy. Briefly describe trends in your industry.

> Don't Worry-- All this information should come from material you have already drafted

> ➤ **Production**
> Describe how you will produce your product. Include the process involved in its production. Identify components that you will subcontract and explain why this is in the best interest of the business.

> ➤ **Management**
> Describe the skills and experience that each of the members of the management team bring to the business. This is critical as investors are very concerned about the strength of the management team.

> ➤ **Financing Required**
> Discuss the amount of financing required and how it will be used. Include information on the amount of money already invested in the firm. Also include what you project that the business will earn in the next several years.

EXAMPLE : EXECUTIVE SUMMARY OF A BUSINESS PLAN

The cleaning products industry has never before encountered a product such as Magic Film bathroom coating. Magic Film is a solution that prevents the growth of mildew on bathroom and floor tile for an entire year. This product was developed by Dr. Sang Kim, Ph.D. in physical chemistry from Tulane University, and currently has a patent pending.

Magic Film, with its moisture and mildew prevention capabilities has no direct competition in the cleaning products industry. The solution consists of silicone polymers which adhere to grout and ceramic tile to prevent the penetration of moisture and preventing the growth of mildew.

The cleaning product market consisted of approximately $1.2 billion in sales in 1994. The market currently has a 4% growth rate. However, due to the unique capabilities of Magic Film, its growth rate is potentially unlimited.

We will begin our marketing efforts in the Central Florida area. This is a growing market and has the warm and humid climate for a mildew prevention product.

Magic Film will be manufactured and distributed by Eastern Coatings, Inc. This company was founded by Dr. Sang Kim in 1994 in Orlando, Florida. EC has been conducting innovative research on coating technology for the past two years. EC is currently selling the product in the Orlando area to some local hotel and motel establishments.

Magic Film will be available in a 12 oz. spray bottle for easy application an also in gallon containers for commercial cleaning services.

We have projected Magic Film to capture approximately 1% of the market within the targeted regions. Within five years Magic Film is expected to have a net income of approximately $84,000 as seen in the prepared pro-forma income statements. The equity holders in the company can expect a rate of return of approximately 55% on their investment.

Magic Film is a breakthrough in the cleaning industry and provides an incredible service for the customer by easing the burden of household cleaning and mildew removal. Inventors can also take advantage of this new product and can expect a profitable return on their investment.

Comment: This Executive Summary clearly explains the product, and includes information on market potential and strategy, production, and finances. It needs to include information about the management team. Otherwise it is a concise and informative Executive Summary that gets the attention of the reader.

EXAMPLE: EXECUTIVE SUMMARY

Java Jumpers Coffee is a mail-order catalog coffee distributor. It will draw on the experience and contacts of its parent company, which has been dealing in coffee for over 17 years. This strategic fusion simultaneously combines the power of the mail-order industry with the smashing popularity of gourmet and specialty coffees.

The gourmet coffee industry has been experiencing consistent growth rates greater than 10% a year. This explosion can be partially attributed to the coffee house explosion that originated in the Seattle area and has since expanded nationally. Approximately 55% if all U.S. households serve coffee during the course of a day—making it a $6.8 billion industry. According to the 1994 Study of Media and Markets, in the United States there are 115,901,000 principal buyer (a quarter of these are classified as "heavy users"). Recently released studies that claim coffee is not harmful are receiving publicity as well.

The size and growth of the direct mail order industry is staggering. Presently it is a $100 billion a year industry—approximately 10% of all retail sales in the United States are through mail order. The founders of Java Jumpers Coffee Company firmly believe that the combination of impeccable service and true convenience of direct delivery will greatly assist the firm in becoming a force in the industry.

Service and deliver, however, are worthless without customers. Through the use of interesting, insightful, colorful catalogs and expertly selected mailing lists, JJCC will accumulate more than 40,000 customers by year five. The management realizes that it is these customers that will ultimately make the company a profitable one. For this reason, the organization is founded around the exemplary service and complete satisfaction.

Java Jumpers Coffee Company will target some of the most exclusive groups of people in the nation. 61% of all coffee drinkers, for example, have incomes greater than $30,000 a year, enabling them to have the buying power to enjoy our high quality products. They also have the income to continue to make regular purchases from JJCC if satisfaction, price, and expectations were successfully met. JJCC plans on including incentives with the customers' first orders to establish a relationship with the customer in an attempt to further increase the possibilities for these valuable repeat purchases.

Comment: Although this Executive Summary has a considerable amount of industry and market data, it lacks key information regarding the competition, the management team, production process, and information about the potential profitability of this venture.

EXAMPLE: EXECUTIVE SUMMARY

Introduction
The Morrison's Medical Corporation (MMC) is a new entrant into the Durable Medical Equipment industry. MMC is introducing an innovative and revolutionary patient lift to the market. A patient lift is a medical product that assists in lifting and moving mobility-impaired individuals. Mobility-impaired persons consist of the elderly, injured, ill, or paralyzed. Traditionally, a mobility-impaired person is manually lifted by one or more people. Manual lifting can result in injuries to both the person being lifted and the assistant(s). The Morrison Lift, requiring only one assistant, will ease this difficult and strenuous task. This lift aids the mobility-impaired person and the assistant by providing a safe and secure lift while preventing injuries.

Product Advantages

Product advantages consist of the lift's size, weight, and price. The size is compact, thus requiring little floor space while is use, and folds to the size of a large briefcase for easy storage. The lift is lightweight due to the plastic of which it is constructed. The combination of the size and weight permits easy portability for use away from the home. Finally, the Morrison Lift has an affordable retail price of $699 compared to the industry average price range of $1,000 to $2,000.

Target Market

The target market is represented by 2,022,000 people in the US who require assistance when getting in and out of a bed or chair. MMC believes the in-home market offers the greatest growth potential and will primarily concentrate on this market. However, MMC will also target institutions for greater market depth to maximize profitability.

Market Share

The projected market share for the Morrison Lift, of the estimated 60,000 patient lifts sold in the US each year, is 250, 2,000, 4,000, 5,000 and 7,000 units for years one through five respectively. Utilizing a conservative growth rate of 3% per year, the five year projection represents approximately a 10.3% share of the current market. This is only 0.34% of the entire potential US market of 2,022,000 people. This market share is conservative since the Morrison Lift is targeting a currently untapped market.

Marketing Objectives

The Morrison Lift will enter the market through a small test market in south Florida. Once the lift is established in this region, MMC will expand nationally by the second year of operation using an aggressive marketing campaign.

Competition

There are many competitors that manufacture patient lifts ranging in price from $900 to $5,000. The most common lift in the market is a sling type lift using overhead arms and slings. These lifts are usually too large for in-home use and are often heavy and difficult to transport without disassembly. The Morrison Lift addresses and resolves these negative attributes.

Manufacturing and Sales

Manufacturing will be out-sourced to Superb Inventions Corporation. The cost to manufacture, package, and ship the product is $160 per unit decreasing to $100 with volume beyond 1,000 units. MMC will use an independent sales firm to sell the lift since outsourcing the sales is initially the most cost efficient measure for maximum distribution.

Financial Data

The breakeven point for the Morrison Lift is 556 units and should be reached within 18 months. This will result in a net profit of $112,746 in the second year. Net profit will increase to $316,952, $412,448, and $604,199 for years three through five respectively. The contribution margin ratio will increase from 31% in year one to 50% in year two leveling off in years four and five.

Investment

MMC requires approximately $125,000 for startup costs and working capital to reach projected manufacturing and selling goals. Investors will be able to cash out earning a 33%-50% return within five years through acquisitions by another company or an initial public offering. The direction of the company will depend on the outlook of the market at that time.

Comment: The Executive Summary for Morrison Medical is thorough and easy to read with its well identified categories.

EXAMPLE: EXECUTIVE SUMMARY

Vision / Mission

In 1996, **JKA Unlimited** was formed to host the operation of a Chili's restaurant that will cater to the huge niche market of students and faculty near the University of North Florida campus. Our restaurant will fill the void that is presently in the market for a casual dining facility closer to the campus.

JKA Unlimited's mission is to be a premier and progressive growth company, with a balance approach towards people, quality and profitability. We will empower our team to exceed all customers' expectations, enhance a high quality of excellence, integrity, and ethics. **JKA Unlimited's** goal is to provide innovative, practical and top-quality products and services that cater to specific niche markets and enhance the casual dining scene. We believe our first responsibility is to be focused, sensitive and responsive to all of our valued customers and investors. Our strong financial position will enable us to grow at a steady rate.

In carrying out our day-to-day business we strive to:

1. Treat our employees as we would like to be treated.
2. Follow the philosophy that our customers are our backbone.
3. Be considered as a leader in the restaurant franchise industry.

Through a long-term commitment to this mission, we will be known as a company that has direction, and the will to succeed.

Background

For many years people that live around campus have been forced to drive across town to enjoy a nice casual dining experience. The only other option for students it to settle for one of the million un-healthy fast food restaurants along Belmont Avenue, or head for the grocery store to stock the fridge.

The legal form of **JKA Unlimited** is a Corporation with limited liability. We have chosen this form of business to reduce the amount of personal liability.

The business location of **JKA Unlimited** Corporate Headquarters is:
    1482 E. Ridgeview Drive
    Jacksonville, FL 32203
The actual location of our Chili's dining establishment is:

1638 Belmont Avenue
Jacksonville, FL 32204

Objectives

Revenues projected for fiscal year 1997 without external funding is expected to be
$1.5 million. Annual growth is projected to be 14.5% per year through 2000.
We fell that within 15 years JKA Unlimited will be in a suitable position for
further expansion into new niche markets around the nation. Our objective, at this
time, is to propel the company into a prominent market position with the addition
of 5 or 6 franchises over the next 15 years if this endeavor flows smoothly.

Capital Requirements

According to the opportunities and requirements for JKA Unlimited described in
this business plan, and based on what we feel are sound business assumptions; our
initial capital requirements for our first year are $1,000,000 by January 1997.

To accomplish this goal we have developed a comprehensive plan to intensify and
accelerate our marketing and sales activities, financial planning and customer
service. To implement our plans we require an investment totaling $1,000,000 for
the following purposes:
Chili's up front Requirement fee's to build the establishment from the
ground up.
Build manufacturing facilities and ramp up production and
inventory to meet customer demands.

Maximize sales with an extensive campaign to promote our
products/ services

We have personally added investment requirements of $255,000 up front from our
own personal savings to purchase the land and cover promotional endeavors for
the first two weeks.

Management Team
In-House Management
John Kenson, President/ CEO / Vice President Finance
Aaron Johnson, President of Marketing
Curtis S. Cannata, President of Administrations

Outside Management Support (hourly / project basis)
Joe Williams, Corporate Attorney
Bob Halstead, Controller
Janice Bryson, CPA

Additionally, our outside Chili's franchise management advisors provide tremendous support for management decisions and creativity.

Comment:
Need to briefly include strengths of this management team and skip outside support in this section. Also need information on market potential for this business. Other sections are well done.

CHAPTER SUMMARY
This is by far the most important section of the business plan. It should clearly and succinctly present the business to the reader in such a manner that they are interested in reading the rest of the business plan. Typically it is less than two pages in length and briefly covers the business concept, market information, management, production, and financing.

MISTAKES TO AVOID
➤ Failure to clearly describe the product or service in such a way that interest is generated.

➤ Lack of sustentative data.

➤ Lack of clarity regarding the amount of money needed and how it will be used.

➤ Failing to highlight the experience and skills of the management team.

➤ Lack of information about the market potential.

➤ Failing to present the business idea in a manner that generates interest in the business plan as a unique opportunity.

➤ Including too much detail. Failing to be concise.

CHAPTER APPLICATION
1. Develop an oral presentation of your business plan (include visual aids).
2. Engage someone to review your business plan and comment on it.
3. Evaluate the Executive Summary of the following business plan. Note its strengths and determine areas that could be improved.

RESOURCES
Business Plan Workbook
http://www.uwadmnweb.uwyo.edu/sbdc/businessplan.doc
Provides a detailed outline of the business plan.

Bizplan

http://www.fascination.com/pub/bellis/bizplan.html

This site provides numerous web sites that will assist in business plan writing.

EXECUTIVE SUMMARY

"The students are fed up with spending all of their money at textbook stores that don't care about them, and now is the perfect opportunity." This conversation was the beginning of a company that would revolutionize the textbook industry. The concept would prove to rattle the very ore of the industry and cause the competition to realize that they had mistreated their customers for too long and in the process has lost them to a company that places the customer's needs first and strives hard to meet all of their textbook needs on a daily basis. This company is RepeatText. Based out of Tallahassee, Florida, RepeatText currently has one location on West Tennessee Street in the heart of where the student population works, lives, and most importantly shops.

The owners of RepeatText, Justin Smythe and Bryan Perez, have spent their time listening to the students complain about other textbook stores overcharging for textbooks and then refusing to buy them back at the end of the semester leaving them high and dry when they need the money the most. This is the sole reason RepeatText was created and in doing so they have invented a concept for selling textbooks that puts the students needs first.

RepeatText is not just another textbook store in a college town, but instead is a book leasing company that provides its customers with a necessary service. The concept is simple, but extremely effective. RepeatText will lease their textbooks for the entire semester much like a video store rents its movies, and at the end of the semester when the students are out of money and trying to scrape enough money to travel home to visit with family, RepeatText will take the textbooks back and return a guaranteed percentage of the textbook price. The price is always guaranteed to be better than the competition and for new textbooks is on average fifty percent of the original price. RepeatText will place money in the hands of the students at a time when they need it most.

Justin Smythe and Bryan Perez have worked hard to create a company centered around satisfying its customer's needs and in doing so have realized that profit and rapid growth are direct results. On a daily basis they strive to constantly meet and exceed the customers expectations. With a solid goal in mind to be the best in the industry locally and nationally, RepeatText spends a considerable amount of time studying their competition to insure that they are providing the best product at all times. David and Sean have place a great emphasis on being the industry leader, which is evident in their company slogan: "RepeatText-Expect Better."

EXECUTIVE SUMMARY WORKSHEET

Product/Service:

What stage of development is the business (start-up, expansion, etc.)?

_____

Describe your product or service.

_____

What form of organization is the business? _____

Why this form?_____

Market:

Describe the market in terms of potential, target market, customer.

_____

_____

_____

_____

Describe your marketing strategy.

_____

_____

_____

_____

Identify major competitors of the business and their strengths and weaknesses.

_____

_____

_____

_____

Management

Identify the key management personnel (include their position and areas of responsibility, and unique skills).

_____

_____

_____

_____

Identify advisors for the business (board of directors or advisors, attorneys, consultants, accountant).

_____

_____

_____

_____

Production:
Describe production process, its stages, and new technology used

_____

_____

_____

Financing:
Detail financing needs and how money will be repaid to investors. What amount of money has already been invested in the business?

_____

_____

_____

_____

If a start-up, when will the business become profitable? If existing business, what is the expected profitability for the next 3-5 years?

_____

_____

SAMPLE PLAN: WARM ' N SAFE BOTTLE COMPANY
EXECUTIVE SUMMARY

Warm 'n Safe Bottle, Inc. (the "Company") was conceived in 1993 and will be incorporated in the State of Florida in 1995. The Company's Primary line of business is the design and manufacture of the Warm 'n Safe bottle, a baby bottle that is equipped with a temperature-indicating device. This device allows the consumers of the product to immediately determine if the liquid within the baby bottle is at the proper temperature for feeding the infant. The temperature-indicating device is unique within the baby bottle industry and the company has a patent pending on the design. Warm 'n Safe has designed a working prototype of the baby bottle, equipped with the temperature-indicating device, that meets all design and safety requirements. The company is in the process of raising seed capital to finance further testing and initial production of the Warm 'n Safe bottle.

The Company believes that an excellent opportunity exists for the sale of the Warm 'n Safe bottle for several reasons:

♦ No other baby bottle manufacturer is producing a bottle that indicates the temperature of the liquid inside.

l

♦ Based on market research, there is a demand for a baby bottle that can indicate the temperature of its contents.

♦ More baby bottles today are heated in microwave ovens vs. in a pot of boiling water. Heating in a microwave oven leads to an uneven distribution of temperature of the contents in the bottle. The Warm 'n Safe bottle design measures the temperature throughout the contents, providing an accurate reading.

♦ The use of microwaves in heating baby bottles has increased because of the convenience and time savings to the consumer. The Warm 'n Safe bottle allows the consumer to heat the bottle quickly with the "peace of mind" that the temperature of the contents is correct.

The company has designated several stages of research and development to be completed before the Warm 'n Safe bottle will be ready to market. Once seed capital is acquired, the Company will develop the molds necessary to mass-produce the Warm 'n Safe bottle. Further testing on the mass-production bottle will then be performed to insure that all quality and safety requirements are met. At this point, production and distribution of the Warm 'n Safe bottle will begin. Initially, the Company has selected the United States as its market. However, expansion internationally is expected.

The Company believes that the unique attribute of our product will appeal to the majority of baby-bottle consumers. The Company has identified its target market and has developed a marketing and distribution plan to reach its target market.

Conservative projections included within this Plan show the Warm 'n Safe bottle reaching two percent of market share within the first year of production. By the end of year five, the Company expects to reach 8.8 percent of the baby bottle market.

The company will manufacture and distribute the Warm 'n Safe bottle using existing baby-bottle manufacturing plants. Warm 'n Safe will sell the product through a master broker who specializes in the retail channels that sell baby bottles. The projected revenues will reach approximately $1.7 million in year one with a gross margin of 58 percent and net income of approximately $196,000. By year five, the projected revenues will reach approximately $7.4 million with a net income of approximately $1.6 million. Although the enclosed financial forecast only covers distribution within the United States, the Company expects additional income from international sales.

Ryan Addison, the creator of the Warm 'n Safe bottle, founded the Company. Mr. Addison is the President of the Company and has identified several other members of his management team. Dan Mays will become Vice President of Marketing, Kevin Harper, Vice President and Chief Financial Officer, and Alex Farmer, Vice President of Manufacturing. The Company believes that all members of the management team add value and expertise in each of their related areas.

The Company realizes the need for outside capital to reach the production and distribution stage of the Warm 'n Safe bottle. The Company seeks $200,000 from an outside investor, to be given in stages only after the Company has successfully completed certain milestones. In return, the Company will offer 20 percent equity in the Company resulting in an approximate 50 percent per annum return on investment. It is expected that at the end of year five, the Company will purchase the investor's portion of the Company, either through an Initial Public Offering or an outright purchase.

CHAPTER 13
SUPPORTING DOCUMENTS

Although this is not a critical section of your business plan, it will allow you to include additional records that back up the main content of your business plan. It will show readers that you have put together a comprehensive and well-planned document. Any exhibits that are included will lend credibility to the business plan and will add to its thoroughness. It will allow the reader to examine detailed information without having them be overwhelmed by extensive details in the body of the business plan. As you complete each section of the plan jot down the documents that you will include in this section. If you have a considerable number of documents organize them according to the sections that they support. Make sure that they are clearly labeled and identifiable. Any supporting documents that are included should be related to and enhance the content of the business plan. Refrain from including documents to add bulk to the business plan. Supporting documents should only be included if they actually add value to the business plan.

What types of documents should you include? This is really a factor of the type of business and the types of services or products that you sell. For example a manufacturing business may include a layout of the plant whereas a new type of service business may have market research data. Let's take a look section by section.

BUSINESS

For the Business section you may have photos of the product itself, your facilities, lease agreements, patents or trademarks, and if you are in the developmental stage of your product you may include research and testing studies that have been completed. You may want to include any non-compete agreements, partnership agreements or articles of incorporation, significant milestones, and lease agreements.

MARKETING

For the Marketing section you will want to include articles about your industry (growth, changes), comparative analysis of your competitors, any charts or graphs with information about market share, demographic market information, and any advertising materials.

MANAGEMENT

Supporting materials for the Management section would include the resumes of your key management staff. Make sure the resumes include not only their relevant work history, education, but also any skills relevant to the business. If you are a sole proprietor you will want to include your personal resume. If you are corporation include resumes for the officers of the corporation, extensive job descriptions for these positions, and an organizational chart.

Include a plan for staff training and any control systems set up for inventory and finance.

PRODUCTION

If you have a manufacturing facility you may want to include a detailed description of the manufacturing process, a flow chart of the process, and a layout of the facility. For a retail operation you may include a floor plan for the store.

FINANCIAL

The Financial section would have lists of equipment and capital expenditures, best and worst case financial statements, graphs of financial data, breakeven calculations by markets or products, and charts or graphs of funding requirements. If you will be applying for a loan to purchase equipment include a equipment purchase agreement or a lease contract. For a new business you could include any letters of intent to purchase. This shows that the business has a source of income. If you are an existing business you can obtain letters of credit from your suppliers.

EXAMPLES

The following pages contain examples of information that would be included in the Supporting Documents section of the business plan. They include a resume, marketing chart, financial graph, distribution agreement, organizational chart, and a timeline.

EXAMPLE: RESUME

Robert Knox
1610 John Knox Road
Nashville, Tennessee
(615-333-0001)

EDUCATION	**NORTH STATE UNIVERSITY** Bachelor of Science in Business Administration, April 1996 • Concentration: Entrepreneurship and Small Business Management
EXPERIENCE	**EASTERN SALES COMPANY, Memphis, Tennessee** • Financed 90% of personal and living expenses as an undergraduate by participating in direct selling/management program
September1994 – August 1995	FIELD MANAGER • Prescreened, interviewed, recruited, and trained students for summer work in direct sales • Educated and motivated 13 salespeople during 1994-19995 school year
February 1994 – August 1995	SALESPERSON • Relocated to run personal business • Learned principles of salesmanship and success (i.e., scheduling, positive mental attitude, goal setting) • Executed all purchasing, inventory, accounting, scheduling, presentation, sales, and delivery of products • Produced revenues of over $45,000 for the two summers combined
September 1989 - December 1992	**RITZ CARLTON HOTEL COMPANY, Naples, Florida** Five Star/Five Diamond resort in southern Florida

Company awarded the Malcolm Baldridge Quality Award in 1993
- Gained invaluable experience in total quality management with a growing service minded company while supporting 100% of personal and living expenses

AWARDS & ACTIVITIES

Eastern Sales Company
- Top First Year Salesperson (finished 72nd out of 3700)

American Marketing Association
- President, 1995-1996
- Vice President of Operations, 1994-1995
- Fundraising Committee, 1993-1994
- Blue Chip member, 1993-1996

EXAMPLE: MARKET CHART

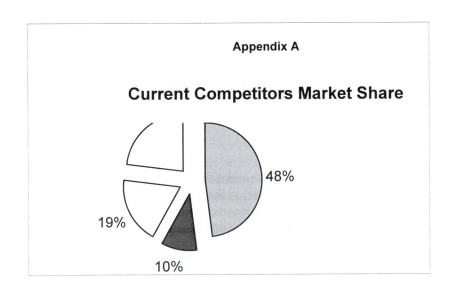

Appendix A

Current Competitors Market Share

48%

19%

10%

EXAMPLE: FINANCIAL GRAPH

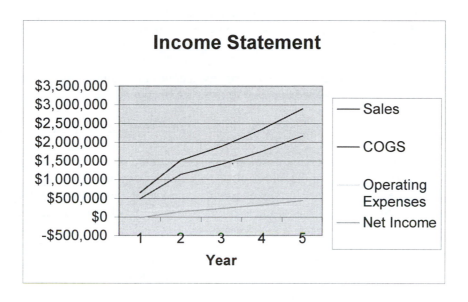

EXAMPLE: DISTRIBUTION AGREEMENT

Distribution Agreement between Access, Inc, 9851 Southwest Drive, Suite 207, Jacksonville Beach, FL 32250 (hereinafter referred to as Publisher) and John A. Andrews, Inc., dba JAACO, 476 Weston Drive, Suite 224, Scranton, PA 18505 (hereinafter referred to as Distributor).

1. APPOINTMENT – Publisher hereby grants unto Distributor the right to market and distribute the publications listed on Attachment A to secondary wholesalers and retail accounts which do not receive the Publications covered under this Agreement directly from the Publisher.

2. TERM – The term of this Agreement shall be for three (3) years commencing with the first issue covered by this Agreement (see Attachment B). Thereafter, this Agreement shall automatically renew for additional one (1) year terms unless written notice is provided to the other party via certified mail at least 90 days prior to any renewable term.

3. DELIVERY – In accordance with Publisher's production schedule (see Attachment B), Publisher shall, at its expense, print and ship copies as specified on individual shipping galleys supplied by Distributor to Publisher's printer.

The total quantities listed on any and all shipping galleys should correspond to the print orders submitted by Distributor.

Upon completion of any and all shipments, Publisher's printer will provide to Distributor a shipping completion notice which shall include the total number of copies shipped to Distributor's customers.

Publisher will notify Distributor of any changes in frequency and/or cover price not less than 60 days prior to any such change(s).

4. PAYMENT – Distributor agrees to automatically render payments, in U.S. funds, to Publisher at the rate of 40% of the cover price for copies sold on a returnable basis. Payments for net copies delivered on a non-returnable basis will also be made at the rate of 40%, based on a guaranteed sale of 62.5%. Payment to Publisher for copies sold outside the United States shall be paid by Distributor to Publisher at the average exchange rate charged by its bank.

100% of the Publishers Payment based upon net sales (i.e., number of copies distributed less number of copies returned) shall be paid within 60 days after the publications off sale date. The off sale date shall be recognized as the on sale date of the subsequent issue.

Initial: _____

Credit for returns of unsold copies for issues which have already been settled, commonly referred to as "priors," may be deducted against payment of any title.

Distributor will, upon request, provide to Publisher a "net sales report" which shall indicate by account: draw, returns, shortages (if any), net sales, and percent sale.

Prior to placing any new account on distribution, Distributor will advise Publisher as to the method (returnable or non-returnable) under which copies are to be sold.

5. RETURN POLICY – Distributor shall receive full credit for all unsold copies which are sold on a returnable basis, via affidavit, up to 365 days after off-sale date.

6. INDEMNIFICATION – Publisher shall indemnify and hold harmless Distributor, its parent, subsidiary or affiliated corporations, their officers, agents, representatives or any of its customers, wholesalers, and their respective retailers against losses, liabilities, damages, fines, judgments, expenditures, or claims, including counsel fees, legal expenses, and other costs (including interest and penalties) actually incurred by them or any of them in connection with the distribution of any publications, or any issue

thereof, or any promotional material provided by Publisher, when same is questioned or objected to by public authorities, or other governmental authorities, or in defending or payment of any claims, civil actions, or criminal prosecutions against them or any legal action arising out of the use of the title of said publication or the contents and printed matter, including advertisements, pictures or photographs contained in the covers or any page of said publication, or in any supplementary or other proceeding or action. In the event that any such claim is made, notice thereof shall be promptly given to Publisher who shall have the absolute right, at its own expense, to defend against such claims, or admit such claims.

Distributor hereby agrees to indemnify, defend, and hold harmless Publisher, its parent, subsidiary or affiliated corporations, their officers, agents or representatives from and against all losses, liabilities, damages, deficiencies, costs or expenses (including disbursements) by reason of any legal claims made by Distributor's customers which are caused by Distributor's breach of any of the terms of this Agreement.

7. GOVERNING LAW – This Agreement shall be construed and governed by the laws of the State of Pennsylvania.

Initial: _____

No waiver by either party of any breach of this Agreement shall be construed as a waiver of any subsequent breach. Any dispute between the parties to this Agreement shall be resolved in the Supreme Court of the State of Pennsylvania, the jurisdiction of which court is hereby consented to. Any action may be commenced via service by certified mail, return receipt requested.

7. CONFIDENTIALITY – All proprietary information exchanged between parties hereto shall be considered confidential. Neither party will release said confidential information to any third party without the written permission of the other. This clause shall survive the expiration of this agreement.

Agreed to and accepted this _____ day of _____, 2002 by:

_____
Arthur King
President
John A. Andrews, Inc.

_____
Brett Johnson
President
Access, Inc.

So You Need to Write a Business Plan!

EXAMPLE: TIMELINE

Smith Medical, Inc.

APPENDIX 2 - PROJECT TIMELINE

Task Name
Mkt. & Bus. Research I
Complete Business Plan
R&D Gen. 1 Product
Seek Investors
Present to Investors
Negotiate 2.0 Funds
Smith Inc.
Bank 2.0 Funds
Find Phase 1 Facility
Est. Offices
Est. labs
Design General Implants
Plan / By Mfg. Equip.
Processes
Design General Externals
Design System
Tooling
Process Validations
Hire VP Market / Sales
Piloting
Add Phase II Facility
Market & Research II
Rev. BP & Seek 1.9 Fund
Negotiate 1.9 Fund
Bank 1.9 Funds
Rev. BP & Seek 2.1 Fund
Negotiate 2.1 Fund
Bank 2.1 Fund
Prepare 510(K)

Timeline quarter headers: Q3 Q4 (1996), Q1 Q2 Q3 Q4 (1997), Q1 Q2 Q3 Q4 (1998), Q1 Q2 Q3 Q4 (1999), Q1 Q2 Q3 Q4 (1999)

242

Task				
Product Validation				
510(K) Approval				
Est. IRB Clinicals			σ	
Commence Mfg.			σ	
Launch Sales				σ
Ship First Product				σ
Publish Clinicals				σ

EXAMPLE: ORGANIZATIONAL CHART

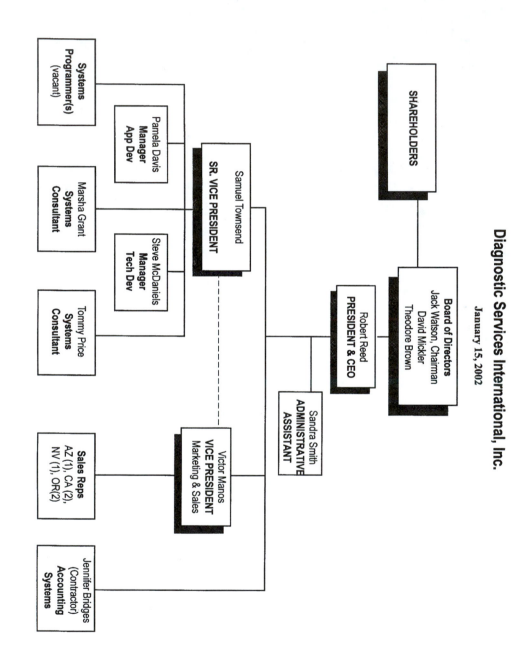

Diagnostic Services International, Inc.
January 15, 2002

SHAREHOLDERS

Board of Directors
Jack Watson, Chairman
David Mickler
Theodore Brown

Robert Reed
PRESIDENT & CEO

Sandra Smith
ADMINISTRATIVE ASSISTANT

Samuel Townsend
SR. VICE PRESIDENT

Victor Manos
VICE PRESIDENT
Marketing & Sales

Pamela Davis
Manager
App Dev

Steve McDaniels
Manager
Tech Dev

Systems
Programmer(s)
(vacant)

Marsha Grant
Systems
Consultant

Tommy Price
Systems
Consultant

Sales Reps
AZ (1), CA (2),
NV (1), OR(2)

Jennifer Bridges
(Contractor)
Accounting
Systems

CHAPTER SUMMARY

This section of the plan provides the reader with additional information regarding your business. This information will lend credibility to your plan. It is critical that the supporting information be understandable and visually attractive.

CHAPTER APPLICATION

> ➢ Review each section of your business plan and determine what additional information could be included in the Supporting Documents.

> ➢ Review supporting documents of other business plans to determine the value added.

MISTAKES TO AVOID

> ➢ Poorly labeled or unlabeled exhibits.
> ➢ Un-referenced articles or articles that have not been highlighted for key areas to read.
> ➢ Graphs, charts that are not understandable.
> ➢ Failing to identify the source of the supporting material if applicable.

APPENDIX

Warm 'n Safe Bottle Company
Business Plan

Crescent City, Florida 34402
(904) 769-2273

March 1995

Executive Summary

Warm 'n Safe Bottle, Inc. (the "Company") was conceived in 1993 and will be incorporated in the State of Florida in 1995. The Company's Primary line of business is the design and manufacture of the Warm 'n Safe bottle, a baby bottle that is equipped with a temperature-indicating device. This device allows the consumers of the product to immediately determine if the liquid within the baby bottle is at the proper temperature for feeding the infant. The temperature-indicating device is unique within the baby bottle industry and the company has a patent pending on the design. Warm 'n Safe has designed a working prototype of the baby bottle, equipped with the temperature-indicating device, that meets all design and safety requirements. The company is in the process of raising seed capital to finance further testing and initial production of the Warm 'n Safe bottle.

The Company believes that an excellent opportunity exists for the sale of the Warm 'n Safe bottle for several reasons:

♦ No other baby bottle manufacturer is producing a bottle that indicates the temperature of the Liquid inside.

♦ Based on market research, there is a demand for a baby bottle that can indicate the temperature of its contents.

♦ More baby bottles today are heated in microwave ovens vs. in a pot of boiling water. Heating in a microwave oven leads to an uneven distribution of temperature of the contents in the bottle. The Warm 'n Safe bottle design measures the temperature throughout the contents, providing an accurate reading.

♦ The use of microwaves in heating baby bottles has increased because of the convenience and time savings to the consumer. The Warm 'n Safe bottle allows the consumer to heat the bottle quickly with the "peace of mind" that the temperature of the contents is correct.

2

The company has designated several stages of research and development to be completed before the Warm 'n Safe bottle will be ready to Market. Once seed capital is acquired, the Company will develop the molds necessary to mass-produce the Warm 'n Safe bottle. Further testing on the mass-production bottle will then be performed to insure that all quality and safety requirements are met. At this point, production and distribution of the Warm 'n Safe bottle will begin. Initially, the Company has selected the United States as its market. However, expansion internationally is expected.

The Company believes that the unique attribute of our product will appeal to the majority of baby-bottle consumers. The Company has identified its target market and has developed a marketing and distribution plan to reach its target market. Conservative projections included within this Plan show the Warm 'n Safe bottle reaching two percent of market share within the first year of production. By the end of year five, the Company expects to reach 8.8 percent of the baby bottle market.

The company will manufacture and distribute the Warm 'n Safe bottle using existing baby-bottle manufacturing plants. Warm 'n Safe will sell the product through a master broker who specializes in the retail channels that sell baby bottles. The projected revenues will reach approximately $1.7 million in year one with a gross margin of 58 percent and net income of approximately $196,000. By year five, the projected revenues will reach approximately $7.4 million with a net income of approximately $1.6 million. Although the enclosed financial forecast only covers distribution within the United States, the Company expects additional income from international sales.

Ryan Addison, the creator of the Warm 'n Safe bottle, founded the Company. Mr. Addison is the President of the Company and has identified several other members of his management team. Dan Mays will become Vice President of Marketing, Kevin Harper, Vice President and Chief Financial Officer, and Alex Farmer, Vice President of Manufacturing. The Company believes that all members of the management team add value and expertise in each of their related areas.

The Company realizes the need for outside capital to reach the production and distribution stage of the Warm 'n Safe bottle. The Company seeks $200,000 from an outside investor, to be given in stages only after the Company has successfully completed certain milestones. In return, the Company will offer 20 percent equity in the Company resulting in an approximate 50 percent per annum return on investment. It is expected that at the end of year five, the Company will purchase the investor's portion of the Company, either through an Initial Public Offering or an outright purchase.

TABLE OF CONENTS

II. THE INDUSTRY, COMPANY AND PRODUCTS

The Industry

The baby bottle industry in the United States is comprised of several major manufacturers, namely Playtex, Evenflo, Gerber, Munchkin, NUK, Chubs and Ansa. See Appendix A. The current baby bottle market in the United States is estimated at $154 million. Of this amount, reusable baby bottles hold 552 percent, $80 million of the market, while the remaining 48 percent is held by disposables. Disposables are defined as baby bottles that are designed for bottle liners and the liners are discarded after each use. The disposable market had grown to a peak of 53 percent of the baby bottle market in the United States, but had shown a steady decline as a percent of the total market over recent years. The Warm 'n Safe bottle will initially be designed as a reusable bottle. However, the Company will evaluate the possibility of entering the disposable market at a later date.

The Business

The Warm 'n Safe bottle was first conceived in 1993 by Ryan Addison recognized an existing market for this type product and established the Warm 'n Safe Bottle Company in 1994. The Company will be incorporated in the state of Florida in 1995. The Company has produced a prototype of the product and has a patent pending on the product. The Company is in the process of raising seed capital to finance initial production and distribution. The Company has identified sources to manufacture the product to strict specifications and is selecting marketing representatives to facilitate distribution of product in the United States.

The Product

During the past two years, Addison has refined his original design in an attempt to produce a baby bottle that would allow the temperature of an internal liquid to be read visually on the outside of the bottle.

Due to the nature of the product, many design requirements and constraints existed which had to be addressed:

(1)   All components must be non-toxic,
(2)   The assembled product must be suitable for use in a microwave oven,
(3)   The assembled product must be suitable for use in boiling water.
(4)   The temperature indicator must be reliable, accurate and easy to read,
(5)   The temperature indicator must have consistent repeatability,
(6)   The entire product must be dishwasher safe and
(7)   The addition of the temperature indicator must not prohibitively increase the bottle cost.

The latest design has been found to meet all of the design requirements and constraints and a prototype has been constructed.

The Warm 'n Safe bottle is designed to provide an indication of the temperature of bottle contents. The bottle utilizes a special polymer spring, which changes in size relative to the temperature. The temperature indicator uses the same principles as an automobile or home thermostat. The spring expands and turns as it is heated. As the spring is fixed at the base, the top turns indicating the temperature. The bottle temperature is read in the indicator window located in the cap of the bottle. The bottle is designed to give an indication of "feed" between 90 and 105 degrees Fahrenheit, the feeding temperature recommended by most pediatricians. Appendix B gives several views of the product.

The very simple design utilizes only three components: the spring, the stem and the cap. All

components lock together permanently on assembly and no fasteners or glues are required. The

assembly contains no small parts and is baby safe. All bottle components are made of recyclable

plastic providing an environmentally conscious design.

The Warm 'n Safe bottle is designed to provide temperature indication regardless of the heating

method. The temperature indicator is designed for consistent repeatability and has a product life

of approximately two years.

All components of the Warm 'n Safe bottle are FDA approved. All of the materials utilized have

been used in the food industry for over ten years. The materials are dishwasher safe and are

easily cleaned. The polymers (plastics) utilized are high impact and have been tested to

withstand falls of ten feet.

The Warm 'n Safe bottle has a patent pending status in the United States and once marketability

is confirmed, worldwide patents will be applied for.

Entry and Growth Strategy

The company's entry strategy is to enter the United States market via a master broker who specializes in servicing the mass merchandisers, food stores and drug stores. The current reusable baby bottle market in the United States is estimated at $80 million. The master broker and their reps will earn a commission on the product sold to these retail channels. By utilizing the master broker network, the Company will gain access to retail accounts without the fixed cost expense of developing our own sales force. The Company expects that the unique attribute of the bottle will gain placement in most accounts.

The growth strategy for the Company is to begin expanding to foreign markets by acquiring foreign patents in those countries with the highest sales potential. The potential for global sales is immense as 98 percent of the births in the world occur outside the United States. The Company will utilize a broker network within each country to sell its product.

III.   **MARKET RESEARCH AND ANALSIS**

Customers

The average customer for a baby bottle product is a female in her late twenties who is, or will be again, employed outside the home. The median family income of the typical baby bottle customer is 36,120. Because the majority of customers of baby bottles work outside the home, time and convenience is heating bottle accurately are of the essence.

Market Size and Trends

After peaking at a post-baby-boom of 4.16 million in 1990, the number of births in the United States is expected to stabilize at approximately 4 million and remain at that level through the turn of the century. The current baby bottle market in the United States is approximately $154 million, or 73 million units a year. Currently, reusable bottles constitute 52 percent of the baby bottle market, or 38.6 million units a year. Reusable bottles have increased their market share over disposable bottles by an average of 2 percent a year over the last years. The trend of reusable bottles capturing a larger share of the baby bottle market is expected to continue over the net several years.

Competition and Competitive Advantages

Although there are several major competitors in the baby bottle industry, none of these are currently marketing a product that indicators the temperature of the liquid in the bottle. The Warm 'n Safe bottle provides this key feature with only a minimal increase in manufacturing cost over standard bottles.

Only one other company has attempted to market a temperature sensitive baby bottle. Ansa Bottling manufactured such a product under the trade name Heat Sensitive and later Comfort

Temp. This product was being produced and marketed when the current owners, according to John Iodise, President of Ansa Bottling, purchased the company.

The Bottle Ansa designed neglected one major fact of baby bottle usage; sometimes bottles are heated from the outside in (boiling water) and sometimes from the inside out (microwave). Their design simply used the bottle's surface plastic to indicate the temperature. An opaque blue or pink plastic would turn white when the contents were too hot. This neglected the fact that microwaves heat from the center so only after the bottle was shaken would it provide an accurate indication. Due to its inaccurate operation, it was withdrawn from the market. Despite their disappointing results, Ansa's efforts confirmed that based on market surveys, there is market for a bottle with a temperature sensor. In addition, Iodise felt their lack of success was the result of a design flaw and not a lack of market. The Warm 'n Safe bottle overcomes this shortcoming in its design of the temperature indicator device.

Estimated Market Share and Sales

According to market information provided by Richard Henry, Vice President of Sales for Munchkin Bottling Company, a leading manufacturer of specialty baby bottles, a manufacturer introducing "just another decorated bottle" without any key features or benefits over current bottles could be expected to capture one to two percent of the total market in the first year of operations. This market share would probably remain at two percent during subsequent years.

Munchkin's market data also indicates that if a company produced a product with significant features or graphics as compared to existing decorated bottles, the company could expect to attain six percent of the market in the first year. That share could grow at 30 percent per year over subsequent years. To achieve these results, however, the product would have to be unique and special.

To present conservative projected pro financial statements, Warm 'n Safe has assumed that the Company will earn two percent and four percent of the total reusable market in the first and second year of operations. A growth rate of 30 percent per year was assumed for years three through five.

Ongoing Market Evaluation

The Company expects to refine the appearance and marketing of the Warm 'n Safe bottle to meet changing demographics of our customers. The Company will install a 1-800 telephone for customers to call with problems or suggestions. In addition, the Company expects to conduct marketing focus groups on a periodic basis t receive input on new graphic and design changes.

IV.   ECONOMICS OF THE BUSINESS

The innovative Warm 'n Safe bottle costs $.35 per unit more to produce than a standard baby bottle. The new feature, however, will allow the Company, and retailers, to market the product at prices comparable to other premium bottles currently available. At a suggested retail of

$3.99, a cost to the retailer of $2.19, and a cost to manufacture and deliver the product of $.92, projected gross margins for Warm 'n Safe and the retailer are 58 percent and 45 percent, respectively.

Initially, the Company will produce a clear, quality plastic bottle to enable the customer to see the difference in the Warm 'n Safe product and other bottles. A decorated bottle would obscure the feature that the Company has developed and result in the appearance of "just another baby bottle." Once the Company and its bottle have achieved recognition and acceptance in the marketplace, Warm 'n Safe will then consider adding graphics to the product which results in little additional cost but is perceived as value added by the consumer.

Continued profit potential and durability exist as births in the United States continue at approximately four million annually. In addition, these four million births comprise only two percent of the world's births. Warm 'n Safe plans to secure patents in all countries where there is a market for the produce once final approval of the United States patent is obtained and full production begins.

Fixed costs for the Company will be low as the product will be manufactured by currently existing plastics manufacturers and shipped directly to the retailer. The main fixed costs will be for office and limited warehousing space. Warm 'n Safe will initially employ three personnel to manage and operate a small office to service the needs of consumers and retailers as well as staff a small warehousing operation to fill small or emergency orders. The use of brokers and sales representatives will significantly reduce the amount of fixed labor cost to the Company.

Warm 'n Safe will not recognize any revenues until stage four of the Overall Schedule shown in Section IX of the business plan. Once full-scale production and distribution begins in January 1997, however, the Company will generate positive cash flow from operations within the first year. Pro forma financial statements contained in Section XI of the Plan present management's worst, best and most likely case projections of the results of operations through year five.

Funding for the start up period in the amount of $200,000 will be drawn in three stages to limit investor risk. Only after specified milestones have been met will additional funds be requested and the next stage started. The initial draw of $66,000 will be required thirteen months prior to full production (year one of the Plan) to fund the design, manufacture and testing of the spring and cap molds. Draw two in the amount of $57,000 will be required six months prior to full production to complete bottle and stem molds. And draw three of $77,000 will be required three months prior to full production to fund an initial production run to produce initial inventory.

V.   MARKETING PLAN

Overall Marketing Strategy

The overall marketing strategy for the Company is to offer our baby bottle as "safe, convenient and worry-free". Our unique temperature-reading indicator will give bottle a strategic competitive advantage over other baby bottles on the market. After final development and testing of the product, we will secure the services of a master broker who will concentrate on selling our product in the United States in the retail channels that sell baby bottles. After significant penetration in the United States market, the Company will aggressively purse patents and distribution in foreign countries.

Pricing

Retail pricing for reusable bottles averages $3.99 for premium bottles and $2.99 for standard bottles. Premium bottles are equipped with a heavier plastic material than standard bottles and may also include a silicone nipple versus a rubber nipple and color graphics on the bottle. The Warm 'n Safe bottle will be equipped with heavier plastic and the silicone nipple. Those features, along with our temperature indicating device, will allow us to retail our bottle at premium prices, or a suggested retail of $3.99. Our cost to retailers will be at $2.19, freight included, which allows the retailer to earn a 45 percent gross margin, comparable to the margin on other baby bottle products.

Sales Tactics

The Company expects that the unique attribute of its bottle will encourage consumers to purchase the product. We will design and develop packaging that emphasizes the temperature indicator on the Warm 'n Safe bottle and market the bottle as "safe, convenient and worry-free". Initially, the Company will distribute the product as a floor shipper in as many retail accounts as possible to expose the consumer to our product as quickly as possible. To help achieve this objective, the Company will offer price discounts to retailers who purchase these shippers. To avoid the costs of recurring, training and employing a full-time sales force, the Company will select a master broker to set up an established, experienced sales force comprised of other sales representatives. The master broker will establish sales territories within the United States for each sales representative and add additional sales representatives as the need arises. The master broker will be compensated ten percent of gross sales and five percent of the sales from the broker's sales representatives. In addition, the sales representatives will earn five percent of the sales from the broker's sales representatives. In addition, the sales representatives will earn five percent on their sales. These sales costs have been included in the projected income statements.

Warranty Policies

The company will offer a money-back guarantee to any customer who is not satisfied with the performance of its products. To assist its customers, Warm 'n Safe will provide a 1-800 number on all packaging. In addition, the Company will guarantee to retailers reimbursement for any returned bottles.

Advertising and Promotion

The Company expects to advertise on a regional, then national basis, in the United States after the first year of sales. Advertising during the first year of sales will be five percent of sales and include point-of-sale materials to place on or near the product in the retail store. For years two and three through five of the plan, the Company projects that advertising expenditures will by four percent and three percent of sales, respectively. The Company expects to use the services of an outside advertising agency to assist in spending advertising dollars as effectively as possible.

Distribution

Shipping of the Warm 'n Safe product will be primarily from the manufacturer to the retailer, which will require the Company to provide only minimal warehouse space. Only minimal inventory will be maintained on hand at the Company's warehouse facilities for emergency shipments. This process will eliminate the need for the Company to finance large amounts of on-hand inventory. In addition, the process will keep shipping costs to a minimum.

VI. DESIGN AND DEVELOPMENT PLANS

A preliminary prototype of the Warm 'n Safe bottle has been manufactured. The prototype provides a functional model of how the final bottle will look and operate. A secondary prototype (Stage 2) will be developed for completion of testing. The initial prototype's spring was manufactured using a cold forming process. This process involves heating the plastic rod a formidable state and then cooling it into a spring shape. The process is slow, costly and produces inconsistent springs. The secondary prototype's spring will be made using an injection molding process. The process is utilized to manufacture 90 percent of all plastic parts. The process provides high production capabilities, low cost, consistent properties and low maintenance.

The main advantage of an injection-molded spring is the consistency in the manufactured product. This same process is presently utilized to manufacture baby bottles. The initial cost of each mold is approximately $25,000 to $30,000. These same molds will be used for the initial manufacturing stage of the project. Experts in the plastic injection-molding field advise that no manufacturing problems are foreseen at this time in light of the simplicity of the molds. Several weeks will be required to perfect the molding process and optimize production.

Since an injection molded plastic spring has not been utilized before, adjustments may be required in the plastics composition to obtain the correct properties. In light of the more than 500 commercially available plastics on the market a substitute for the existing polymer will be available if needed.

Testing will require the new spring to be operating in environments replicating overheating and microwaves, exposure to detergents and extended heating and cooling cycles. Each test will subject the spring to extreme conditions. The present plan is to utilize plastic polymers presently used in baby bottles and microwavable containers (i.e., Tupperware).

The injection molding and testing of the thermostat spring is the only technical hurdle for the product. No other moving parts exist in the very simple design of the Warm 'n Safe bottle. The manufacturing of this critical component will be performed first to limit risk. The other components will follow sequentially. No delays are expected in the manufacturing of other components as several plastic molders are currently producing them.

Over time, the Company plans to work in proving the aesthetics of the product with colored plastics, varied bottle shapes and bottle graphics. These changes will increase product variety resulting in increasing sales.

The overall schedule (Section IX) details the cost for bringing the bottle to market. It is broken down into stages to show cost during each stage and the milestone to be achieved during each stage. The schedule shows the capital required at each stage and is a tool for illustrating the level of risk throughout the project. The majority of the "funds sought" will be required only after a fully functional product has been developed and tested.

To date no product exists on the market that provides the functions of the Warm 'n Safe bottle. In light of this a patent application has been made and there is a current patent pending.

The cost of manufacturing the completed Warm 'n Safe bottle is as follows:

Premium bottle including silicone nipple, standard ring and disk	$.50
Warm 'n Safe Temperature Sensor	
Spring	$.15
Stem	.08
Cap	.10
	.35
Total Warm 'n Safe Manufactured Cost	$.85

Economics of scale should reduce a minimum of five percent once production exceeds 500,000 annually, which should occur during the first year of sales (cost reduction not taken into effect in financials).

VII.   MANUFACTURING AND OPERATIONS

The Warm 'n Safe baby bottle during the initial four years will be most likely manufactured in the Far East, where most bottles for the United States market are produced today. The component manufacture will be contracted only through manufacturers identified as quality injection molders. Firms experienced in providing service worldwide will also perform the assembly, packaging and shipping.

Alternative suppliers have been identified in the United States, although manufacturing costs are expected to be higher. These sources would have the advantage of shorter delivery time due to its closer proximity. The United States manufacturers will be kept as a secondary source in case supply problems occur. Since the investment castings (molds) will belong to the Company, injection molding can actually take place anywhere worldwide where injection-molding capabilities exist.

Manufacturing will occur year round. When manufacturing reaches sufficient levels, bulk purchasing of plastic will be performed during seasonal price drops. This should lead to a materials cost savings of at least five percent.

Operations during the initial years will be based in Northwest Florida. This area, having both an international port and airport, will be sufficient during the early years. The area also provides a location base with low labor and warehouse costs. The initial warehouse space selected has ample space for growth and is available at fixed, long-term, low rates. The initial staff will consist of only three permanent employees to operate the office and warehouse. Other employees with needed expertise will join the Company in year two of operations. When sufficient qualities justify the relocation of warehousing, a more central nationwide location will be selected.

Initially distribution will occur only in the United States. However, since only two percent of the births worldwide occur in the United States, an incredible potential for future expansion exists. The Company plans to seek foreign patent protection within one year of obtaining its United States patent. To date, no conflicting patents have been identified on the worldwide cross search though the United States Patent Office.

VIII.   MANAGEMENT TEAM

The management team will be built in stages. Initially, Ryan Addison will be the only employee at Warm 'n Safe Bottle Company. His diverse expertise in engineering and manufacturing will be sufficient for all tasks in the early start up stages of the Company. Addison will hold the position of President and Chief Executive Officer. Dan Mays will be brought on board as the Director of Marketing as the Company enters stage four. May's experience in retail will be required once the Company begins its initial production phase. Kevin Harper will join the Company as Director of Finance at the beginning of year two. Harper's experience in accounting and finance for a major convenience store chain will provide the required financial support as the

Company expands and accounting issues become more complex. Alex Farmer will also join the Company at the beginning of year two as Director of Manufacturing.

Financial compensation for the management team can be found in Section XI of the Plan. In addition, each of these employees, the board members and other professional advisors will be compensated through the issuance of stock of the company. The following table outlines proposed distribution of stock:

	Initial	Year 2	Year 4
Investor	20%		
Board Members	6%		
Attorneys	2%		
Ryan Addison	22%		
Dan Mays	2%	2%	3%
Scott Tilden	2%	2%	
Kevin Harper	2%	2%	
Alicia Whitney	2%	2%	
Alex Farmer	1%	2%	1%
Unissued Stock	41%	31%	27%

Unissued stock will be reserved for future financing needs, as incentives for attracting new key personal and other needs as agreed upon by the board of directors. In the event that the Company is sold, unissued stock will be divided among the employee owner according to their percentage of the employee ownership.

The board of Directors will consist of Addison, Dan Mays, Bennett Marshall, Ph.D. and the investor. Dr. Marshall is currently a professor of finance at West State University. Professional advisors to the board will consist of Lester Gordon, Esq., Doug Kessler of Star Commerce Bank and Anita Downs, CPA.

IX.   OVERALL SCHEDULE

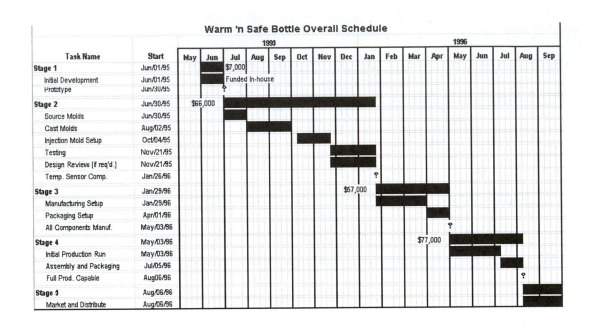

Warm 'n Safe Bottle Overall Schedule

Task Name	Start	1995									1996								
		May	Jun	Jul	Aug	Sep	Oct	Nov	Dec	Jan	Feb	Mar	Apr	May	Jun	Jul	Aug	Sep
Stage 1	Jun/01/95		▮	$7,000														
Initial Development	Jun/01/95			Funded In-house														
Prototype	Jun/30/95		♀															
Stage 2	Jun/30/95	$66,000		▮▮▮▮▮▮▮▮▮▮▮														
Source Molds	Jun/30/95			▮▮▮														
Cast Molds	Aug/02/95				▮▮▮													
Injection Mold Setup	Oct/04/95						▮▮											
Testing	Nov/21/95								▮▮▮									
Design Review (if req'd.)	Nov/21/95								▮▮▮									
Temp. Sensor Comp.	Jan/26/96									♀								
Stage 3	Jan/29/96								$57,000		▮▮▮							
Manufacturing Setup	Jan/29/96										▮▮▮▮							
Packaging Setup	Apr/01/96												▮▮					
All Components Manuf.	May/03/96													♀				
Stage 4	May/03/96												$77,000		▮▮▮▮			
Initial Production Run	May/03/96													▮▮▮				
Assembly and Packaging	Jul/05/96															▮▮		
Full Prod. Capable	Aug/06/96																♀	
Stage 5	Aug/06/96																▮▮	
Market and Distribute	Aug/06/96																▮▮	

24

X.   CRITICAL RISKS

The only critical point remaining for the manufacture of the Warm 'n Safe bottle involves the change from a cold rolled spring to an injection-molded spring. The dynamics of all solids are such that upon heating they expand, therefore the principle that leads to the spring's growth should not falter. Plastics have been used years in dishwashers, microwaves and for food storage as they are safe and dependable.

The property of thermal expansion simply has not been tested on a tested on an injection-molded spring. At least there is no published data, which can be found. Plastic containers are used for heating in microwaves and time and time again return to the original size without distortion. The repeated heating and cooling has not shown to have a degradable effect on food storage containers through thousands of cycles. Therefore, this principle of repeatability should transfer to the spring. Since testing of a spring heated and cooling in various liquids has not been performed, a risk exists.

In light of the fact that over five hundred plastics are presently widely used, a suitable substitute able to resolve an unexpected problem would be likely. Due to the simplicity of the design, the ability to engineer a spring with repeatable characteristics should not be insurmountable.

In the event the injection molded spring fails and an alternative solution not found the exposure to the investor has been limited.

XI. THE FINANCIAL DATA

According to market information provided by Richard Henry, Vice President of Sales for Munchkin Bottling Company, a leading manufacturer of specialty baby bottles, a manufacturer introducing just another decorated bottle without any key features or benefits over current bottles be expected to capture one to two percent of the total market in the first year of operations. This market share would probably remain at two percent during subsequent years. This assumption is the basis for the worst-case scenario presented in the projected financial statements for Warm 'n Safe Bottle Company.

Munchkin's market data also indicates that if a company produced a product with significant features or graphics as compared to existing decorated bottles, the company could expect to attain four percent of the market in the first year. That share could grow at 30 Percent per year over subsequent years. To achieve these results, however, the product would have to be unique and special. These are the assumptions that Warm 'n Safe has used to project the Company's best-case scenario financial results.

To present conservative projected pro forma financial statements, Warm 'n Safe has assumed that the Company will earn only two percent per year is assumed for years three through five. Based on the above projected market share percentages, the current U.S. reusable bottle market of approximately 38.6 million units and a selling price of $2.19 for the Warm 'n Safe bottle. Projected sales were calculated for all three scenarios. Based on industry practices of retailing premium bottles at $3.99, Warm 'n Safe established its cost at $2.19 to provide a 45 percent gross margin to the retailer.

The most likely case scenario pro forma financial statements are, in management's opinion, a conservative, yet realists, projection of Warm 'n Safe's first five years of production. These statements reflect positive cash flow in the first year of full production (year one of the Plan). The Company will also generate a profit after taxes in the first year of operation. Under this scenario, the Company will generate cash and grow in value sufficiently to allow Company to purchase an investor's ownership and allow the investor to realize a 50 percent return investment by the end of year five.

Pro Forma Income Statement Assumptions

Sales To present a conservative view of pro forma results, the assumption was made that market share will be captured only from existing U.S. reusable market. In actuality, however, worldwide patents, the vast markets available outside the U.S. and the desirability of the product will result in greater sales than used in these financials.

To convert dollar bottle market to units for projection purposes:

	Dollar Sales	Units	Avg Selling Price	Calculations
U.S. bottle mkt	154,000,000			
U.S. reusable mkt	80,000,000	38,605,000	2.076,	175,000+32,430,000
U.S. premium reusable mkt	20,000,000	6,175,000	3.24	20,000,000/ ((2.99+3.49)/2)
U.S. standard reusable mkt	60,000,000	32,430,000	1.85	60,000,000/ ((1.80+1.90)/2)

Warm 'n Safe's pricing structure allows retailers 45% gross margin based on a suggested retail of $3.99, while providing Warm 'n Safe a 58.0% gross margin.

Cost of Goods Sold

Bottle including silicone nipple, standard ring & disk, shipping	$0.57
Warm 'n Safe Modifications	0.35
Cost of Warm 'n Safe bottle	0.92

Master Broker engaged to set up established, experienced sales force. Master broker is paid 10% of his sales and 5% of his reps sales. The reps are each paid 5% of their sales. All pay their expenses and the master broker is anticipated to make 20% of the total projected sales.

Salaries and Wages

	Year 1	Years 2-5
Ryan Addison-President and CEO	60,000	60,000
Dan Mays-VP of Marketing	55,200	55,200
Warehouse Manager	24,000	24,000
Chief Financial Officer		50,000
Manufacturing Director		50,000
Secretary/Clerk		20,000
	139,200	259,200

Payroll Taxes

OASDI	6.20%	to 61,200 per employee
Medicaid	1.45%	no limit
FUTA	.8%	to 7,000 per employee
FL SUI	2.50%	to 7,000 per employee

Worker's compensation insurance is based on 1.01% of payroll expense.

Health insurance is based on a rate of $3,600 per family per year and is paid entirely by the

Company.

Advertising is estimated at 5% of sales in year 1, 4% in year 2 and 3% in years 3 through five.

Bad Debts are estimated to be 3% of sales.

Depreciation is for office equipment and furniture with a cost of $20,000 and manufacturing equipment with a cost of $111,000 depreciated straight-line over 5 years.

Dues and Subscriptions based on estimated cost of trade journals, etc. to keep abreast of industry trends and activities.

Insurance expense is estimated to be 2.12% of sales and includes product liability and Directors and Officers coverage.

Miscellaneous expense is estimated t be .15% of sales.

Rent is based on .60% per square foot per month * 1,000 square feet * 12 months. This estimate is based on currently available office space in the Panama City business district. An additional $.30 per square foot per month * 10,000 square feet * 12 months is estimated at the same site for inventory storage.

Supplies are based on $.355% of sales.

Travel is estimated at .37% of sales per year for trade shows.

Utilities – Electricity costs are based on $.89 per square foot per month * 1,000 square feet * 12 months. This estimate is based on current utility charges in the Panama City area. Telephone expense is estimated to be $6,800 per year to include a 1-800 number for consumers and retailers.

Pro Forma Balance Sheets Assumption

Accounts Receivable assumes sales are constant over the year (1/12 each month) and the accounts receivable balance at any balance sheet date is December's sales less an allowance for bad debts of 3%. (1/12 * Annual Sales * .97)

Inventory assumes that although major orders will be shipped direct from manufacturer, equivalent of 1 month's sales will be kept in inventory at Company's office for emergencies. (1/12 * Annual Cost of Goods Sold)

Fixtures and Equipment assumes a $20,000 purchase of office furniture and equipment (PC's) and an $111,000 purchase of manufacturing equipment with depreciation computed on a 5 year straight-line method.

Accounts Payable and Accrued Expenses assumes sales are constant over the year (1/12 each month) and the accounts payable balance at any balance sheet date is December's cost of goods sold.

Common Stock assumes 100,000 shares of stock, par value $.10, are authorized and issued.

Additional Paid in Capital assumes that $30,000 shares of the above stock is issued to an investor at $6.67 per share.

Retained Earnings is the prior year's retained earnings balance plus the current year's net income.

Warm 'n Safe Bottle Company
Pro Forma Income Statements
Most Likely Case

	Start Up Period	Year 1	Year 2	Year 3	Year 4	Year 5
Sales	$0	$1,690,680	$3,381,360	$4,395,768	$5,748,312	$7,438,992
Cost Of Goods	$0	$710,240	$1,420,480	$1,846,624	$2,414,816	$3,125,056
Gross Margin	$0	$980,440	$1,960,880	$2,549,144	$3,333,496	$4,313,936
S, G & A Expenses						
Sales Reps						
Master Rep	$0	$101,441	$202,882	$263,746	$344,899	$446,340
Others	$0	$67,627	$135,254	$175,831	$229,932	$297,560
Total	$0	$169,068	$338,136	$439,577	$574,831	$743,900
Salaries & Wages	$29,000	$139,200	$259,200	$259,200	$259,200	$259,200
Payroll Taxes	$2,681	$11,341.00	$21,214	$21,214	$21,214	$21,214
Worker's Comp Ins	$293	$1,406	$2,618	$2,618	$2,618	$2,618
Health Ins	$2,700	$10,800	$21,600	$21,600	$21,600	$21,600
Advertising	$0	$84,534	$135,254	$131,873	$172,449	$223,170
Bad Debts	$0	$50,720	$101,441	$131,873	$172,449	$223,170
Depreciation	$0	$26,200	$26,200	$26,200	$26,200	$26,200
Dues & Subscriptions	$0	$400	$400	$400	$400	$400
Insurance	$0	$35,842	$71,685	$93,190	$121,864	$157,707
Miscellaneous	$326	$2,536	$5,072	$6,594	$8,622	$11,158
Patents	$5,000	$60,000	$40,000	$0	$0	$0
Rents	$0	$43,200	$43,200	$43,200	$43,200	$43,200
Supplies	$4,000	$5,917	$11,835	$15,385	$20,119	$26,036
Travel	$6,000	$6,256	$12,511	$16,264	$21,269	$27,524
Utilities	$0	$17,480	$18,179	$18,906	$19,662	$20,448
Total S, G & A Exps	$50,000	$664,900	$1,108,545	$1,228,094	$1,485,697	$1,807,545
Income Before Taxes	($50,000)	$315,540	$852,335	$1,321,050	$1,847,799	$2,506,391
Income Taxes	($19,000)	$119,905	$323,887	$501,999	$702,164	$952,429
Net Income	($31,000)	$195,635	$528,448	$819,051	$1,145,635	$1,553,962

32

Warm 'n Safe Bottle Company
Pro Forma Balance Sheets
Most Likely Case

Current Assets	Start Up Period	Year 1	Year 2	Year 3	Year 4	Year 5
Cash	$2,000	$130,172	$548,156	$1,311,409	$2,373,914	$3,817,412
Accounts Receivable	$0	$136,663	$273,327	$355,325	$464,655	$601,319
Inventory	$44,000	$59,187	$118,373	$153,885	$201,235	$260,421
Total Current Assets	$46,000	$326,022	$939,856	$1,820,619	$3,039,804	$4,679,152
Property & Equip @ Cost						
Fixtures & Equip	$111,000	$131,000	$131,000	$131,000	$131,000	$131,000
Less Allowances	$0	($26,200)	($52,400)	($78,600)	($104,800)	($131,000)
	$111,000	$104,800	$78,600	$52,400	$26,200	$0
Total Assets	$157,000	$430,822	$1,018,456	$1,873,019	$3,066,004	$4,679,152
Current Liabilities						
Accrued Expenses	($19,000)	$59,187	$118,373	$153,885	$201,235	$260,421
Long-Term Debt	$0	$0	$0	$0	$0	$0
Stockholder's Equity						
Common Stock	$10,000	$10,000	$10,000	$10,000	$10,000	$10,000
Additional Paid in Capital	$197,000	$197,000	$197,000	$197,000	$197,000	$197,000
Retained Earnings	($31,000)	$164,635	$693,083	$1,512,134	$2,637,769	$4,211,731
Total Stockholder's Equity	$176,000	$371,635	$9,000,083	$1,719,134	$2,864,769	$4,418,731
Total Liabilities & Equity	$157,000	$430,822	$1,018,456	$1,873,019	$3,066,004	$4,679,152

Warm 'n Safe Bottle Company
Pro Forma Cash Flows
Most Likely Case

	Start Up Period	Year 1	Year 2	Year 3	Year 4	Year 5
Net Income	($31,000)	$195,635	$528,448	$819,051	$1,145,635	$1,553,962
Add Items Not Requiring Cash						
Depreciation	$0	$26,200	$26,200	$26,200	$26,200	$26,200
Cash From Operations	($31,000)	$221,835	$554,648	$845,251	$1,171,835	$1,580,162
Sources of Cash						
Issuances of Stock	$207,000	$0	$0	$0	$0	$0
Increase in Accounts Payable	($19,000)	$78,187	$59,186	$35,512	$47,350	$59,186
Total Sources of Cash	$188,000	$78,187	$59,186	$35,512	$47,350	$59,186
Uses of Cash						
Increase in Accounts Receivable	$0	$136,663	$136,664	$81,998	$109,330	$136,664
Increase in Inventory	$44,000	$15,187	$59,186	$35,512	$47,350	$59,186
Increase in Fixed Assets	$111,000	$20,000	$0	$0	$0	$0
Total Uses of Cash	$155,000	$171,850	$195,850	$117,510	$156,680	$195,850
Increase in Cash	$2,000	$128,172	$417,984	$763,253	$1,062,505	$1,443,498
Beginning Cash	$0	$2,000	$130,172	$548,156	$1,311,409	$2,373,914
Ending Cash	$2,000	$130,172	$548,156	$1,311,409	$2,373,914	$3,817,412

Warm 'n Safe Bottle Company
Pro Forma Income Statements Highlights
Worst Case

	Start Up Period	Year 1	Year 2	Year 3	Year 4	Year 5
Sales	$0	$845,340	$1,690,680	$1,690,680	$1,690,680	$1,690,680
Cost of Goods	$0	$355,120	$710,240	$710,240	$710,240	$710,240
Gross Margin	$0	$490,220	$980,440	$980,440	$980,440	$980,440
S, G & A Expenses	$50,000	$487,464	$770,577	$714,397	$715,153	$715,939
Income Before Taxes	($50,000)	$2,756	$209,863	$266,043	$265,287	$264,501
Income Taxes	($19,000)	$1,047	$79,748	$101,096	$100,809	$100,510
Net Income	($31,000)	$1,709	$130,115	$164,947	$164,478	$163,991

Pro Forma Balances Sheet Highlights

	Start Up Period	Year 1	Year 2	Year 3	Year 4	Year 5
Current Assets	$46,000	$102,502	$288,411	$479,558	$670,236	$860,427
Property & Equip, Net	$111,000	$140,800	$78,600	$52,400	$26,200	$0
Total Assets	$157,000	$207,302	$367,011	$531,958	$696,436	$860,427
Current Liabilities	($19,000)	$29,593	$59,187	$59,187	$59,187	$59,187
Stockholder's Equity	$176,000	$177,709	$307,824	$472,771	$637,249	$801,240
Total Liabilities & Equity	$157,000	$207,302	$367,011	$531,958	$696,436	$860,427

Pro Forma Cash Flow Highlights

	Start Up Period	Year 1	Year 2	Year 3	Year 4	Year 5
Cash From Operations	($31,000)	$27,909	$156,315	$191,147	$190,678	$190,191
Total Sources of Cash	$188,000	$48,593	$29,594	$0	$0	$0
Total Uses of Cash	$155,000	$73,925	$97,925	$0	$0	$0
Increase in Cash	$2,000	$2,577	$87,984	$191,147	$190,678	$190,191
Beginning Cash	$0	$2,000	$4,577	$92,561	$283,708	$474,386
Ending Cash	$2,000	$4,577	$92,561	$283,708	$474,386	$664,577

Warm 'n Safe Bottle Company
Pro Forma Income Statements Highlights
Best Case

	Start Up Period	Year 1	Year 2	Year 3	Year 4	Year 5
Sales	$0	$3,381,360	$4,395,768	$5,748,312	$7,438,992	$9,636,876
Cost of Goods	$0	$1,420,480	$1,846,624	$2,414,816	$3,125,056	$4,048,368
Gross Margin	$0	$1,960,880	$2,549,144	$3,333,496	$4,313,936	$5,588,508
S, G & A Expenses	$50,000	$1,019,775	$1,311,325	$1,484,941	$1,806,759	$2,224,922
Income Before Taxes	($50,000)	$941,105	$1,237,819	$1,848,555	$2,507,177	$3,363,586
Income Taxes	($19,000)	$357,620	$470,371	$702,451	$952,727	$1,278,163
Net Income	($31,000)	$583,485	$767,448	$1,146,104	$1,554,450	$2,085,423

Pro Forma Balances Sheet Highlights

	Start Up Period	Year 1	Year 2	Year 3	Year 4	Year 5
Current Assets	$46,000	$773,058	$1,602,218	$2,821,872	$4,461,708	$6,650,274
Property & Equip, Net	$111,000	$104,800	$78,600	$52,400	$26,200	$0
Total Assets	$157,000	$877,858	$1,680,818	$2,874,272	$4,487,908	$6,650,274
Current Liabilities	($19,000)	$118,373	$153,885	$201,235	$260,421	$337,364
Stockholder's Equity	$176,000	$759,485	$1,526,933	$2,673,037	$4,227,487	$6,312,910
Total Liabilities & Equity	$157,000	$877,858	$1,680,818	$2,874,272	$4,487,908	$6,650,274

Pro Forma Cash Flow Highlights

	Start Up Period	Year 1	Year 2	Year 3	Year 4	Year 5
Cash From Operations	($31,000)	$609,685	$793,648	$1,172,304	$1,580,650	$2,111,623
Total Sources of Cash	$188,000	$137,373	$35,512	$47,350	$59,186	$76,943
Total Uses of Cash	$155,000	$367,700	$117,510	$156,680	$195,850	$254,605
Increase in Cash	$2,000	$379,358	$711,650	$1,062,974	$1,443,986	$1,933,961
Beginning Cash	$0	$2,000	$381,358	$1,093,008	$2,155,982	$3,599,968
Ending Cash	$2,000	$381,358	$1,093,008	$2,155,982	$3,599,968	$5,533,929

XII. PROPOSED COMPANY OFFERING

Desired Financing

The management team has projected that Warm 'n Safe Bottle Company will need capital of $200,000 to begin operations. These funds will be primarily used to secure patents, fund initial plastic mold manufacture and complete development and testing. Anticipated immediate sales should generate sufficient cash to fund operating activities once actual production begins and no additional funding needs are expected.

Offering

In exchange for the seed capital in the amount of $200,000, Warm 'n Safe Company is prepared to surrender 20 percent ownership in the Company. Warm 'n Safe Bottle Company anticipates that an investor willing to provide these funds will require a return on investment of 50 percent per year and be able to liquidate his investment in the Company in five years. At a 50 percent return rate, this investment at the end of five years will be $2,010,000.

Based on most likely case scenario pro forma financial statements and using five times after tax earnings as a basis for valuing Warm 'n Safe Bottle Company, a 20 percent ownership in Warm 'n Safe Bottle Company will be worth approximately $1,554,000 at the end of five years. Assuming ten times after tax earnings as an approximate basis for valuing Warm 'n Safe Bottle

Company, a 20 percent ownership in the Company will be worth approximately $3,108,000 at the end of five years.

In the event that Warm 'n Safe Bottle Company is not prepared or desirous of issuing an initial public offering at the end of the five-year period, the financial situation of the Company would allow Warm 'n Safe Bottle Company to purchase the initial investor's stake in the Company at the same rate mentioned above.

Appendix A

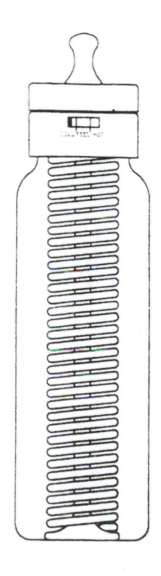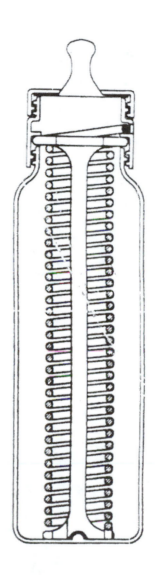

ASSEMBLY VIEW   SECTIONAL VIEW